Colorado
Weather Almanac

Colorado
Weather Almanac

Mike Nelson

Johnson Books
BOULDER

Published by Johnson Books
a Big Earth Publishing company

3005 Center Green Drive, Suite 220, Boulder, CO 80301.
E-mail: books@bigearthpublishing.com
www.bigearthpublishing.com
1-800-258-5830

This book was created in conjunction with Front Range
Community College students, Jake Ryan, cover and book
design, and Linda Ford, illustrator, through the Westminster
Campus Multimedia Graphic Design program. Elaine Betts,
MGD Faculty, was the Intern Coordinator and design advisor.
Ryan Girard, Math and Meteorology Faculty, initiated FRCC
participation and was consultant on technical illustration of
this project.

9   8   7   6   5   4   3   2   1

Library of Congress Cataloging-in-Publication Data
Nelson, Mike P., 1957–
    Colorado weather almanac / Mike Nelson.
        p.   cm.
    ISBN-13: 978-1-55566-401-5
    1. Colorado—Climate—Observations. 2. Almanacs,
American—Colorado. II. Title.
    QC999.N45 2007
    551.69788—dc22   2007019304

Printed in Thailand by Imago

Contents

Acknowledgments

Writing a second book on Colorado weather was both a task and a privilege. I have long enjoyed talking and teaching about our wild and wonderful weather, so creating a book provides a terrific opportunity to put it all together into one source. At the same time, there is a pretty good chunk of discipline needed to actually get down to business and write, especially when the very weather you are describing in text is just outside the window, compelling you to go out and enjoy it. Since my first book, there have been many memorable storms, fires, and weather events, plus more research on the changes in our climate, so it was time to put it all together in a new, bigger, and more in-depth book about our state.

In this project, I have been truly fortunate to partner with some excellent, hard-working people who have been a pleasure to work with. At the top of my list is my lead researcher Chris Spears. I first met Chris when he served as an intern in the weather center, and his enthusiasm for weather led to a friendship and earned Chris a stint as our weather producer at 7News. Chris has helped put together all of the climate charts and has coordinated the development of the wonderful graphic elements on the pages to follow. Thanks also to my friend Richard Ortner, who has helped write many of the sidebars that appear in the pages to follow.

The students and staff at Front Range Community College have done an amazing job in the design and creation of the book, all part of a college credit program. Special thanks to Jake Ryan and Linda Ford, and instructors Elaine Betts and Ryan Girard.

Mark Montour-Larson, the art director at KMGH and graphic artist Andrew Williams, have been extremely helpful in creating and fine tuning many of the graphics in the book. Both are gifted artist and have been both gracious and generous with their much sought after time and talent.

Johnson Books, and especially Mira Perrizo, Linda Doyle, and Rebecca Finkel, have given a balanced level of support and freedom to me, allowing me to develop this book in the way I envisioned, but also providing plenty of guidance and suggestions.

Gregory McNamee, my copyeditor, has been valuable in helping us shape the text into a very readable and accurate format—and managed to save a few trees by cutting down on some lengthy passages.

Thank you to the management at KMGH-TV, especially Darrell Brown, Byron Grandy, and Linda Bayley, for their complete support of this project in particular and for their overall support of the 24/7 Weather concept in general. In thirty years of doing television, my time at 7News has truly been the most fun, with the freedom to build a weather department in the manner that I have long envisioned.

I am indebted to the many talented photographers, amateur and professional, who have provided the outstanding pictures in the pages to follow. A special thanks to Gregory Thompson for the incredible shot of lightning that graces the cover.

My gratitude goes out to the many local experts that gave of their time to read over the text, add comments and offer suggestions. Nolan Doesken and the staff at the Colorado Climate Center, Mickey Glantz, Kevin Trenberth, Pieter Tans, and the staff at NCAR have all been very helpful in proofing and critiquing—especially the latest information on our changing climate. Thanks to stormchasers Tim Samaras, Roger Hill, Verne Carlson, and Ken Langford for their expertise on severe weather. And a special thanks to Tony Laubach, not only for his knowledge on storm chasing, but his technical skills in helping with many of the pictures and graphics.

My dear friend and mentor in television weather, Terry Kelly, president of Weather Central, has provided so much guidance to me. Over the extent of my career, no one has taught me more about TV weathercasting than Terry Kelly.

I want to thank my family for their support: my daughter Christiana is an excellent writer in her own right, and my son Anders enthusiastically helped with this project. I am so very proud of both of you.

Thank you to my parents, John and Arliss, for all of their love and support throughout my life. I miss you both so very much.

I dedicate this book

to my wife Cindy,

my partner, friend, and guide

for thirty years.

Together we have traveled

along this journey,

and I would not have arrived

at this point without her

vision and intuition

on when not only to accept change,

but also to embrace it.

I love you.

CHAPTER ONE

COLORADO CLIMATE:
THE BASICS

Colorado's weather is a source of beauty, wonder, and danger. Our state enjoys—or, sometimes, endures—just about every kind of weather on the planet except hurricanes, and features a climate best characterized by the word contrast.

There are many days when a simple drive across the state on I-70 will take you through two, three, and sometimes all four seasons. In April and May, it is not uncommon to have a blizzard in the mountains and severe thunderstorms with tornadoes on the plains—all in the same afternoon. Other days can feature extreme differences in temperature over just a few miles. For example, sometimes shallow arctic air masses slide down from the northern Great Plains and bank up against the eastern slope of the Rockies, leaving Denver cloudy, cold, and damp while foothill locations as close as Evergreen and Conifer, sitting above the shallow layer of cold air, are several degrees warmer and basking in sunshine. Still other days can bring thick clouds and very heavy snow to the mountains and strong, warm winds with sunshine to the plains, or vice versa.

Temperature extremes range from readings of less than 60 degrees below zero to over 110 degrees above. Colorado has held the record for the most intense snowfall in twenty-four hours, but it has also had many winters with little or no snow in certain high valleys or on the far eastern plains. Some places in Colorado receive little more annual precipitation than the deserts of Arizona, while only a few miles away, the annual total runs upward of 50, even 60 inches.

We see our share of unsettled weather in the Centennial State, but sunshine and mild temperatures are most often the rule. This makes our climate a delightful one for outdoor activities. But when stormy weather does decide to strike the state, it can be a nightmare, not only for business and travel, but also for those trying to predict the weather.

Colorado Geography

Where does one begin to understand the weather in Colorado? It starts with a simple geography lesson. Colorado is located between 37 and 41 degrees north of the equator, in an area known as the midlatitudes. Each of the earth's hemispheres can be divided into upper, middle, and lower latitudes. If you enjoy weather with lots of variety, the place to be is the midlatitudes, where cold polar air from the north meets and wrestles with warm equatorial air from the south, setting the stage for atmospheric excitement.

Another important feature of Colorado is its interior continental location, meaning we are a landlocked state, more than 1,000 miles from the nearest major body of water. Moisture is precious in Colorado. Our great distance from the oceans means that winds must bring humidity hundreds of miles to our state. Usually, we are lucky enough to have the storm track bring us heavy winter snows and adequate summer rains, but dry weather patterns are always a concern.

Prolonged dry weather patterns, or droughts, are of even greater concern to Colorado. Careful studies of tree rings and of ice and seafloor core samples show that droughts come in

cycles. Evidence of recurring drought can also be found in historical and anecdotal records that stretch back hundreds and even thousands of years. In Colorado, our dry periods seem to come about every twenty to thirty years. Noteworthy droughts of the recent past occurred around 1900, in the 1930s, the 1950s, and the mid-1970s, as well as at the turn of the millennium. The dryness often lingers for several years before the large-scale weather pattern shifts and wetter conditions return. Drought has always been a worry in our state, perhaps now more than ever before, due to greater population and the increased strain on water resources.

Colorado's midlatitudinal, midcontinental location is key to understanding our overall climate on the large scale, such as when studying both wet and dry weather patterns. But the most important factor that really drives weather on the small scale is the local topography.

This example from Lake Granby is what can happen when Colorado enters a long dry period.

Upslopes and Downslopes

The weather in our state is mainly influenced by the Rocky Mountains, which dominate the western half. As winds blow into Colorado, the air is pushed up, over, and around these mountains, creating huge contrasts in rain and snow patterns. When the winds blow up a mountain slope, the air is forced to rise. This rising air cools and moisture condenses out to form clouds and precipitation. As the air sinks on the other side of the mountain, the air warms and dries out. Because the main flow of wind is from the west to the east, the mountains intercept most of the moisture, leaving the eastern plains much drier. The wettest area in the state, on average, is in the Park Mountains east of Steamboat Springs. The annual precipitation in this area falls mostly in the form of snow during the cold season months, and is equivalent to about 60 inches of liquid.

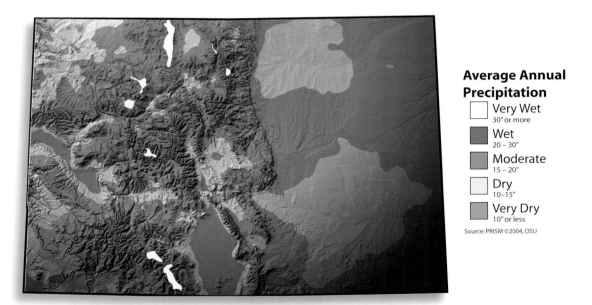

Average Annual Precipitation

- Very Wet
  30" or more
- Wet
  20 – 30"
- Moderate
  15 – 20"
- Dry
  10–15"
- Very Dry
  10" or less

Source: PRISM ©2004, OSU

The annual precipitation in Colorado varies widely due to terrain-driven local weather patterns.

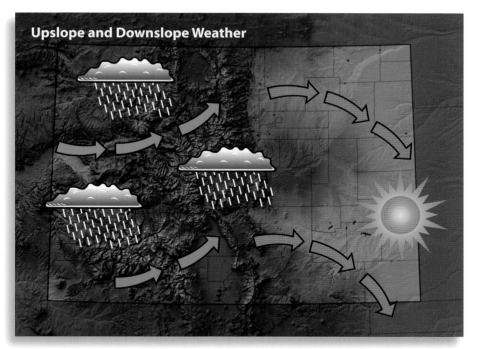

Upslope and Downslope Weather

By contrast, most of the eastern plains will average just 12 to 16 inches of liquid equivalent precipitation per year, mostly from summertime thunderstorms. The driest part of Colorado is in the San Luis Valley, where moisture is blocked from three directions by mountains. The driest areas average less than 8 inches of precipitation annually.

The spine of tall mountains that divides the state can play all kinds of havoc with our weather. Weather forecasters on radio and television often speak of "upslopes" and "downslopes" during their weather reports, but what exactly do these terms mean?

As the winds blow against a mountain, the air is forced to rise over the peak. This rising air is moving "up" the slope of that mountain. When air rises, it cools at a rate of about 5.4 degrees Fahrenheit for each 1,000 feet of ascent. This temperature change is called the "dry adiabatic lapse rate." The cooler air cannot "hold" as much water vapor as warm air, so the vapor condenses out to form clouds. If the air continues to rise

An upslope wind blows up the side of a mountain, bringing cloudy, cool, and wet weather. A downslope wind blows down a mountainside, bringing clear, warm, and dry weather.

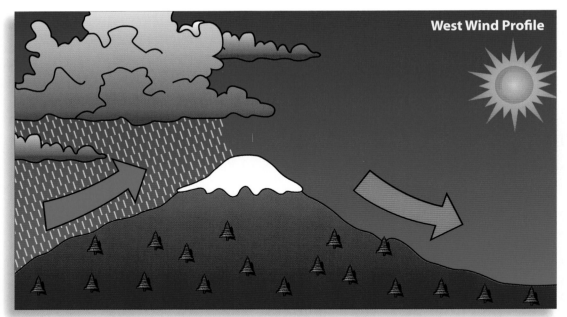

West Wind Profile

A west wind blowing across Colorado usually brings unsettled weather to the west and dry weather to the east.

up the mountain, more and more moisture will condense and the clouds will thicken and eventually produce precipitation.

Let's take a situation where a fairly moist westerly wind is pushing into western Colorado. The air will be forced to rise up as it travels into the mountains. This rising air will cool, the moisture will condense out, clouds will form, and rain or snow will develop over the west-facing slope of the mountain. This is the upslope.

A downslope is just the opposite. As the air reaches the crest of the mountain and begins to move downhill, it will begin to warm up, due to the air being compressed as it descends. The molecules of air are being pushed closer together as the air moves down into the thicker atmosphere at lower elevations. This compression warms the air, causing the relative humidity to drop and the clouds to evaporate. Thus a downsloping wind will generally bring clearing skies and warmer temperatures.

The same weather pattern that can bring snow to the western side of a mountain can bring dry and mild weather to the opposite side of the mountain. That is why it is sometimes

East Wind Profile

snowing on the western side of the Eisenhower Tunnel, but not on the eastern side. In fact, it can be sunny, breezy, and warm in Denver with a strong westerly wind, while the mountains west of the Continental Divide are being hammered with heavy snow.

In Denver and along the Front Range, our upslope winds are from the east. An easterly wind will have to travel "up the hill" from the 4,000-foot elevations near the Kansas border to our mile-high elevation in Denver. Easterly winds bring an increase in clouds and often a chance for rain or snow to the Denver area, especially since that air moves west of Denver and backs up against the mountains, gradually forming clouds and precipitation over the foothills and then out across the eastern plains. In this instance, the upslope winds will often cause rain or snow here, but dry weather will hold west of the Continental Divide (remember, they would have an easterly downsloping wind there as the air blows down from the Continental Divide toward the west).

An east wind blowing across Colorado usually brings unsettled weather to the east and dry weather to the west.

High Altitude Sickness

Colorado is the nation's highest state, with more than fifty mountain peaks stretching above 14,000 feet. Even Denver, the state's capital, is located 5,280 feet above sea level, or roughly a mile higher than Miami, New York City, and New Orleans.

Regardless of the season, the Rocky Mountains provide a paradise for tourists and outdoor enthusiasts from across the country. The lure of mountain snow and summer sun can be dangerous for visitors not used to Colorado's elevation. Atmospheric pressure decreases, and the sun's ultraviolet rays are stronger. The air is colder and drier, and less oxygen is available. The combination can be deadly for anyone not acclimated to the mountain environment.

High altitude sickness (HAS) can be subtle enough to be dismissed by anyone unfamiliar with the danger signs: faster and deeper breathing, shortness of breath, headache, nausea, increased heart rate, and difficulty sleeping. Simply traveling to a lower elevation can alleviate the symptoms and help victims feel better. Left untreated, the condition can worsen and develop into more dangerous conditions called high altitude pulmonary edema (HAPE) and high altitude cerebral edema (HACE).

HAPE occurs when fluid begins collecting in the victim's lungs. Shortness of breath and *continued ▶*

It may sound a little confusing, but that is why Colorado weather is such a challenge to predict. Just remember, upslopes tend to bring clouds and precipitation, and are therefore sometimes referred to as "upslops." Downslopes, conversely, tend to bring windy, dry, and mild weather.

Upslopes and downslopes are not experienced only over the higher mountains of our state; even relatively gentle slopes can create this effect. In fact, southwest of Greeley, the terrain is about 150–200 feet higher than it is in town. Because of this slight edge in elevation, the southwest side experiences more precipitation, especially snow.

It is common for folks who have lived along the Front Range for a few years to note that it seems to be drier in the Fort Collins, Longmont, Berthoud, and Loveland area than in Denver. It is, on average. The higher terrain just to the south and west of Denver helps to increase any upslope component from a northerly wind. This aids in squeezing more moisture out of the clouds—especially over the western and southern suburbs. Areas farther to the north along I-25 do not get this benefit of forced lifting. There is actually a slight downsloping component to a northerly wind crossing Fort Collins and vicinity. The Cheyenne Ridge is a slightly elevated area just south of Cheyenne, Wyoming, and the terrain dips southward toward Fort Collins and Loveland. According to Nolan Doesken, the Colorado State Climatologist, Denver gets about 61 inches of snow in an average winter, while Longmont gets only about 48 inches, Berthoud and Loveland get a little over 50 inches, and Fort Collins normally receives about 52 inches.

Geographical Features

So why is there so much variation in the weather in Colorado? How can one location just a matter of miles away have such a different climate? The answer can easily be summed up with a real estate analogy—location, location, location. The type of weather one experiences when a storm system moves into Colorado largely depends on the local wind direction and the surrounding terrain. For Denver, which sits in a bowl and is surrounded by higher terrain on three sides, precipitation type and amounts can vary greatly from one suburb to the next. There are many other geographical features in Colorado that affect the weather, but a few of the terms mentioned most often include the Continental Divide, Front Range, the foothills, and the Palmer Divide. Other features that affect local weather patterns include the Grand Mesa, the Raton Ridge, and the Cheyenne Ridge.

Newcomers often ask what the Palmer Divide is. If you check a topographical map of Colorado, you will notice a west-to-east ridge of higher terrain running from just north of Colorado Springs out to around Limon. In fact, many people don't realize that Limon is actually higher than the city of Denver by nearly 100 feet.

The Palmer Divide (or Palmer Ridge) is about 1,500 feet above the surrounding area and has a very large effect on weather conditions as the winds blow over and around it. Winds from the north push moisture onto the northern flank of Monument Hill, sending clouds, rain, and snow back into the Denver metro area as the moisture piles up against the ridge. In contrast, a wind from the south can bring rain and snow to the Colorado Springs side while leaving areas north of the Palmer Divide much drier.

The Palmer Divide also creates some interesting swirling wind patterns that can stir up severe weather in Denver. During the spring and summer, when the winds are blowing across the state from the southeast, the air must pass over and down the Palmer Divide as it moves toward Denver. This motion often causes a large-scale swirling movement in the air known as the "Denver Cyclone." More detailed descriptions of this local weather pattern will be found in Chapters 3 and 4.

The Cheyenne Ridge is a similar, although less dramatic, west-to-east ridge that has much the same effect as the Palmer Divide. The Cheyenne Ridge extends from

a wet cough are the warning signs, and immediate descent and medical attention are necessary to treat the illness. HACE occurs when the brain begins to swell, a condition that can occur quickly and subtly. Victims suffering from HACE will appear confused and tired, and may appear to be drunk. Vomiting, hallucinations, seizures, and eventually coma and death are possible with this disorder. Immediate descent and medical attention are necessary.

Preventing High Altitude Sickness

- The human body has the ability to acclimate to higher elevations, but it needs time to adjust. One should move to increasingly higher elevations gradually. Out-of-state visitors on their way to Colorado's mountains will benefit from spending a night at lower elevations before heading into the high country.

- The signs of HAS can be subtle and may masquerade as other maladies. Be familiar with the warning signs and descend to lower elevations if you suspect its onset.

- Drink plenty of water, and limit alcohol consumption.

- Be prepared for changing weather conditions and dress appropriately.

- Sunscreen is essential. The sun's ultraviolet rays are more intense at higher elevations.

the mountains west of Cheyenne eastward right along the Colorado-Wyoming border, east to the southern edge of the Nebraska Panhandle. Much like its southern counterpart, the Cheyenne Ridge induces a variety of upslopes and downslopes, depending on the wind direction. These air motions cause clouds and precipitation to be greater on the windward side and lighter on the lee side.

To the south, the Raton Ridge extends west to east along the Colorado–New Mexico border. Best known for Raton Pass, a sometimes perilous place to drive on I-25 in the winter, the Raton Ridge teams up with the Palmer Divide and the Cheyenne Ridge as less widely known, but still important, regional weather makers.

The Grand Mesa is the very large flat-topped mountain just to the south and east of Grand Junction. This elevated terrain is quite effective in grabbing moisture from the clouds pushing into western Colorado, at the expense of areas nearby. Snowpack on the Grand Mesa often piles to the 200-inch level, while nearby lower terrain will remain dry, with little or no snow for the season.

The Front Range extends from the Summit County area to the north and east and includes the higher terrain west of Denver, Boulder, and Fort Collins. The rapid drop in height from the top of these mountains west of the I-25 corridor is most pronounced near Boulder. In this area, the Continental Divide is only about 20 miles west of the flat plains east of Boulder. Being so close to tall mountains gives the Boulder area some uniquely wild weather fluctuations, especially when it comes to winds during the winter months. More details about winter winds will follow in Chapter 2.

Weather forecasts often mention the foothills, especially when it comes to predictions about heavy snow or strong winds. The foothill locations are essentially areas with elevations between 6,000 and 9,000 feet along and just west of I-25. In the Denver Metro area, the foothills include much of western Jefferson, Boulder, Clear Creek, and Gilpin Counties; higher terrain west of Fort Collins in Larimer County; and the northeastern parts of Park County. Elevations between 6,000 and 9,000 feet west of Colorado Springs, Pueblo, and Trinidad are considered the southern foothills, while those west of the Denver Urban Corridor (Castle Rock to Fort Collins) are the northern foothills. Often the higher elevations south of Denver in Douglas County also receive similar weather to foothill locations, so if you live around or above 6,000 feet in Parker, Castle Rock, or Larkspur, you can often expect much the same type of wind, rain, and snow as the other foothill locations. The higher elevation of the foothills tends to enhance snowfall during upslope events and can bring very strong downsloping winds called chinooks, which will be explained further in Chapter 2.

You hear these terms all the time in weather forecasts—probably more so in the snow season than at other times of the year. So where does one end and another begin? And just what is considered the foothills versus the mountains? Where are the plains? And who lives in the Front Range? The easiest way to define each region is to assign an elevation. Keep in

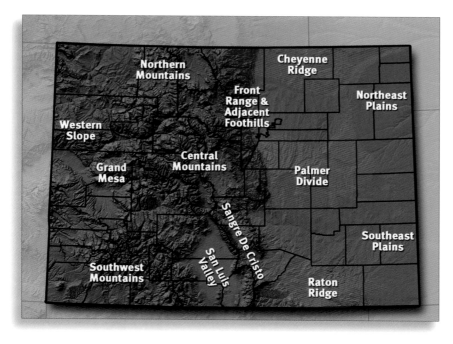

In addition to the Rocky Mountains, several geographical features affect the climate of Colorado.

mind that these definitions are tailored to Colorado and can vary in other mountainous states.

- **Mountains.** In general, locations above 9,000 feet in elevation are considered mountains. Some cities below that elevation are still considered to be in the mountains because of the surrounding terrain, such as Aspen, Steamboat Springs, and Durango.

- **Foothills.** The foothills are locations between 6,000 and 9,000 feet that parallel a mountain chain. During localized weather events, the foothills west of Denver may be divided into the northern and southern Front Range foothills, with I-70 as the dividing line. Cities and towns in the foothills include Evergreen, Conifer, Pine, Bailey, Georgetown, Idaho Springs, Estes Park, Nederland, Red Feather Lakes, Central City, Black Hawk, and Fairplay. There are also foothills in southern Colorado west of Pueblo, Trinidad, and Colorado Springs. Note that some of the southern suburbs of Denver have areas that exceed 6,000 feet in elevation and can have weather similar to the foothills due to the terrain enhancing precipitation, yet they are not technically considered to be in the foothills.

- **Eastern Plains.** Sometimes just called "the plains." This general term refers to almost all areas east of I-25 in Colorado. In general, it refers to locations below 6,000 feet in elevation. It includes cities and towns such as Greeley, Sterling, Akron, Yuma, Wray, Bennett, Byers, Limon, Burlington, Lamar, Springfield, and La Junta.

- **Western Slope.** The area of Colorado west of the Continental Divide, generally in elevations below about 7,000 feet, is called the Western Slope. Western Colorado doesn't really have any foothills of the kind that are found on the eastern slope of the Rockies. Outside of the mountains, the terrain is made up of numerous mesas and plateaus. Cities and towns identified as being on the Western Slope include Grand Junction, Delta, Montrose, Meeker, Craig, and Rangely.

- **Front Range.** This is technically the front mountain range, or the easternmost range, of the Rocky Mountains. This mountain range, the foothills, and locations along the I-25 corridor are all within 50 to 75 miles of one another, so the entire area is often collectively termed the Front Range. It may be helpful to picture everything from just east of the Continental Divide to I-25 as the Front Range.

- **Palmer Divide.** This ridge of land extends from the Front Range of the Rockies in central Colorado eastward toward the city of Limon. It sits right in between the cities of Denver and Colorado Springs. The elevation of the Palmer Divide runs roughly between 6,000 and 7,500 feet, peaking at Monument Hill. This terrain feature is the cause of several small-scale, or microscale, weather patterns and can make a world of difference in the weather between Denver and Colorado Springs. Although this elevation technically makes it qualify for the foothills category, it does not parallel a mountain chain as the foothills do. The Palmer Divide is perpendicular to the mountains. Because of the orientation of the Palmer Divide with respect to the eastern plains, the weather can be similar to the foothills during active weather with enhanced precipitation, especially during snowstorms. Cities and towns within the Palmer Divide include Castle Rock, Franktown, Elizabeth, Kiowa, Monument, Black Forest, Sedalia, and Palmer Lake. Parts of the Denver Metro area along C-470 from Chatfield to I-25 and along E-470 from I-25 to Smoky Hill Road are on the extreme northern fringe of the Palmer Divide. Interestingly enough, Limon sits on the eastern fringe of the divide, at an elevation higher than Denver.

- **Denver Metro Area.** Includes all or parts of the nine counties that make up the metropolitan area: Denver, Boulder, Jefferson, Arapahoe, Adams, Broomfield, Douglas, Elbert, and Weld. These counties encompass portions of the plains, the foothills, and the Palmer Divide—hence the reason precipitation from storm events, particularly snow, can vary so much in a relatively short distance.

We defined the foothills as being elevations between 6,000 and 9,000 feet and the plains as areas east of I-25. So what about the small strip of land east of the foothills but west of I-25, including Boulder, Longmont, Lakewood, Arvada, Wheat Ridge, Loveland, Fort Collins, Golden, and Highlands Ranch? These areas can go either way, foothills or plains, but tend to have climate characteristics closer to the foothills, especially when it comes to wind.

Humidity and Dew Point

One weather variable sets Colorado and the central Rockies apart from the Midwest and East: our low humidity. Visitors often comment on how dry the air is, in both the winter and summer. The cold season is filled with plenty of static electricity, dry skin, and chapped lips. The warmer months moisten up somewhat, but still are extremely dry compared to the Midwest, East, or South. Our air is so dry thanks to the combination of altitude and distance from major bodies of water.

The moisture in our air can be measured in a number of different ways. Relative humidity is the measurement that is most commonly displayed on television weather reports. The relative humidity is a percentage comparison between how much moisture is actually in the air and what the air could possibly hold at a given temperature. Dry air has a low relative humidity; humid air will have a much higher percentage—up to 100 percent.

The dew point is the temperature at which the air becomes saturated with water vapor—in other words, at which dew

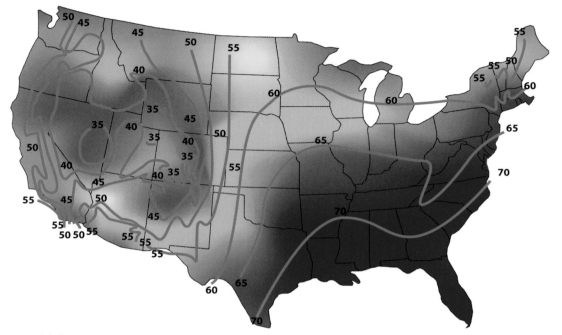

would form. Once the air is saturated, any additional moisture added to the air will result in clouds, dew, frost, fog, or precipitation—depending on the given weather pattern. The dew point is always less than or equal to the air temperature. It cannot be higher—when the temperature and the dew point are the same, the air is said to be saturated. When the air is saturated, the relative humidity is 100 percent.

One of the reasons that Colorado is so nice a place to be is because we have a "friendly dew point." Our high elevation and greater distance from the oceans means that our atmosphere is fairly dry, and the dew points are often much lower than those of cities farther to the east and south. In the summertime, our dew point is often just in the 40s during a hot summer afternoon. This means that the actual air temperature would have to cool from, for example, the mid-80s all the way down to the 40s in order for the air to become saturated. In contrast, summertime dew points in St. Louis or Dallas might be in the upper 60s or even the mid-70s. That means the air would have

The average July dew point in the United States. It is an important factor in summertime thunderstorms, as well as outdoor comfort.

17

to cool only to the upper 60s or mid-70s for the air to become saturated and dew or clouds to form. This is the reason why we often have little or no morning dew here, especially compared to our muggy neighbors to the east.

Our lower dew points also mean that we have a lot less moisture in the air to help fuel thunderstorms. The storms that develop in Colorado have to "pull" moisture in from a large area in order to blossom into heavy rainmakers. Our storms tend to be small and more widely scattered, as there is limited moisture available. In the Midwest, the South, and the East, the dew points are higher and there is a great deal more moisture available to feed large squall lines or big clusters of thunderstorms.

One of the things that meteorologists watch for is the difference between the temperature and the dew point. If there is a large difference (temperature is much higher than the dew point), then the air is obviously quite dry. If the dew point spread is getting larger, the air is getting drier (the relative humidity is getting lower). If the dew point spread is getting smaller, then the air is getting more humid and there could be a chance of fog, clouds, or even precipitation. Pilots are especially watchful of the dew point spread; if it is getting progressively smaller, that means that the air is getting more humid and there is an increasing risk of low clouds, poor visibility, and possible icing conditions.

Rare indeed is the weather forecaster who has not heard, "Boy, it must be great to have a job where you can be wrong half the time and not get fired."

The dew point is measured by using a combination of a "dry bulb" thermometer (just a regular thermometer) and a "wet bulb" thermometer (a thermometer that has a moistened piece of cloth over the bulb or bottom of the tube). The wet bulb thermometer will read lower due to the cooling of evaporation of the moisture on the bulb. The drier the air, the more powerful the cooling will be and the lower the wet bulb will read. If the dry bulb and the wet bulb were the same, the air would have to be saturated (relative humidity = 100 percent).

Under saturated conditions, there is already so much moisture in the air, there can be no more added through evaporation.

In Colorado, most of the time our wet bulb temperatures are much lower than in other, more humid parts of the country. The dry bulb (or regular temperature) may be in the 90s or even low 100s, but it is still much more comfortable than a hot day would be in another part of the nation where the wet bulb temperatures are higher. In those places, weather reporters often speak of the heat index—a combination of the heat and the high humidity that makes it feel even hotter than what the thermometer reads.

In Colorado, we sometimes have a negative heat index. In other words, the air is so dry that even with a temperature of 100 degrees, it doesn't feel that hot. This is thanks to the very effective cooling that the human body achieves through perspiration. Your shirt may stay dry, even on a very hot day, as the sweat quickly evaporates, keeping you cooler. In other parts of the country, working outside on a hot day would leave you drenched in sweat. In Colorado, the same work would leave you warm, but with a dry shirt. The downside is that we have to watch out for signs of dehydration, as we lose so much water through sweating. All in all, our friendly dew point is just one more thing that makes Colorado such a great place to live.

Forecasting Challenges

Rare indeed is the weather forecaster who has not heard, "Boy, it must be great to have a job where you can be wrong half the time and not get fired." That's a harmless bit of humor, but it is important to remember what it is weather forecasters are trying to do. The weather report is the only aspect of a local newscast that attempts to predict the future rather than report the past. If the purpose of the news and sports reports were to predict the following day's events, or perhaps the events to come in the next few days, we would have a lot of folks frustrated about the accuracy of news and sportscasters as well.

Blueice, an IBM super-computer at the National Center for Atmospheric Research. It is capable of performing 12 teraflops, or 12 trillion floating-point operations per second.

Predicting the weather is an attempt to foretell the future, and that is always a difficult task. Weather forecasters combine science and art, using the very latest in high technology and supercomputing to track the current weather conditions and project them into the future. Adding to the complexity of the task, any given weather pattern can have many different outcomes. One example would be tracking a low pressure system that is poised to bring an accumulating snow of 6 to 8 inches to Denver and the Front Range. A slight shift just 75 to 100 miles either north or south from the forecasted path could mean anything from no snow to a crippling snow. Another example occurred in January 2007 across eastern Colorado. Forecasters were watching a departing area of low pressure over Kansas and an approaching area of low pressure in the Pacific Northwest. Snow was in the forecast, expected at only 1 to 3 inches. Suddenly, overnight on January 21, the low pressure over Washington sped up and dropped into southern Utah by sunrise the next day. The close proximity of the low pressure west of Colorado and east of Colorado put Denver and the plains in prime positioning for gusty wind and moderate to heavy snow. Within a period of just twelve hours, the 1- to 3-inch snowfall grew to 5 to 10 inches.

A skilled forecaster takes all of the resources available and brings them together in an attempt to choose the most likely scenario that will play out. Different forecasters may often come up with very different projections about how the weather will unfold over the course of hours and days.

Forecasting weather involves extensive studies, including high-level mathematics, physics, and chemistry, along with high-powered radar and satellite equipment to monitor the atmosphere. This combination of knowledge and equipment is matched with skilled analysts and research scientists whose job it is to predict how the weather will change with time.

Printed weather maps allow meteorologists to analyze weather patterns and potential outcomes.

Forecasting is done in steps. First, measurements and readings are made by a variety of instruments. Second, the data are fed into very complex numerical models, using massively parallel supercomputers that can crunch numbers at a rate of over several trillion calculations per second, creating basic forecasts. Third, the final results are plotted on the maps, tables, and charts. When these maps and numerical analyses are completed, they are sent to various government agencies, the military, private forecasting companies, and Wall Street analysts, as well as to television and radio stations, where forecasters interpret the information and translate it into user-friendly forms for the public.

Scanning the Skies

The weather maps that are most often used in forecasting are created at different pressure levels. Scientists most often use the millibar scale for measuring air pressure. One bar is considered to be the average atmospheric pressure (weight of the air) at sea level. A millibar is one-thousandth of a bar. The commonly used 850 mb, 700 mb, 500 mb, and 300 mb ranges are roughly equivalent, respectively, to 5,000 feet, 10,000 feet, 18,000 feet,

A radiosonde, or weather balloon, gathers important weather information as it climbs through the atmosphere. Temperature, wind, and humidity are among the data reported.

and 30,000 feet above sea level (surface). Pressure levels are easily determined by weather balloons that carry barometers and other weather sensors from the surface all the way to the edge of outer space. These balloons are released twice each day from more than a hundred locations across the United States and hundreds more around the world. In Colorado, weather balloons are released each day from Denver and Grand Junction. These balloons carry a small package of weather instruments called a radiosonde. The data from the radiosondes are incorporated along with surface weather observations and plotted on a variety of weather maps to provide an overall view of the weather around the world.

In forecasting, meteorologists incorporate all of those maps to understand the whole state of the air, since the conditions aloft and at the surface interact to create atmospheric dynamics—a fancy phrase for motion. To add to the complexity of forecasting in Colorado, the surface for places like Denver and Fort Collins is not found on the 850 mb map, because those spots are already higher than 5,000 feet above sea level. In fact, many mountain locations are not even on the 700 mb map. This makes forecasting more of a challenge in Colorado because so much atmospheric action takes place in the lowest levels, nearest the ground. When air masses move into Colorado, all of the low-level information that was easy to interpret at sea level is quickly crunched into a very narrow layer right near the ground. As a result, our weather can be very different over a small change in location or elevation.

Fronts That Affect Us

The maps used for forecasting are drawn mostly on a regional to national size, or what meteorologists call a synoptic scale. This scale involves North America and its surrounding oceans to give us a whole picture of the air movements. By observing the air movements, one can see the cold fronts, warm fronts, and stationary fronts that show the temperatures and flows. In addition, the maps show the wind speed and direction as well as precipitation. All of this information is drawn on the map with symbols and various lines. Lines of equal air pressure, or isobars, and symbols such as high and low pressure indicate different information that takes a little practice to read and interpret.

Looking at a weather map and trying to figure out the forecast can be a daunting task for the non-meteorologist, especially a busy weather map full of various weather symbols. The weather maps on TV and in the newspaper are often crisscrossed with various red, blue, and black lines that forecasters use to denote changes in air masses. These are the warm, cold, and stationary fronts, as well as something called a "trough."

Cold fronts are denoted by solid blue lines with points indicating the direction of movement. The cold front usually moves into Colorado from the north or west, bringing cooler air behind it. Sometimes cold fronts swing into Colorado from the northeast. These are nicknamed "backdoor" cold fronts. Showers and thunderstorms often occur along and near the front. In the winter months, arctic cold fronts can race southward across the plains of eastern Colorado in just a few hours. These fronts may bring several inches of snow and drop temperatures 50 to 60 degrees in twelve hours or less.

Air pressure in Colorado is lower than at sea level because of the elevation. The higher you climb, the lower the air pressure.

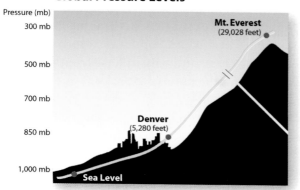

Global Pressure Levels

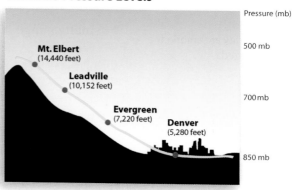

Colorado Pressure Levels

Cold Front

A cold front marks the leading edge of an approaching colder air mass.

Warm Front

A warm front marks the boundary of warmer air that is replacing cooler air.

Stationary Front

A stationary front marks the boundary between two air masses that aren't moving.

Trough

A trough is a boundary that marks a wind shift between two air masses. There is usually little temperature change.

Warm fronts are drawn as solid red lines with rounded lobes that indicate the direction of movement. A warm front usually moves into Colorado from the south or southwest, bringing in warmer and, on occasion, more humid air. Sometimes warm fronts move into Colorado from the southwest. These fronts can bring very warm, dry air from the deserts of Arizona and increase fire danger statewide.

A stationary front is indicated by a combination of the blue pointed lines and the red lobed lines. This type of front marks a boundary between warm and cool air that is not moving. If a stationary front stays near Colorado for a number of days, we will probably have a lot of rain or snow. Because of our mountains, it is common for a cold front to move southward into Colorado from the Dakotas, Montana, and Wyoming, but then stall and become stationary in Colorado. The chilly air easily slides over the flat terrain of the eastern plains, but the colder, denser air literally has trouble climbing over the mountains to the west. If you watch the weather maps, especially during the winter months, you will often see a front draped across the state from the northwest to the southeast. On the east side of the front, the plains will be shivering in the grip of a cold, dense arctic air mass. To the west of the Continental Divide, the air will be much warmer as the front stalls in the mountains. Denver may have low, gray skies, with snow and bitter cold temperatures, while Aspen and Vail are sunny and pleasant and it's downright warm in Durango, Glenwood Springs, and Grand Junction. The impact of a stationary front was clearly shown during the arctic outbreak in late December 2006. Denver and the eastern plains had temperatures in the single digits, while readings were in the 30s and 40s over the mountains and western valleys.

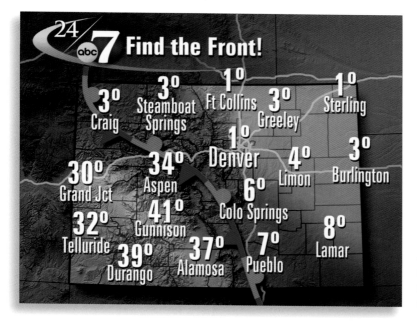

An arctic cold front moving south across Colorado stalled over the mountains and became stationary.

The black dashed line that sometimes appears on the weather map indicates a trough. This is an elongated area of lower air pressure, but little change in temperature. Troughs are "light" fronts, with not quite enough contrast in the air from one side to the other to qualify as a warm or cold front. The trough line marks a zone where wind, humidity, or pressure will shift, and it can indicate a region that is likely to have thunderstorms in the warm season or gusty winds in the cold season.

Why the Winds

The weather maps most often seen by the public are those from the local TV forecasts. In addition to the fronts, there are two other symbols often seen on a weather map that represent not only what kind of weather one can typically expect but also how the winds will behave: the big red L and blue H, denoting low and high pressure systems.

Air pressure is the weight of the atmosphere pushing down on the surface of the earth. It is measured with a barometer. The overall air pressure around the world is constant: that is, the weight of our atmosphere does not change when taken as a whole. In that light, the high and low pressure areas are like huge waves in the average air pressure around the world. Wind is simply air in motion, caused by differences in air pressure. Air moves from high pressure toward lower pressure; anyone who has ever had a flat tire has witnessed this fact of physics. In meteorology, air pressure is measured at all weather stations, and then the reading is "corrected" to sea level. In this way, the pressure readings at Denver (5,280 feet above sea level) can be compared with cities such as St. Louis (at about 535 feet above sea level) and New York or Los Angeles (at sea level). If we did not make this correction in the pressure readings, Denver would always show up as a low pressure area on the weather map, since our atmosphere at 1 mile high is about 15 percent thinner than that along the coast. Corrected sea level pressures are used to find the relative high and low pressure systems on weather maps, and

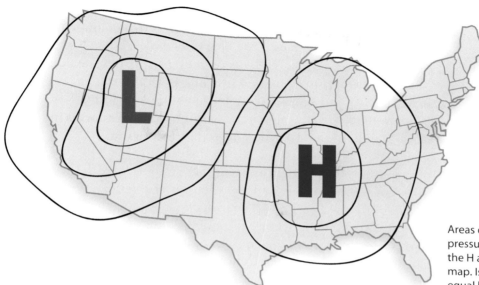

Areas of high and low pressure are indicated by the H and L on the weather map. Isobars are lines of equal barometric pressure—much like contour lines on a topographic map.

meteorologists study pressure changes to help in forecasting the movements of weather systems.

The thin, black, swirling circles seen on some weather charts are called "isobars," defined as lines of equal barometric pressure. Meteorologists chart the pressure patterns over the United States by drawing lines that connect various places that have the same "corrected" barometric pressure. By connecting the dots between weather stations, forecasters can determine areas of high and low pressure.

High pressure systems, the big blue H on the weather map, are characterized by slowly sinking and diverging air motion through the lower atmosphere. This often means that highs have dry, quiet weather, since any clouds will be "pulled apart" by the diverging air motion.

Low pressure systems, the big red L on the weather map, illustrate the principle that nature abhors a vacuum. Therefore, if the surface pressure is lower in any area, the air motion will be toward that center of low pressure to attempt to fill it in. Thus, low pressure areas at the surface of the earth tend to have air moving in toward the center of the low. That air cannot

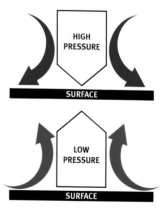

A low pressure area has rising air motion in the atmosphere. In most parts of the country it means unsettled weather.

A high pressure area has sinking air motion in the atmosphere. In most parts of the country, it means fair weather.

go into the ground, so it is forced to rise. The combination of the surface convergence and the rising air means that low pressure areas, in general, are characterized by clouds and precipitation.

The basic motion from high pressure toward low pressure would be nice and simple except for a few crucial issues. Earth is not a smooth, flat, stationary, frictionless surface. Because it is a rough, round, spinning object, the motion of air from high to low pressure is not direct. Instead, the combination of mountains, plains, oceans, and other landforms, with their different temperatures, and the rotation of the planet—the Coriolis effect—create a vast swirling dance among high and low pressure systems around the globe. At the surface, in the northern hemisphere, the air spins into a low in a counterclockwise direction and out from a high in a clockwise fashion. Just to make it more interesting, these motions are the exact opposite in the southern hemisphere.

The atmospheric drama between high and low pressure becomes even more intriguing in a rugged state such as Colorado. As we have seen, the main factor in whether the weather is hot or cold, wet or dry in our state is the terrain. The winds that spin around a high or low pressure system as it moves across or close to Colorado will have to contend with getting around those mountains. The big high pressure system over the upper Midwest will likely bring fair skies and quiet weather to the Dakotas, Nebraska, and Kansas. But the winds swirling around that high will swing into Colorado from an easterly direction. For the eastern plains and the Front Range, that means an upslope wind—one that can create clouds, rain, or snow. In the case of a low pressure system, one state's cold snowstorm can bring warm and dry weather to Colorado. Imagine a low pressure area centered over southeastern Wyoming. The counterclockwise flow around the low will spin clouds, rain, or snow over western Nebraska, South Dakota, and much of Wyoming. The same low pressure system will sweep a westerly wind across Colorado. Our mountains may get some snow with this wind, but in Denver, we will have a strong downsloping wind,

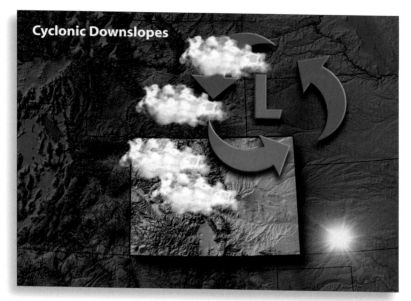

Cyclonic Downslopes

In most of the country, low pressure is associated with unsettled weather. In Colorado, the type of weather low pressure brings depends on where it is located.

Anticyclonic Upslopes

High pressure typically means fair weather. But some high pressure centers bring cold and snow to Colorado.

with the air becoming warmer and drier as it descends from the Continental Divide. The weather can be counterintuitive in Colorado—high pressure systems can bring snow, while a nearby low brings sunshine and warmth.

What Is Normal?

Sometimes a forecast will undergo a dramatic change over the course of a couple of days. The reasons can be as simple as an air mass taking a different track on its journey over North America. That is a fairly straightforward process, but it plays havoc with the resultant forecast. If an arctic air mass shifts in its path by 100 miles, Denver and the mountains may never get in the cold air, while Greeley, Fort Morgan, Limon, and the eastern border counties turn very cold. In that light, it is possible—and even fairly common—that an extended outlook can change from mild and dry to cold and snowy, or vice versa. Now, meteorologists could couch all of their forecasts by saying, "This might occur, or it could be just the opposite," but that would not serve the public very well, either. So forecasters give their best estimate of what is going to happen in the future—just as a stockbroker or a mortgage banker would do. Meteorologists do their best to provide the most accurate and erudite reports possible, but given the task of trying to forecast weather, especially in a state like Colorado, there will always be some tough days.

Did you know that water in Denver boils at 202° instead of 212°?

When talking about weather, not just here in Colorado but anywhere, meteorologists often compare the current forecast information to the average. On the daily weather reports on 7News, we display the average temperatures for any given date. Sometimes weathercasters refer to these temperatures as the "normal" readings for that date. One can see how "normal" and "average" can create confusion, but in meteorology informally, we use them interchangeably.

More precisely, in meteorology, the term normal is defined as a thirty-year smoothed average. These numbers are updated with new data every ten years. So, even though they are averages in the strict sense, the common usage is to call them normals.

El Niño and La Niña

Sometimes weather patterns shift on a large, or global scale, and can cause observed weather conditions to vary greatly from what we know as the thirty-year average. One such case is when El Niño or La Niña influences global circulation.

The term El Niño first became familiar to the public in the early 1980s. A very strong El Niño event in the winter of 1982–1983 resulted in heavy, wet storms pounding California, and television newscasts around the country showed flooding and mudslides night after night. Before that stormy winter, scientists knew about the periodic warming of the sea surface in the Pacific, but this phenomenon had not really been explained to the average American. Today, "El Niño" is probably right up there with "email," "Google," and "Internet" in recognition and acceptance. But just like the Internet, most folks know what it is, but are not sure how it works.

ENSO, the acronym for El Niño Southern Oscillation, consists of a cycle of warming and cooling of the sea surface in the equatorial Pacific. The temperature change in the water is not simply right at the ocean surface, but actually sinks down hundreds of feet below the waves. The cycle is not on a strict timeframe, but may occur every three to five years on the average. The warm phase of the cycle is called El Niño—Spanish for "the Christ child," since the warming of the ocean was often noticed by early winter, around the time of Christmas. The term dates back at least a couple of hundred years. Although we have had intense study of the phenomenon only in the past few decades, there are anecdotal references to events along the western coast of South America that date back for centuries, observations made by fishermen who noted the substantial effects the weather feature had on fishing conditions locally.

The opposite of El Niño is a cooling of the ocean surface known as La Niña. This warming and cooling flips back and forth on a more or less three- to five-year cycle. The in-between

ENSO, the acronym for El Niño Southern Oscillation is a cycle of warming and cooling of the sea surface in the equatorial Pacific.

period is simply called the "neutral phase." In this case, the sea surface temperatures are neither unusually high nor low.

The main effect of the periodic warming or cooling of the ocean surface is to change the way the jet stream blows across the Pacific and into North America. When an El Niño is in progress, large numbers of thunderstorms form in the air above the tepid ocean water. These storms release vast amounts of energy into the skies and help fuel a strong jet stream flow that can blast central and southern California like a fire hose. Intense storms roar in from the Pacific and hammer the coast with huge waves. Heavy rains soak inland areas and deep snows pile up in the Sierras. During a La Niña episode, the jet stream winds are often in a different pattern, swinging storms down from the Gulf of Alaska and bringing very wet and stormy weather to British Columbia and the Pacific Northwest.

There are not simple, straightforward connections between El Niño, La Niña, and the weather we can expect in Colorado. There are several reasons for this, the main one being that each ENSO episode is different. The Pacific is a big place, and the exact location of the warm or cold pool of water can be shifted east or west by hundreds, even thousands of miles. In addition, the strength and longevity of the event is seldom the same. We only have a dozen or so El Niño events that have been truly scrutinized, so the study is still in its youth. And finally, the crystal ball for Colorado is cloudy concerning

El Niño, the periodic warming of the equatorial waters in the eastern Pacific Ocean, can significantly affect the global weather pattern and economy. It is measured by the difference between the observed surface temperature and normal temperature of the ocean's surface.

Notable El Niño Events Since 1950

1957–1958:
Scientists from around the globe gathered to study natural phenomena at the International Geophysical Year. It was observed that the salmon population in the Pacific Northwest was negatively affected.

1965–1966:
The first decline in fish landings was recorded in Peru and linked to El Niño.

1972-1973:
Interest from American scientists grew about the El Niño phenomenon. The potential effects of El Niño on the global economy became a driver for additional research.

1982–1983:
Known as the "El Niño of the Century," the 1982–1983 El Niño episode drew large interest from the U.S. government, and of many other governments now known to be directly affected by droughts, floods, and fires generated by El Niño, among them Australia, Indonesia, and Zimbabwe.

what El Niño brings, since our state is more than 1,000 miles from the ocean. In California and along the West Coast, it is easier to associate a type of weather with either El Niño or La Niña, since they are right there next to the ocean. For our state, an awful lot can happen to those western storms before they arrive in Colorado.

El Niño winters and early springs usually bring heavy storms into the southern and central parts of California, and eventually those storms can make it into southwestern Colorado. The really heavy snows hit in the San Juan Mountains and favor Telluride, Durango, and Wolf Creek. This is not an absolute, however, as the storms can slide from California into Arizona and New Mexico and miss Colorado altogether. During winters with El Niño conditions, there is a tendency for the first half of fall to be a little more moist—evidence being the huge October storm during the El Niño event in 1997. The late fall and early winter can often be drier than average for Denver, the Front Range, and the eastern plains, so December through February can be moisture-challenged. Of course, there are few absolutes in weather, so the series of heavy winter snows over eastern Colorado in December 2006 and January 2007 did not follow that pattern of El Niño. By March and April, El Niño events more often than not help to fuel big soggy storms that can greatly boost snowpack and soil moisture for Summit County, the Front Range mountains and foothills, and

1986–1987:
Although not a major El Niño season, this marked the first time that El Niño researchers communicated to the American public the possible effects of the weather system.

1991–1992:
This El Niño episode was a controversial one in that some researchers argue that it actually lasted until 1995, while others saw it as two separate events in that five-year period. Australia was among the hardest-hit areas, with a severe multiyear drought.

1997–1998:
Now called the biggest of the century, this episode made the term El Niño a household word around the globe. Glantz calls this the "El Niño of the People." It challenged the notion that there could be only one particularly strong event each century.

La Niña Conditions

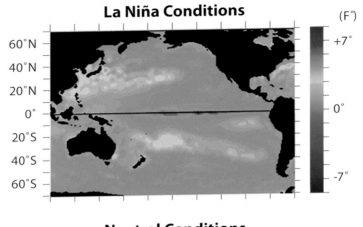

During a La Niña year, the temperature of ocean water decreases at the equator, as shown by the blue area in the illustration.

Neutral Conditions

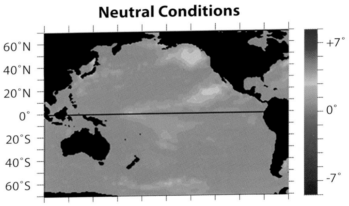

Neutral conditions are periods when sea surface temperatures are neither warmer nor colder than average.

El Niño Conditions

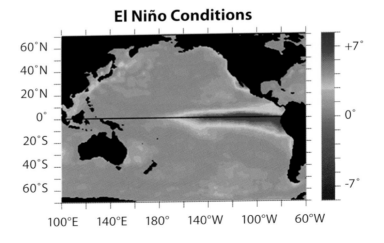

During an El Niño, the sea surface temperatures in the Pacific are unusually warm near the equator.

the eastern plains. In the mountains of central and southern Colorado, El Niño winters typically are good ones for skiers and snowboarders as the storms favor the Elk, West Elk, San Juan, and La Garita Ranges.

La Niña events tend to favor the northern mountains of Colorado with an abundance of snow. The storms that hit Washington and Oregon will spin down across Utah, often dropping good snow at Snowbird and Alta, and then glide into northwestern Colorado. Steamboat often enjoys a wonderful season during La Niña, but the rest of the high country, especially the San Juans, can often use more snow.

Along the Front Range, it is difficult to pin down just what ENSO will do to our weather. For the most part, the effects are more noticeable in the cold weather season as the jet stream winds play a greater role in our winter weather than in the summer. The summer season usually features light winds aloft over Colorado, so any effect El Niño or La Niña has on the jet stream is minor for our daily weather. There is some evidence that the late summer monsoon—the annual arrival of moisture flowing into Colorado from Mexico—is influenced by El Niño and is wetter when the Pacific sea temperatures are warmer.

The stronger connection is in the winter. La Niña winters tend to be dry and windy ones; indeed, 1999–2000 proved to be that way. El Niño winters can bring a few good storms; for instance, 1997 was an El Niño year, as was 2006, but for the most part, the eastern plains do not feel the biggest effects from the El Niño/La Niña phenomena. One possible impact is with Arctic cold fronts. During an El Niño event, the stronger jet stream blowing from west to east across the nation tends to block very cold air masses from moving south from Canada. So—and keep in mind, this is quite a generality—El Niño winters tend to be warmer over Colorado as a whole and wetter for the central and southwestern parts of the state. El Niño often means a wet spring for Denver and the eastern plains. La Niña winters can be colder, especially over the northern areas of the state, and usually will bring their heaviest snows to the mountains around Steamboat. La Niña winters tend to

There is some evidence that the late summer monsoon is influenced by El Niño and is wetter when the sea surface temperatures are warmer.

bring plenty of strong northwestly winds to Denver and the eastern plains, but not too much snow.

When there are near-normal ocean temperatures in the Pacific, other factors enter into the long-range forecast equation. These include temperature fluctuations in the northern Atlantic and surface pressure oscillations in the Arctic. Other factors include the amount of snowpack over the plains of northern and central Canada, southward into the northern Great Plains of the United States. All of these factors are important, but they tend to be much weaker indicators of the type of winter we will have—especially compared to strong indicators like El Niño or La Niña.

In Colorado, we may not always withstand the worst of El Niño, but we are at the forefront on research about the phenomena. Scientists from the Climate Diagnostic Center in Boulder do an excellent job of tracking and predicting what ENSO will do next. These forecasts are used not only in Colorado, but also around the world.

Clouds to Consider

"Welcome to Colorful Colorado," signs at our state's borders proclaim. Certainly the colors are varied and brilliant, from the golden aspen leaves to the cerulean blue of our skies to the gleaming white of our snow-capped peaks. Some of the most beautiful and colorful parts of Colorado are found in the clouds above.

Some of the most beautiful and colorful parts of Colorado are found in the clouds above.

Clouds in Colorado are not only very colorful and can be often tweaked, turned, and twisted into wild art forms by strong mountaintop winds, but also can be excellent tools for weather forecasting as they are usually a good indicator of the weather we can expect in the coming hours or days. Here are a few of the cloud basics for Colorado.

Cirrus clouds are high, thin clouds composed of ice crystals. Cirrus clouds are sometimes called "mares' tails," since the long, thin cloud filaments can resemble the curling tail of a horse. These clouds are often the first feathery forerunners of an approaching storm system.

Altostratus and altocumulus clouds are found at the middle levels of the lower atmosphere, about 3 to 5 miles above sea level. The altostratus clouds appear like thick cirrus clouds and may produce very light rain or snow. The altocumulus clouds are puffier in shape and are indicative of some turbulence or unstable air aloft. In the warm season, altocumulus clouds seen early in the day can be a sign that thunderstorms will occur in the afternoon.

Stratus clouds are low-level clouds found near the earth's surface, up to heights of about 5,000 feet. Stratus clouds bring a low, gray sky and sometimes steady rain or snow. Correctly referred to as "nimbostratus," stratus clouds are often only a few hundred feet thick. Denver and the eastern plains may be overcast, while the mountains are sunny above the clouds.

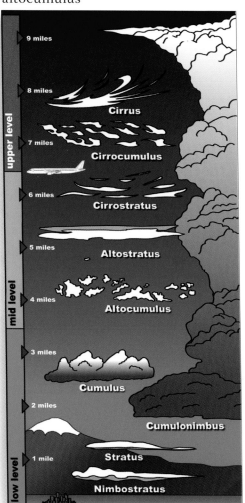

Cumulus clouds are the puffy white cotton-ball clouds that form when warm air near the ground rises and the moisture condenses. These clouds are most common during the warm season, when there is enough heating of the ground to create strong rising currents in the lower atmosphere. These clouds often have flat bottoms, marking the exact height at which the rising column of air has cooled enough for the moisture to condense. Cumulus clouds are rare at night, since the cooling atmosphere takes away the rising air and the clouds either dissipate or flatten out into a deck of stratus clouds.

Cumulonimbus, the thunderstorm clouds, often pile up 8 to 10 miles above the earth and are signs of extreme turbulence and instability in the atmosphere. Cumulonimbus clouds are nicknamed "CB" and usually bring very heavy rain, hail, and sometimes tornadoes.

A rapidly building "CB" or cumulonimbus cloud blossoms over Weld County.

Mammatus clouds are ominous-looking, bubble-shaped clouds associated with thunderstorms. These clouds look threatening, but do not cause tornadoes. They are good indications of extreme turbulence and very heavy thunderstorms. Mammatus clouds are especially photogenic at sunset, when the low angle of the sun casts an eerie red and orange glow upon the pendulous protrusions on the underside of a departing thunderstorm.

Lenticular clouds are the famous flying-saucer clouds that often grace the Colorado skies during the cold season. These twisted and sculpted mid-level clouds are created by the turbulent flow of strong upper-level winds as they bounce and blow over the rough mountain terrain. Like mammatus clouds, the lenticular clouds can be painted with some amazing colors as the late-day glow of the sun coats them in hues of orange, fiery red, and glorious gold.

Colorful Colorado

In addition to colorful clouds, our skies are graced by many other beautiful colors—not just the cobalt blue of a clear day, but also a variety of colorful phenomena that frequently show up throughout the year. The rainbow is a lovely and familiar guest in our skies, especially during the summer months. Rainbows are caused by the light rays from the sun passing through the water droplets of a passing storm. The sun must be at a low angle in the sky, so usually the storm has already passed by to the east and the late-day sun shines in from the west. The opposite can happen early in the morning and foretell an approaching storm—but early morning thunderstorms are rare in the Rocky Mountains.

A rainbow sighted near Nederland during a round of afternoon thunderstorms.

As the light shines through the water droplets, the light is bent or refracted, similar to when light travels through the glass in a prism. The light moves more slowly through the prism or the raindrop and is therefore spread out into the various colors that make up visible light (red, orange, yellow, green, blue, indigo, and violet, represented by the mnemonic acronym ROYGBIV). The light is refracted once as it enters the drop, then reflected off the back of the drop, and finally refracted again as it exits the drop. Secondary rainbows are often seen and are the result of the light being reflected again off the inside of the raindrop before it exits. The results of all of this optical bouncing around are the lovely rainbows that we enjoy.

Because the rainbow is such a dramatic and easy-to-see feature in our skies, it is not surprising that the ancients had many beliefs about them. Not all cultures felt the same about the rainbow. In Genesis 9:16, the rainbow signifies "a covenant between God and every living creature."

A rainbow near Barker Reservoir.

The ancient Greeks thought that the rainbow was "Iris," the messenger of the gods, who bore news of war and death. Many African and American tribes saw the rainbow as a giant and deadly serpent. The Shoshone people, for instance, thought that the rainbow was a snake that arched its back against the icy dome of the sky and brought forth the destructive hailstorms that are so common on the high plains.

Coronas

Another colorful display in our Colorado skies is called the corona, a ring of faint color that is sometimes seen at night around the moon when a few clouds are present. When the moon is close to full, ragged clouds drifting in front of it may produce a colorful display. The colors may take on a striking mother-of-pearl cast. On occasions when the clouds are uniform in thickness, the colors will form a ring around the moon, the corona, which comes from the Latin word meaning "crown."

The corona is caused by the diffraction of light as it moves around tiny water droplets in the cloud. It is important to note

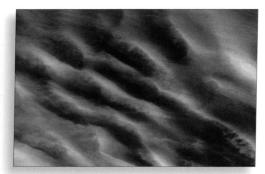

that under certain conditions, water can stay in a liquid state at temperatures well below freezing. This type of water is called "supercooled." To explain diffraction, think of light as a series of waves on a lake. Imagine some of the waves as they pass by a pole sticking out of the water. Each side of the pole would create a disturbance as the waves pass by. This disturbance would change the angle of some of the waves, and very soon the initial "straight" waves would be crashing into the waves that curled around the pole. In some places the crests of the two waves would pile up to form a larger wave; in other places a crest and a trough would cancel each other out. In physics this is known as constructive and destructive interference. The same thing happens as the light waves move around a supercooled water droplet. The constructive interference is seen as a bright light and the destructive interference as a darker light. Because the different wavelengths of light bend around the droplets differently, we see the various colors. The colors will change in a given sequence over and over, growing fainter as they extend farther from the source of the light—the moon.

(top) Water droplets in a cloud can diffract sunlight passing through and make for a beautiful sight. (bottom) Iridescence seen in the clouds near Fort Collins.

The sun can also create a corona, a common sight in our skies when high, thin clouds are moving through the area. On occasion, the colors will appear not in a ring around the sun but along the edges of the clouds. These clouds are called iridescent clouds and are a sight that often sends folks scrambling for their cameras. The constructive and destructive interference caused by the diffraction of light passing through tiny water droplets creates the iridescence. This phenomenon is quite similar to the bands of color seen on a puddle of water that has a touch of oil in it. The tiny droplets of oil diffract the light, causing the colorful bands and swirls.

The corona and iridescent clouds are beautiful sights, but they also can be somewhat useful. The presence of the super-cooled droplets indicates, of course, water in the atmosphere. That water can be associated with an approaching storm system. Our pioneering ancestors used these indicators to help them prepare for a change in the weather. Just as now, the prediction did not always pan out—sometimes the storm would develop somewhere, just not in that particular area.

The term halo is generic for all rings, arcs, and spots produced by the reflection and refraction of light by ice crystals in the atmosphere. There are two major types of ice crystal, the hexagonal (six-sided) plate and the hexagonal column, which account for almost all observed halos. They can create a variety of shapes—rings, arcs, and the like—because the tiny crystals are swirled around in different ways by the motions of the air.

(above) Ice crystals have many flat surfaces that act like tiny mirrors, which is why the pillar follows a vertical line. (below) Rings of light, or sundogs, form when light is refracted by ice crystals in high, thin clouds.

Sun Pillars and Sundogs

Reflection is a familiar concept to everyone as we see our reflection in a mirror or on the surface of a calm lake. When light hits a flat, smooth surface, it bounces off that surface at the same angle as it approached. Ice crystals of the hexagonal plate type behave like millions of tiny flat mirrors that reflect the image of the sun or moon. This can create a false sun or moon that can be seen to the side of the actual object. If the ice

Colorado skies afford an abundance of color. This sun circle was observed near Steamboat Springs.

crystal is shaped into six-sided columns instead of flat plates, they reflect the light differently as they tumble through the atmosphere and may create a column of light. We call this a sun pillar. Sometimes these pillars can be seen in the winter during extremely cold weather as tiny ice crystals float above streetlights and create a similar effect.

Refraction is a phenomenon that occurs when light penetrates the surface of a flat water or ice surface and the light rays bend slightly. This is because the light travels at a slightly different speed in air compared to liquid water or ice. Because the amount of bending that occurs depends upon the wavelength of the light (blue light is bent more strongly than red light), white light can be separated into its component colors. A prism is a familiar example of this and the hexagonal shape of ice crystals can act as tiny prisms. When ice crystals refract light, the light is bent from its original direction and fans out away from the light source to create an arc of light around the sun or the moon. Depending upon the density, size, and type of ice crystal (plates or columns), the arc may be a complete circle, a partial circle, or even two circles, one close to the sun and another farther outside.

Sundogs are created when some of the ice crystals become large enough to line up in the atmosphere to refract the light in a less random pattern. Instead the light is refracted to cause a mock sun to the left or right (or both) sides of the sun. These mock suns are scientifically called "parhelia." Sundogs are not as common as halos, but they can be seen a few dozen times a year, especially in the winter months. They can be forecasting tools, since the thin clouds of ice crystals are often associated with an approaching storm system.

Crepuscular and Anticrepuscular Rays

One of the most glorious sights in our skies are the beams of light that stream out from clouds as if they were sent from heaven. These light rays often take on a subtle beautiful golden color in the late afternoon sky as they fan out from between the clouds. The light beams are called crepuscular rays, yet another fascinating optical effect. The rays are visible because of dust in the air that reflects the light from the sun. The golden color is produced by late afternoon or early morning filtering of the incoming sunlight as it travels through more of the atmosphere (due to the low angle of the sun). The greater amount of atmosphere the light has to traverse, the more the shorter wavelengths are filtered out by the dust, leaving only the longer yellow, orange, and red light. The light rays seem to fan out from a central point, but it is really just an illusion—they are actually parallel. The best way to think of this is to

(top) A beautiful display of crepuscular rays seen from Erie. (above) Crepuscular rays are most common at sunrise and sunset.

envision a pair of railroad tracks. If you look way down the tracks into infinity, the tracks seem to converge in the distance. Of course they do not; they remain parallel, but to our eye it would appear that the tracks are fanning out from a point way in the distance. The same illusion is what creates the fanning out of the crepuscular rays.

Other phenomena that are seen on rare occasions are anticrepuscular rays. These take a little imagination to figure out. If the sun has already set from your vantage point (or has yet to rise), you may see beams of light and shadow seeming to come together along the opposite horizon (180 degrees from the sun). This is caused by the sunlight and shadows cast by clouds in front of the sun. At the cloud level (higher in the sky), the sun is still above the horizon. The light from the sun shines onto the clouds, casting parallel beams of light and shadow across the sky. In the distance behind you, those beams seem to converge just like the railroad tracks.

Meteors and Fireballs

Other colorful characters are the meteors that occasionally streak across our nighttime skies. These shooting stars can come in association with several annual meteor showers, or they may simply be pieces of cosmic sand that streak to a fiery end in our atmosphere. The meteor showers are periods of increased meteoric activity caused when the earth is moving through a particularly dusty part of space. The cosmic grit is a mix of ice, dust, sand, and gravel left by a passing comet or asteroid. As the earth spins through this celestial litter, the tiny grains burn through our atmosphere at speeds of 20,000 to 70,000 miles per hour and quickly flame out. Most of the meteors burn brightly for a second and are gone as the tiny space fragment is quickly consumed. Larger meteors the size of a golfball or baseball can burn for several seconds and may illuminate the sky as brightly as a lightning flash; these are called fireballs.

In general, most of these fireballs burn up quite high in the atmosphere, often 10 to 20 miles above the surface of the earth. The brilliant light is caused by the material vaporizing as it hits the atmosphere at high speed. The greenish colors that are often reported are actually the glow of ionized oxygen. Rarely, these fireballs are not sent by nature. On January 4, 2007, early morning commuters along the Front Range marveled at the bright arching trails left by dozens of "shooting stars." The cause of the light show was the lower stage of a Russian rocket motor burning up as it descended back to earth from a launch in late December.

Few of these objects ever actually reach the ground, even though it often appears that they have hit quite close by. It is not uncommon to have reports over half of Colorado or even several states, and each witness is quite certain the object must have hit nearby. Most of these meteors are small, only the size of a golfball or baseball when they hit our atmosphere, so that less than 1–2 percent of the mass, if any at all, typically survives to the ground.

Larger meteors can burn for several seconds and may illuminate the sky as brightly as a lightning flash.

45

Sunrise, Sunset

The sunrise and sunset times are about the only things in our atmosphere that are entirely predictable. Yet there are often questions about them, especially around the equinox periods in the spring and fall. Interested observers often ask why the sunrise and sunset are not exactly twelve hours apart on the exact day of the equinoxes. The answer is that because of the shape of the earth's orbit and its tilt on its axis, the sun's apparent motion through the heavens varies slightly through the year. In essence, the real sun runs up to twenty minutes fast or slow, depending on the season.

(below) The dramatic colors from this Centennial sunset only lasted a few minutes. (bottom) Beautiful red, pink, and orange sunrise from Bittersweet Park in Greeley.

The phenomenon of the "real" equinoxes—twelve hours of sunshine, twelve hours of darkness—preceding the actual beginning of spring and following in the fall is due to the index of refraction of the atmosphere. There is some effect that the atmosphere has on the apparent sunset and sunrise as the air tends to "bend" the

light rays slightly (something that would not happen without an atmosphere—on the moon, for instance).

The atmosphere bends sunlight over the horizon, making the sun appear to rise up to a couple of minutes before it has theoretically cleared the horizon. At sunset, the refractive effect causes the observed sunset to occur up to a couple of minutes later than theory would allow. This of course causes those days of twelve hours of sun and twelve hours of darkness to occur a few days before the equinox in spring and a few days after in fall.

Sunrise and sunset are the most predictable elements in the skies over Colorado, but with increasing research, technology, and a greater understanding about how our atmosphere works, we are making great progress in our ability to forecast the weather. Twenty years ago, a forecast was reasonably accurate for a day or two; now a forecast is much more precise. Now, meteorologists can predict three to four days out, with about the same degree of accuracy we had on a forty-eight-hour forecast just a few years ago. As advancements are made in how we observe and measure the weather, especially in places where observations are hard to come by, such as over the oceans, there may be a day in the future when the seven-day forecast will not just communicate a weather trend, but will be reliable enough to make definite plans.

(left) The sun setting over the Rocky Mountains as seen from Broomfield. (top) A lake can often add to the beauty of a Colorado sunset. This picture was taken at Lake Arbor in Arvada. (above) Beautiful start to the day at Addenbrook Park in Lakewood.

CHAPTER TWO

THE COLD SEASON

The image of Colorado that comes to mind for most includes snowcapped peaks, frosted evergreens, and skiers happily cruising down the slopes. Certainly this vision is what our tourist industry likes to project—and, fortunately, we do have a winter season that offers much more cold weather enjoyment than in many other parts of the country.

Our cold season extends far longer than most, thanks to the fact that Colorado is the state with the highest average elevation. The first hints of winter often appear at the same time many neighboring states are still sweating out the dog days of summer. By the beginning of September, the weather in Colorado starts the annual shift from a summer pattern to a mix of fall and winter. Just a week or two after Labor Day, something seems to be missing in our Colorado weather routine—the nearly daily round of afternoon summer thunderstorms! The shorter days and lower sun angle bring an end to the thunderstorm season, as the decrease in daytime heating prevents the strong convective lifting that helps afternoon storms to pop up. In

(top) Alpenglow on the Indian Peaks. (above) A snowboarder carving turns through fresh powder at Winter Park. (right) Gliding through "champagne powder" on a perfect day at Steamboat.

addition, the middle and upper levels of the atmosphere are comparatively warm after the long summer, so the air becomes relatively stable—cooler near the ground and warmer aloft. Although the official end of summer is not until the third week of September, for most in Colorado, the real psychological end of summer is marked by the Labor Day weekend. After Labor Day, weather thoughts turn away from thunder and lightning and start to center on the annual golden glow of the aspen and the fall of the first snow. Usually the gilded glory of the forest is accompanied by light, early snowfalls in the high country; one morning, usually just shortly after the start of football season, a thin veil of fresh snow will suddenly show up on the high peaks along the Continental Divide. Often it disappears by midday, but it marks the beginning of a new snow season for our mountains and serves to remind us that the warmth of summer is drawing to a close and that the cold season will soon be upon us.

Aspen Gold

For most Coloradoans, September truly is one of the best months of the year to be outdoors. The bright blue skies, cool nights, and warm, quiet days are perfect enough, but perhaps the best part of the month is the gold to be found in the mountains. As the days grow shorter in August and September, the decrease in sunlight turns off the mechanism in the leaves that creates

(top) Storm clouds roll over Poncha Pass. (bottom) An aspen grove along Highway 62 near Telluride.

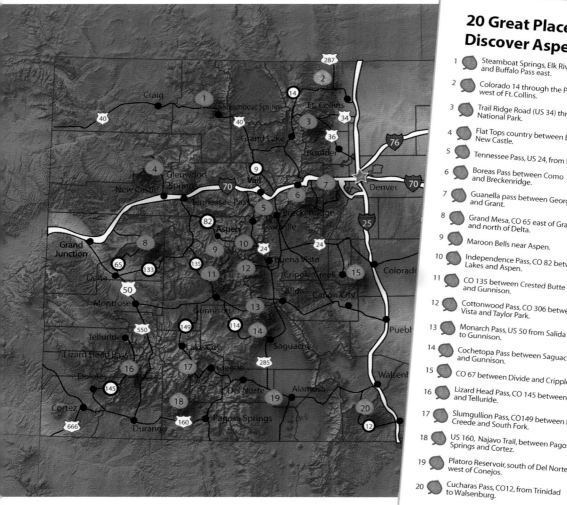

20 Great Places to Discover Aspen Gold

1 Steamboat Springs, Elk River country north and Buffalo Pass east.

2 Colorado 14 through the Poudre Canyon west of Ft. Collins.

3 Trail Ridge Road (US 34) through Rocky Mtn. National Park.

4 Flat Tops country between Buford and New Castle.

5 Tennessee Pass, US 24, from Leadville to Vail.

6 Boreas Pass between Como and Breckenridge.

7 Guanella pass between Georgetown and Grant.

8 Grand Mesa, CO 65 east of Grand Junction and north of Delta.

9 Maroon Bells near Aspen.

10 Independence Pass, CO 82 between Twin Lakes and Aspen.

11 CO 135 between Crested Butte and Gunnison.

12 Cottonwood Pass, CO 306 between Buena Vista and Taylor Park.

13 Monarch Pass, US 50 from Salida to Gunnison.

14 Cochetopa Pass between Saguache and Gunnison.

15 CO 67 between Divide and Cripple Creek.

16 Lizard Head Pass, CO 145 between Dolores and Telluride.

17 Slumgullion Pass, CO149 between Lake City, Creede and South Fork.

18 US 160, Najavo Trail, between Pagosa Springs and Cortez.

19 Platoro Reservoir, south of Del Norte and west of Conejos.

20 Cucharas Pass, CO12, from Trinidad to Walsenburg.

chlorophyll—the green color in the leaf. As the green fades, the gold color dominates until the dying leaf flutters to the ground. The best years for aspen viewing are those with consistent summer rains and no major fall storms. A very dry summer will send the leaves falling quickly, while a very wet summer tends to make them darken to brown or black. The best weather conditions for a brilliant display combine a mild late summer with periodic rain and a dry September free of big windstorms or early snows. The first signs of aspen gold begin to appear over the higher forests of northern and central Colorado as early as the last week of August. By the second and third week of September, many groves are worth a day's drive to see. The peak for aspen viewing is around the last weekend of September. After that, incoming autumn storm systems knock down many of the leaves, while others simply drop away by themselves.

Some folks from the East feel that the lack of variety in color makes Colorado's fall display second-rate, but there is something about that deep blue sky, the gold mixed with the evergreens, a touch of snow on the peaks, and a perfect autumn day that makes a trip to our mountains so special.

First Snow

The winter season does not follow a traditional calendar, often beginning well ahead of schedule compared to the rest of the country. In the mountains, snow may fall even in the summer. Some years A-Basin skiers have enjoyed fresh powder on the Fourth of July.

Along the Front Range, the first snow can often come as early as mid-September. Usually, these early storms are quick and quite light, but once in a while we get dumped on with a heavy, wet snow that takes our trees by surprise. On September 21, 1995, an intense low pressure system formed over the plains of eastern Colorado and dropped over 6 inches of wet, sloppy snow on Denver. The trees, still in leaf, suffered ter-

One of the first autumn snows covers the high country near Estes Park.

ribly, with many branches and limbs broken by the weight of the slush. Those branches crashed down through power lines and caused large-scale outages over the metro area. A similar early snow hit on October 10, 2005, with nearly a foot of snow on the southern and eastern parts of the Denver Metro area. The northern and western sides of town barely saw any snow, while over 2 feet fell across portions of central Adams,

7 Top September Snowfalls in Denver		
Date		**Amount**
September 26-28,	1936	16.5 inches
September 16-19,	1971	15.6 inches
September 21-22,	1895	11.4 inches
September 28-29,	1959	10.6 inches
September 28-29,	1985	8.7 inches
September 20-21,	1995	7.4 inches
September 25-26,	1908	6.5 inches

Arapahoe, and Elbert Counties. Ironically, that storm was the first snow of the season and ended up being the only heavy snowfall for the entire winter in Denver.

Once in a while, a very early snow will visit the Front Range cities. The earliest on record for Denver was September 3, 1961, when about 4 inches of snow fell over the western suburbs of the city.

The wonderful secret to our early snows is how fast the drifts usually disappear after the storm is over. Newscasts from around the nation may show us shoveling deep piles of snow well before Halloween. What the television viewer misses in other parts of the country is that we are not left snowbound for weeks by these big storms. Instead, the rest of the nation stops paying attention while the snow quickly melts. In just a couple of days, golfers and gardeners are back outside enjoying warm sunshine and deep blue skies.

Snowfall in Colorado, particularly at the lower elevations, disappears quickly thanks to our high and dry atmosphere. As soon as the storm is over, the skies generally clear and the intense high altitude sunshine takes over. The solar energy quickly begins to eat away at the snow, and the low humidity means that the moisture from that snow evaporates very fast.

In more humid parts of the country, such as the upper Midwest and the Northeast, storms are frequently followed by days of cloudy, damp, dreary weather, and the lack of sunshine and high humidity do not allow the drifts to diminish. It is rare in eastern Colorado to be left with those gray-black piles of snow and grit that cling to the streets and sidewalks in cities such as Chicago and Minneapolis.

First Frost

The average date for the first frost in Denver is October 7, while the average first measurable snow is October 19. In this case, frost means the first time the air temperature reaches 32 degrees. The terms frost and freeze are often used interchangeably in meteorology, but they have different meanings. A frost can occur with temperatures at or slightly above freezing and with light to calm wind, usually less than 5 mph. Frost forms when low-level moisture freezes onto surfaces, such as cars and rooftops. In this scenario, there is usually a surface inversion in place, meaning the air actually warms in temperature with increasing height. The 32-degree air is very shallow, sometimes as little as just a few hundred to a thousand feet above the surface. Generally, the temperature will be at or near the freezing mark for only a few hours. Many garden plants, even tomatoes, can withstand a light frost, but cautious gardeners are wise to cover those plants just in case.

During a freeze, or heavy frost, the temperature falls to freezing or below for several hours, and can be dangerous to unprotected plants. The cold air is usually deeper, meaning not trapped against the immediate surface as it is during an inversion. Winds can be as high as 10 mph or greater with frost observed. A hard freeze generally occurs when the temperature dips into the upper 20s and remains below freezing for several hours, ending the growing season.

Fall across Colorado can be a tough time for plants, with periods of warm followed by cold.

Average First Frost and Freeze Dates

Location	Elevation	Average First Frost (32° Temp)	Average First Freeze (28° Temp)
Akron	4,540	9/27	10/7
Alamosa	7,533	9/10	9/21
Aspen	7,913	9/4	9/21
Bailey	7,730	9/8	9/14
Colorado Springs	6,181	10/6	10/13
Craig	6,440	9/10	9/23
Crested Butte	8,851	8/17	9/4
Denver—Downtown	5,286	10/15	10/29
Dillon	9,800	8/10	8/27
Durango	6,554	9/21	10/4
Eagle	6,497	9/8	9/16
Fort Collins	5,004	9/28	10/9
Fraser	8,560	8/3	8/12
Gunnison	7,694	8/29	9/12
Idaho Springs	7,569	9/16	9/26
Leadville	10,177	8/27	9/14
Meeker	6,242	9/10	9/22
Mesa Verde NP	7,070	10/14	10/22
Monte Vista	7,665	9/11	9/22
Monument	7,400	9/22	10/2
Nederland	8,233	9/4	9/13
Pueblo	4,639	10/8	10/17
Salida	7,060	9/14	9/29
Steamboat Springs	6,770	8/23	9/9
Trinidad	6,030	10/7	10/18
Walsenburg	6,221	10/6	10/13
Winter Park	9,121	9/5	9/15

The First Major Storm

Most years stay frost- and snow-free in Denver and along the I-25 corridor through September, but October is a very different story. In October the first significant low pressure storm systems of the season start to form over Colorado. These storms bring easterly upslope winds along the Front Range and more times than not, provide for the first days for shovels and snowblowers along the I-25 corridor and over the eastern plains.

October 1997 was highlighted by one of the deadliest and most destructive snowstorms of the 1990s. A strong jet stream swept a low pressure system down from the Pacific Northwest on the twenty-third of the month. This low had produced strong winds and rain on the West Coast, but as it moved toward Colorado, two other factors began to come together. To the north, cold Canadian air was funneling down through the Dakotas. To the south, warm, moist air drifted northward from the Gulf of Mexico. As the low pressure system struggled over the mountains of Colorado, the low weakened and became disorganized crossing the rugged terrain. Moderate snows fell in the high country, but nothing exceptional. By the night of October 24, the low was beginning to leave the mountains and spin off over the eastern plains of Colorado. At the same time, chilly air from the north and the muggy southern air were closing in on Colorado, setting the stage for a major storm. By the next morning, all the ingredients came together to swirl up a huge storm system. As the storm spun up, very heavy snow began to fall over the Front Range and northeastern plains. To the southeast, a bone-chilling rain covered areas from Colorado Springs to the Oklahoma Panhandle. The low continued to deepen, the winds began to increase, and soon a full-blown high plains blizzard was in progress.

As the storm system continued to grow in size and strength, very cold air was pulled down from Wyoming. The snow

In October the first significant low pressure system provides the need for shovels and snowblowers along the I-25 corridor and over the eastern plains.

Denver's Consecutive Days With Snow Cover	
Days	Dates
63	November 26, 1983 —January 27, 1984
61	December 21, 2006 — February 19, 2007
60	December 1, 1913 —January 29, 1914
48	December 24, 1982 — February 9, 1983
43	December 19, 1973 — January 30, 1974
39	November 21, 1992 — December 29, 1992
38	December 24, 1987 — January 30, 1988
35	January 2, 1949 — February 5, 1949
33	December 17, 1918 — January 18, 1919
27	January 28, 1989 — February 23, 1989

continued to accumulate over northeastern Colorado, while rain changed to snow in the southeast. The result was a deadly combination for ranchers on the plains. Over the northern areas, farmers and ranchers had to contend with huge drifts and subzero wind chills. Across the southeastern plains, the rain wetted down most of the cattle, and the snow and sharply colder temperatures brought the threat of hypothermia. Tens of thousands of cattle died from the storm, the worst losses in many years for Colorado ranchers. Such a large loss of livestock was not seen again until the massive eastern plains blizzard in December 2006.

The low pressure center of the storm stalled over southwestern Kansas for nearly twenty-four hours before moving on across the central plains. The pedestrian pace of the system meant that eastern Colorado was under the influence of a deep upslope flow for a long time. The huge snow totals were the result of this pattern as heavy snow fell at a rate of 1 to 2 inches per hour and occasionally 3 inches per hour for nearly a day.

Along the Front Range, the snow piled up 2 to 3 feet deep, one of the worst blizzards in Denver since the infamous Christmas Eve storm of 1982. Streets and highways were impassable from the deep drifts. Denver International Airport (DIA) was closed down for many hours because crews could not get to the airport.

The Denver Broncos nearly missed their flight to Buffalo. The Broncos did manage to get out of Denver and win their game; ironically, the weather in Buffalo—famous for its big snowstorms—was sunny and mild. The huge storm finally moved out by the morning of October 26, with clearing skies, fresh snow, and low temperatures tumbling into the teens. Although sunshine followed, it took many days to melt all the deep drifts; snow boots and heavy coats went with many a trick-or-treater on Halloween.

Halloween Weather

It is interesting to note that Halloween in the minds of many is always snowy in Denver. A look at the data shows that our memories are playing tricks on us. According to the National Weather Service in Boulder, since the mid-1950s, snow has fallen on Halloween only a small percentage of the time. However, there have been many years in which snow has fallen just before Halloween—such as in 1997—or on November 1. Because Halloween is a memorable time and a holiday that requires parental attention to what the kids are wearing, we tend to remember those snowy, cold times and forget the nice, dry, and mild ones.

An autumn snow adds to the local Halloween decorations.

Halloween Weather in Denver

Year	high	low	precip	snowfall Oct 31	depth at 5pm	ave temp 5–8pm	snowfall Nov 1
2006	38	23	0	0	0	30	0
2005	55	31	0	0	0	45	0
2004	55	24	0.27	1.4	0	39	1.8
2003	30	23	0.07	0	0	28	0
2002	19	15	0.03	1.2	2	18	0.6
2001	71	37	0	0	0	54	0
2000	46	33	0.07	0	0	43	0
1999	77	31	0	0	0	59	0
1998	38	34	0.06	0	0	36	T
1997	59	38	T	0	0	41	0
1996	32	28	T	T	0	30	0.1
1995	45	27	0	0	0	35	0.9
1994	59	27	0	0	0	53	0
1993	65	27	0	0	1	46	0.5
1992	53	35	0.42	0	0	40	0
1991	32	10	0	0	3	24	2.3
1990	72	37	0	0	0	63	0
1989	59	24	0.24	3.4	0	36	1.1
1988	73	34	0	0	0	58	0
1987	62	47	0	0	0	54	0
1986	44	33	0.51	1.2	0	37	2.8
1985	59	36	0.38	0	0	39	0
1984	67	24	0	0	0	50	0
1983	71	41	T	0	0	58	0
1982	53	34	0.04	0	0	46	0
1981	53	36	0	0	0	46	0
1980	76	36	0	0	0	58	0
1979	40	23	0	0	T	32	T
1978	59	32	0	0	0	46	0
1977	56	28	0.39	3.3	0	34	0
1976	61	31	0	0	T	48	T

Year	high	low	precip	snowfall Oct 31	depth at 5pm	ave temp 5–8pm	snowfall Nov 1
1975	55	37	T	0	0	48	0
1974	56	28	0	0	0	45	0
1973	62	38	0	0	0	39	0.8
1972	30	15	0.53	8	2	28	5.8
1971	53	21	0	0	0	40	T
1970	54	24	0	0	T	34	T
1969	45	24	0	0	T	36	2.7
1968	63	37	0.23	0	0	44	0
1967	63	33	0	0	0	50	0
1966	48	26	0.16	1.4	0	32	0
1965	66	29	0	0	0	47	0
1964	66	35	0	0	0	46	0
1963	45	27	0.16	1.1	0	36	0
1962	71	31	0	0	0	41	0
1961	56	29	0	0	1	48	T
1960	61	34	0	0	0	53	0
1959	48	21	0	0	4	36	T
1958	52	28	0	0	0	37	0
1957	70	39	0	0	0	54	0
1956	65	32	0	0	0	56	4.7
1955	65	35	T	T	0	38	T
1954	58	24	0	0	0	26	0

Halloween Summary and Averages Number of years = 53	high	low	precip Oct 31	snowfall Oct 31	depth at 5pm	snow-fall Nov 1	average temp 5–8pm	10/31 & 11/1 Totals
Max value	77	47	0.53	8	4	5.8	63	
Min value	19	10	0	0	0	0	18	
Total Days Measurable			15	8	7	12		20
Total Days Trace Only			5	2	4	8		10
Average or Total	55.3	30.0	20	10	11	20	42.2	30
Percent			37.80	18.80	20.75	37.80		55.50

NOAA's National Weather Service

Indian Summer

Autumn is not just a waiting period for the inevitable onslaught of winter; it also features a delightful stretch of warm, sunny days known as Indian summer. This beautiful time is perhaps the nicest weather we experience during the whole year in Colorado. Brilliant blue skies, highs from 60 to 70 degrees, light winds—in other words, perfect weather. Indian summer does not have a formal definition, but is casually considered to be the warm, dry, quiet period of weather that follows the first killing frost. This weather pattern usually occurs during late September or the first two weeks of October. It is especially delightful because it often coincides with the peak of the aspen gold. There really is no meteorological significance to Indian summer—it does not foretell anything about the upcoming winter or reflect on the summer just past. Indian summer is simply a time to savor one's good fortune at living in Colorado.

The First Cold Wave

As autumn grows deeper into October, the first strong Canadian cold front will usher in the first frosty taste of winter. As the days begin to grow shorter in Colorado, they are really getting short in northern Canada. Sunlight drops down to just a few faint hours, and even that is with a dim glow, low on the horizon. Warmth quickly escapes from the atmosphere over the northern latitudes. As snow begins to pile up over northern Canada, the ground temperatures drop below freezing and then much colder. The chilly air becomes a dense, stable air mass that slowly grows over the flat tundra of northern Canada and Alaska. The growing weight of the air creates a high pressure area over the region. Anyone that has had a flat tire knows that air flows from high pressure (inside the tire) toward lower pressure (outside the tire). As the high builds in Canada, the pressure difference becomes large enough to cause the air mass to bulge southward toward the United States. The leading edge of this cold air mass is marked by the blue pointed lines on the weather map—the cold front.

As the front edges southward, the frigid facts about the impending cold begin to make headlines. "Low temperatures in North Dakota and Montana dipped below zero early today," a meteorologist might say at the beginning of the weather report. Although the average citizen may not be too thrilled about an approaching cold wave, most weather forecasters start to get quite excited about these events, since they mark a dramatic change after the long, often quiet early fall season.

Often, weather forecasters can see signs of the approaching arctic outbreak a week to even ten days ahead of time. By watching the position and intensity of a large high pressure system over Alaska and Siberia, meteorologists can have a pretty good handle on when the Polar Express is planning a visit. If you are not equipped with a full home version of the "24/7 Weather Center" or are not monitoring weather reports on TV and radio, you might not notice the subtle signs that the weather is about to turn a cold shoulder. Ahead of the front, the weather is often warm and sunny, with little indication of impending trouble. But watch the skies for signs of wispy cirrus clouds to the north. There won't be many, but a few may offer a clue. A home barometer will signal a change in the weather as it gradually falls ahead of the approaching front. Winds may shift from southwesterly and blow lightly from the southeast, but the signs are subtle.

The approach of a Canadian Cold Front is not well marked, but once the front goes by, the story is very different.

The approach of a Canadian cold front is not well marked. Once the cold front goes by, the story is very different. As the bitter cold air pours down across Wyoming and into Larimer and Weld Counties, the sky to the north darkens and billowy clouds gather. Those clouds are often not just full of moisture, but also of swirling dust from the dry plains of Wyoming and Montana. When the cold front roars down the Front Range, winds suddenly switch and howl in from the north, whipping up to 40 mph or more. Clouds rapidly lower, dust and tumbleweeds sweep by, and within an hour or so comes the snow.

This type of arctic cold front often races through Colorado in just three or four hours. Snow will fall for several hours after the front passes and may pile up to 4 to 6 inches in a hurry. After that, the skies clear and the temperatures tumble as the center of the cold high pressure area settles in for a couple of days.

The passage of a Polar Express front in the fall can bring some amazing temperatures drops in a very short time. In October 1992, eastern Colorado was basking in the warmth of 80-degree temperatures along the Front Range. A particularly potent push of polar air rocketed across the region, tumbling temperatures from a high in Denver of 90 degrees the previous afternoon to a snow-laden low of 17 degrees by the next morning. That bitter blast caused extensive tree damage on the eastern plains as the moisture inside the trees froze so quickly. Some cottonwoods literally exploded from the rapid expansion of the icy sap. Thousands of trees were killed or damaged by that early rush of arctic air.

Chinook Winds

Colorado's cold season weather is not about snow alone; often the main weather worry is wind. Wild westerly winds often rocket down the mountains and roar onto the plains. Gusts may exceed 100 mph in places such as Boulder, Golden, and Fort Collins. These warm, dry zephyrs are called chinook winds. They not only serve up great gusts, but they can also quickly pull us out of a deep freeze and put temperatures into the 50s and 60s in a matter of hours. As the winds blow over the mountaintops and down onto the plains, the descending air is warmed by compression. Think of how a bicycle pump gets hot when you are inflating a tire. The warmer air has the capacity to hold more water vapor—this means that the relative humidity in the air drops quickly as the air warms, sometimes down to a "desert dry" 10 percent. The very low humidity these winds bring can make fast work out of a pile of snow.

Colorado's Wild Winds

Colorado may be famous for its snow, but it is notorious for its wind.

Seasonally, hurricane force winds blow across the Front Range of the Rocky Mountains, and wind speeds approaching 150 mph—equivalent to a category 4 hurricane —have been measured at the National Center for Atmospheric Research in Boulder. These Rocky Mountain hurricanes are most likely to occur during the winter, during a time of year that can be defined as Colorado's wind season.

Colorado's wind season begins around the middle of November and goes through the middle of April, says wind expert Anthony Rockwood, during a time of year when severe thunderstorm weather is unlikely in Colorado. The westerly-flowing winds cross the Rocky Mountains and descend on the lee side, or eastern slope, of the Rockies. These downslope winds occur throughout the year, but tend to be stronger during the colder winter months, when cold fronts pass through the state.

Downsloping winds transport either warm or cold air into the Front Range foothills and the urban corridor. This difference defines the type of wind event as either Chinook or Bora. As air descends the leeward side of a mountain range it compresses, which causes the air to warm up and dry out. By definition, Chinook winds are warmer, while Boras are colder. The air associated with a Bora wind remains cold despite undergoing the same adiabatic compression as its Chinook sibling. Bora winds are most common during the fall and spring, and Chinook winds are more likely during the winter months. Boras occur after the passage of a strong cold front. Rapidly rising high pressure over western Colorado and low pressure along eastern Colorado provide the primary mechanism that drives the cold, blustery winds across the state. Boras therefore tend to affect a larger area than Chinooks and can spread well out onto the eastern plains.

Chinook and Bora winds are associated with strong westerly winds. The difference is in how the westerly winds are generated. Chinooks are more closely associated with strong jet stream winds aloft. Under the right conditions, these high-altitude winds flow up and over cold, stable air that is trapped west of the Continental Divide and cascade down the Front Range like water spilling over a dam. While the Chinook winds can blow over 100 mph, their impact tends to be limited to the Front Range and cities west of I-25.

City	Date	mph
Boulder*	25 Jan 1971	147
	11 Jan 1972	120
	22–24 Dec 1977	54hrs with gusts ≥ 65
	17 Jan 1982	137
	24 Sept 1986	131
	6 May 1988	110
	9 Dec 1992	120 (Winter Park ski area shut down)
	5 July 1993	92
	8 Mar 2000	101
	17 Feb 2003	100
Fort Collins**	24 Jan 1982	95
	2 Apr 1982	89
	19 Sept 1988	91
	14 Mar 1989	89
Other notable windstorms	25 Oct 1997	20,000-acre tree blowdown, Mt. Zirkel Wilderness, Routt County; Blizzard, Front Range & eastern plains

* Winds measured atop the NCAR Mesa Lab building located in Boulder on Table Mesa (except as noted)
** Winds measured at CSU Foothills Campus, three miles west of downtown Fort Collins
Courtesy Anthony Rockwood

Chinook winds are very common along the Front Range, especially in January and February, when strong jet stream winds aloft race over the state. The jet stream creates a great deal of momentum in the atmosphere as it blows over the mountains. In certain places, such as near Boulder, the winds are concentrated as they squeeze over and around the mountains and down onto the plains. A good analogy is to think about how strong the winds become in between downtown high-rise buildings—the Venturi effect. Chinook winds are quite powerful just to the east of the mountains in places where there is a dramatic change in elevation over a fairly short distance. For this reason, the chinook winds really hammer Boulder and areas along Highway 93 north of Golden. Some of the chinook wind events can create wind gusts in excess of 125 mph. The record gust recorded at the National Center for Atmospheric Research in Boulder is 147 mph in January 1971. Orientation to the foothills makes all the difference in the world when a downslope windstorm is in progress. Here in Denver, the wind speeds along and east of I-25 are 50 percent less than the speeds experienced in Boulder and Golden. This is because of the close proximity of the flat plains east of Boulder to the Continental Divide, which lies only 20 miles west as the crow flies. This rapid drop in elevation is such a steep slope that it allows the momentum from the high-altitude winds over the mountains to concentrate over Boulder and Golden, especially along Highway 93. Farther to the north and the south, the elevation change from the divide to the plains is more gradual, and the strong winds occur with less frequency.

> *Because of the close proximity to the Continental Divide and the rapid drop in elevation, high-altitude winds over the mountains concentrate on Boulder and Golden.*

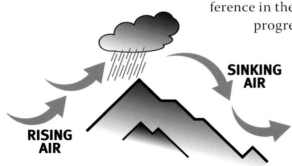

RISING AIR

SINKING AIR

Rising air cools and loses moisture as it blows over the mountains. The drier air warms up and gains momentum as it descends onto the plains.

Bora Winds

A second type of windstorm we can see along the Front Range is called a bora wind. Boras are cold winds, usually ones that come behind the passage of a strong cold front. They tend to be more abundant in the fall and spring, and to reach beyond the areas immediately adjacent to the foothills. Boras can affect a much larger area, though, and are often felt on the eastern plains. Bora winds are not usually as strong as chinooks, but still may bring gusts of 50 to 70 mph. Boras are typically dry, blowing from the northwest and arriving as a downsloping wind over northeastern Colorado. Any snow that is on the ground when the winds increase will be picked up and blown about, sometimes creating hazardous driving conditions and significant drifting—often with a cream-colored mix of dirt and snow.

The Jet Stream

The jet stream is a major weather maker for the central Rockies during the cold season. The strongest winds aloft form above areas where there is a large temperature gradient over a relatively short distance. This temperature contrast creates pressure differences that work their way high into the atmosphere. Such a temperature contrast occurs along a front, warm or cold. In the summer months, the main zone of temperature contrast is usually well north of the Canadian border, as the sun has warmed most of the northern hemisphere and pushed the boundary between the warm and cold air well north of the U.S.-Canadian border. In the fall and winter, the decrease in solar energy means cooling for the northern hemisphere, so the main boundary between warm and cold air sinks southward over the United States. In essence, think of that dividing line between the cold air and warm as something that annually migrates north and south, like the birds. As a result, the jet stream (officially known as the polar jet stream) tends to be

Rivers of Air

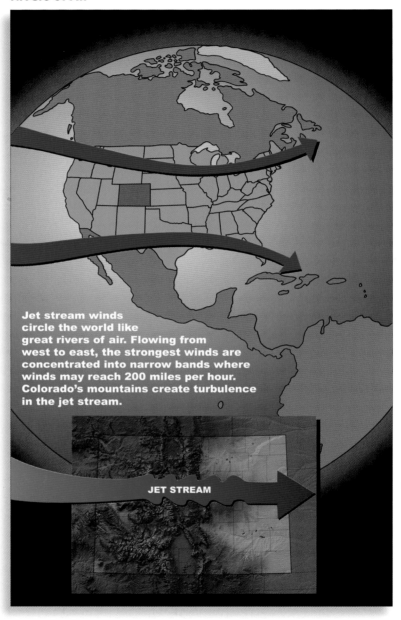

Jet stream winds circle the world like great rivers of air. Flowing from west to east, the strongest winds are concentrated into narrow bands where winds may reach 200 miles per hour. Colorado's mountains create turbulence in the jet stream.

JET STREAM

far to the north of Colorado in the summer, but drops back south and often over Colorado during the fall and winter. As the winds aloft increase over the Rockies, the potential for stronger storm systems and major fluctuations in temperature increase as well. Cold fronts start to roll down from the north with more vigor, and the result can often be gorgeous summery weather one day and several inches of snow the next.

The jet stream has a major effect on our weather as the powerful winds roar up, over, and around the mountains. The peaks may be well below the altitude of the strongest winds aloft—typically 25,000–30,000 feet—but the mountains create a tremendous amount of turbulence in the wind flow. A good way to visualize this is to look at the effect that rocks and boulders have on the water in a mountain stream. The water flow is disrupted and diverted over and around the rocky surface. In the mountain stream, the rough streambed causes a great deal of turbulence in the flow. In the atmosphere, the rough terrain of Colorado's mountains creates a great deal of turbulence in the wind flow over the state. This turbulence stirs up active weather, strong wind events, and often major storm systems.

Where the Storms Form

Because of the rugged terrain of the Rocky Mountains, Colorado serves as the birthplace for some of the most powerful winter storms that pummel the central and eastern United States with sleet, freezing rain, and heavy snow. Low pressure storm systems frequently develop just to the eastern (or lee) side of the Rockies. Strong winds aloft must squeeze over the mountain peaks and then blow over the plains. As the air moves out away from the mountains, the pressure falls, creating a low pressure area. If conditions are right, this low will begin to pull cold air down from the north and swirl moisture into the region from the Gulf of Mexico. The cold air and the moisture are whipped into clouds, rain, and snow, and before long, a storm is born. Such storm systems first dump heavy snow over eastern

Colorado and then churn to the northeast. Heavy wet snow, sleet, freezing rain, and even thunderstorms mark the path of these storms as they roll on toward the Mississippi River and the Great Lakes. The storm systems can form over Wyoming and New Mexico as well, but Colorado is centrally located to serve as the staging ground for both the chilly northern air and the muggy air from the south. In addition, the mountains of Colorado are higher and the transition to the flat plains is more abrupt than in neighboring states, which creates more turbulence in the wind flow.

The soggy storm systems that spin out of eastern Colorado can give a false impression to the rest of the nation. Often, those eastern plains storms dump heavy snow on Denver, Colorado Springs, Limon, and other cities on the plains while leaving the mountains with a much smaller accumulation. Television weather reports around the country show all the snow in Denver, leading viewers in other parts of the nation to think, "If Denver has a foot of snow, the mountains must really have been clobbered!" In fact, the moisture from eastern plains storms tends to be blocked off by the mountains, while the areas along and east of I-25 get snow. This was the case on the night of Monday, October 15, 1984, when the Broncos and the Green Bay Packers played in a blizzard at Mile High Stadium. The national TV audience saw all that heavy snow in Denver and promptly flooded the ski resorts with calls for reservations. Being good businesspeople, the ski resort staff probably did not make mention of the fact the skies were mostly clear at the time in Vail and Aspen.

Pacific Fronts and Southeastern Lows

There is an old saying about Colorado weather that is very helpful when trying to figure out if a storm system will bring heavy snow: "Pacific front, mountains bear the brunt; southeastern low, Denver gets the snow." The storm systems on the eastern plains spin their heavy snow over the Front Range and adjacent plains but may miss the mountains. In contrast, a moist storm from the Pacific Coast may dump very heavy snow on the mountains but have little moisture remaining by the time the storm finally slips down into Denver. The Pacific fronts have a tough time traversing the Cascades and Sierra Nevada mountains, then struggle to cross the Wasatch Range in Utah and finally stagger over the Continental Divide. When the once-potent storm finally tops the last of three or four mountain ranges, there often is not even enough moisture left to bring a flake of snow to Denver.

These depleted mountain storms can often regenerate once they get east of Colorado. As the weakened low pressure area wanders out into Kansas, the counterclockwise circulation slowly begins to pull moisture back into the storm from the southern plains and the Gulf of Mexico. As the storm system feeds on that humidity, it will again intensify and begin to bring rain, freezing rain, sleet, and snow to Nebraska, Kansas, and the Mississippi Valley. Eventually, this same storm can turn into a real winter monster for the Ohio Valley, the Appalachian mountains, and New England. Thus, a big storm can spin in from the Pacific, dumping heavy snow over the Cascades, the Sierras, the Wasatch Range, and the mountains of Colorado. That same storm is pretty well out of gas when it moves over Denver and the eastern plains but then is refueled in Kansas and hammers the rest of the country. In essence, everybody gets snow—except Denver.

"Pacific front, mountains bear the brunt; southeastern low, Denver gets the snow." Alberta Clipper storms generally bring wind but little snow to Colorado.

Bitter Cold

Snow is certainly not the only thing that falls in Colorado during the winter; our temperatures can certainly take a tumble, too. The coldest reading on record for Colorado is -61 degrees at Maybell on February 2, 1985. According to Nolan Doesken, the state climatologist, there are some unofficial reports of readings as low as -70 from some of the ranches around Taylor

Everybody talks about the weather, but nobody does anything about it.
Charles D. Warner 1897

Skiing is big business: annually, more than ten million skiers and snow boarders make the trek to Colorado's ski resorts, spending millions of dollars that mountain communities have come to depend on. A lack of snow can be disastrous, so rather than relying on the whim of weather, ski resorts rely on technology to make the snow they need. Even when Mother Nature is generous with natural snow, resorts are better able to control the quality of the snow by making it. By supplementing natural snow, Colorado's resort managers are able to lengthen the ski season, create better skiing conditions for their customers, and add an element of predictability to an otherwise finicky force of nature—the weather.

Making snow is not unique to Colorado. Winter enthusiasts can ski and snowboard year round, even during the summer, and yes, even indoors. Snowmaking technology makes it possible to turn spring, summer, and fall into winter, and many business ventures are capitalizing on the public's desire to hit the slopes in the most unlikely places. Vacationing in Dubai, United Arab Emirates? Bring your snowboard. Two indoor ski resorts are located in this desert oasis, and whether you are in Dubai or Shanghai, or even England, Germany, or Spain you can hit the slopes year-round in the great indoors thanks to snowmaking technology.

Snowmakers are able to create artificial snow that is no different than its naturally forming sibling by mimicking Mother Nature. Clouds and precipitation form when water vapor in the atmosphere cools and condenses into water droplets or ice crystals. Initially, these droplets and crystals form clouds, and then eventually precipitation as the droplets and crystals grow to be too heavy for the atmosphere to support. This process is facilitated by condensation nuclei—tiny particles in the air that provide a surface for water vapor to condense. These condensation nuclei are the center of the water droplet or ice crystal. As droplets and crystals move through the cloud, surrounding water droplets and ice crystals condense onto them and eventually the droplets and crystals grow large enough to fall as precipitation. Whether it rains or snows depends on the ambient air temperature. Snowmakers mechanically reproduce this process by combining water and condensation nuclei, such as protein or bacteria, and then forcing the mixture through snow guns. The snow guns atomize the water into a fine mist, and the condensation nuclei provide a surface for the water to condense into ice crystals—in other words, snow.

Just as naturally occurring snow is dependent on surrounding weather conditions, so is artificial snow. Snowmakers need to consider whether the weather will support snow making operations. If the ambient air temperature is too warm, then water droplets will form rather than ice crystals. If the relative humidity is too high, then it may be too difficult to make snow because water cools more slowly when the humidity is high. Rain, and not snow, may be the result. The cold, dry conditions in Colorado's mountains during the winter can be ideal for making snow. Colorado snowmakers can make snow when the air temperature is several degrees above freezing—if the relative humidity is low. They can also determine whether the snow is dry or wet by controlling the amount of water they use to make snow. Snowmakers use less water when they want to make dry, powdery snow for ideal skiing conditions, and they use more water to make heavier, wet snow for developing and maintaining the snow base on a ski slope.

We may not be able to control the weather, but without elaborate ceremony or sacrifice we can at least appease the snow gods enough to make Colorado's legendary snow just a bit better for the annual winter pilgrimage.

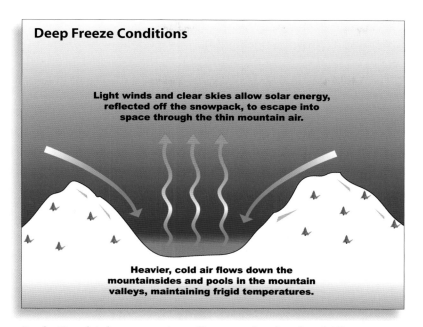

Deep Freeze Conditions

Light winds and clear skies allow solar energy, reflected off the snowpack, to escape into space through the thin mountain air.

Heavier, cold air flows down the mountainsides and pools in the mountain valleys, maintaining frigid temperatures.

Park. Our high mountain valleys tend to be the chilly spots as the thin mountain air allows the heat of the day to rapidly escape into space after sunset. This is called radiational cooling, since the heat radiates from the ground into the atmosphere. The cold, dense air then begins to pool in the valley, leaving the mountainsides a bit milder. Gunnison, Alamosa, Taylor Park, Fairplay, and Fraser all plummet to readings of -40 to -50 at times during January and February. This air is very stable and can sometimes get stuck for days in the valleys. Just a few hundred feet above the cold, heavy surface air, the temperatures are warmer, sometimes by 20 to 30 degrees. This condition is called an inversion, since it is the inverse of the normal condition in the atmosphere where temperatures get cooler with height. The best combination for extreme cold is a deep snowpack, clear skies, and light winds. The broad mountain valleys, such as the Gunnison, North Park, Middle Park, South Park, and San Luis, are the best kind of places for the really cold temperatures to occur. In sharper, narrow valleys, there tends to be more turbulence in the wind flow and the strong inversions are less likely to form.

The eastern plains can get their share of bitter air in the weeks around and following the holidays. The record low for Denver is -29, set on January 9, 1875. January takes the prize as the month with the greatest number of days in Denver with a temperature of -20 or lower. That icy threshold has been reached fourteen times since 1870. In February, the temperature has tumbled to -20 nine times, and December has featured that frigid figure on a half dozen icy mornings. Many of these marks were made in the nineteenth century, though, and we have had very few truly bitter cold waves in recent years. The last time the temperature fell that low was in December 1990.

Brown Cloud

One of the least attractive but still important aspects of cold season weather is the infamous "brown cloud." This unwelcome guest is a result of temperature inversions and population growth along the Front Range. Trains, planes, and automobiles, along with industry and wood-burning fireplaces, result in trillions of tiny particles being released into the air. These microscopic bits of air pollution swirl daily around the Front Range throughout the year, but under certain cold weather conditions, they are trapped over the metro area and build up over a period of days. The worst-case scenario for the brown

Poor air quality in the winter produces a brown cloud over Denver. Smoke and steam rising into the stagnant air from a power plant can be seen.

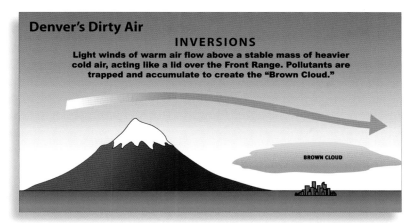

Denver's Dirty Air

INVERSIONS

Light winds of warm air flow above a stable mass of heavier cold air, acting like a lid over the Front Range. Pollutants are trapped and accumulate to create the "Brown Cloud."

BROWN CLOUD

Warm air aloft traps cold air near the ground. The stagnate air gradually becomes more polluted.

cloud is a combination of warm temperatures aloft with cold temperatures and light winds at the surface—an inversion. Under these circumstances, the cold air at ground level is heavy and stable, minimizing mixing of the air. The light winds mean little change will occur in the overall pattern if no major weather fronts are on the way. Day after day the air fills with more and more pollution, and the cloud grows thicker. The brown cloud is a cold season phenomenon because the sun is low in the sky and does not effectively heat the ground enough to create mixing of the low-level atmosphere. In the summer months, strong daytime heating helps create plenty of up and down motions in the atmosphere that help swirl in fresher air. In addition, the frequent summer showers help to wash out the particles of pollution. So much for clean rainwater.

The brown cloud is nothing new, for Native Americans told the early pioneers of a brown-colored cloud that developed from their campfires during the cold season. In addition, there are times when the brown cloud can develop even with very strong winds over the mountains. In this case, the winds roar over the mountain peaks, blow high above Denver, and then drop down east of the metro area. Limon, Fort Morgan, and Akron may have very strong westerly winds, while Denver and vicinity are caught in a light easterly "backwash" of air and remain with a sluggish brown cloud pattern, while every other town on the eastern plains has cleaner air but people holding onto their hats.

Big Contrasts

Thanks to the mountains, some weather patterns can leave Colorado with a very wide range of conditions all at the same time. Strong jet stream winds may slam into the mountains, bringing strong winds and snows to the high country. Those same winds are forced up and over the peaks and then blow down toward Denver as warm, dry chinooks. Boulder and the Fort Collins area batten down for the strong blasts of wind, but then the air currents bounce off the surface and back up higher in the skies over Denver. Thus the cities of Denver and Aurora are left with light winds and bad air. Meanwhile, the air currents return again to the surface east of Denver and bring gusty conditions to the eastern plains, under mostly cloudless but dust-laden skies. Thus snowing, blowing, bad air, clear skies, and a dust storm can all come from just one weather feature, all thanks to the topography of Colorado.

Flying Saucer Clouds

(below) Lenticular clouds during the late afternoon at Russell Gulch. (below, right) Looking up at lenticular clouds at sunset in Fort Collins.

There are some amazing cloud formations that are a frequent sight in our fall and winter skies. Strong winds blowing over the mountains can create lenticular, or flying saucer clouds. These clouds occur at the mid-levels of the troposphere (about 20,000 feet above sea level). The best way to understand how

lenticular clouds are formed is to think again of the water flowing in a mountain stream. The current swirls into eddies and standing waves just downstream from the rocks. These features may stay in more or less the same location for an extended period of time. In the atmosphere, the air is pushed up over and around the mountains. The wind currents respond by forming eddies and standing waves in the atmosphere on the lee side of the mountains. Moisture in the air condenses to form the mid-level clouds that are carved and twisted into a tapered shape like that of a lens or a saucer. These clouds are especially beautiful in the evening and early morning, when the low angle of the sun casts a haunting gold and reddish hue to them.

Lenticular clouds at sunset over the Twin Sisters near Estes Park.

The official meteorological name for flying saucer clouds is "altocumulus standing lenticularus." This meteorological mouthful is shortened by weather forecasters to just "ACSL." Lenticular clouds are a good indicator of a developing chinook wind event along and east of the mountains. Since they are created by strong westerly winds aloft, it follows that some of the momentum from on high will sweep down the eastern flanks of the Rockies and blow into chinook-prone places, especially Boulder and northern Jefferson Counties. Because the chinook is driven by strong winds aloft, some meteorologists like to call this weather pattern "a shove from above." The appearance of lenticular clouds can also be an indicator of an approaching snowstorm. The jet stream winds that first create the ACSL clouds can then aid in the development of a strong low pressure system over Colorado. So remember, when you see those flying saucer clouds, be ready for some changes in the weather—first strong winds and warming and then maybe snow.

Rotor Clouds

Another result of strong winds along the Front Range can be rotor clouds, which are just what their name implies—rotating clouds, but not tornadoes. While a tornado rotates on a vertical axis, a rotor cloud spins on a horizontal axis, like a pencil

Lenticular vs. Rotor Clouds

Strong winds blowing over the mountains can create a variety of cloud formations due to turbulence. Lenticular clouds form eerie shapes east of the mountains of Colorado, sometimes looking like flying saucers. Rotor clouds (right) are less common, but are indications of extreme low level turbulence that can be very hazardous to aircraft.

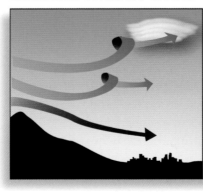 

A true "flying saucer" lenticular cloud along Highway 93 northwest of Denver.

rolling off a desk. Once again, go back to the analogy of the mountain stream. In certain areas, the water in the stream may develop into a standing rapid that has the water swirling over and over on itself. If you have been whitewater rafting, this is one thing the guides warn you about. In the atmosphere, the winds descend from the mountaintops and may develop into a swirling band about halfway down from the top. Any moisture in this swirl of air will form into a cloud that rolls over and over, while staying at about the same location on the mountainside. Rotor clouds are of special concern to pilots since the descending air currents can trap a helicopter or airplane into a deadly fall, even at full power. Wintertime pilots are especially wary of rotors, and they watch lenticulars very carefully, because the same conditions that create them can create rotor clouds. There is evidence that a United Airlines 737 crashed in Colorado Springs in March 1991 after being caught in a rotor wind circulation. Despite the immense power of jet engines, the aircraft could not escape the rapidly descending air currents.

Avalanches

One of the most dramatic winter sights in Colorado is the avalanche. Heavy mountain storms may pile 2 or 3 feet of snow on the peaks in just a matter of a day or two. This snow surface may become very unstable for a variety of reasons. The sheer weight of the fresh snow may cause numerous slides in the first few hours after a major storm. This is especially true on slopes of greater than 30 degrees. In addition, strong winds that often accompany a snowstorm pack the snow into drifts and cornices that can suddenly break free and race downhill. As a snowslide thunders down, it gains momentum and volume and can become hundreds of feet wide. Look carefully at mountain forest patterns and you will see the effects of

On average, about 2,300 avalanches are reported to the Colorado Avalanche Information Center each year. It is estimated that up to ten times that number occur but go unreported.

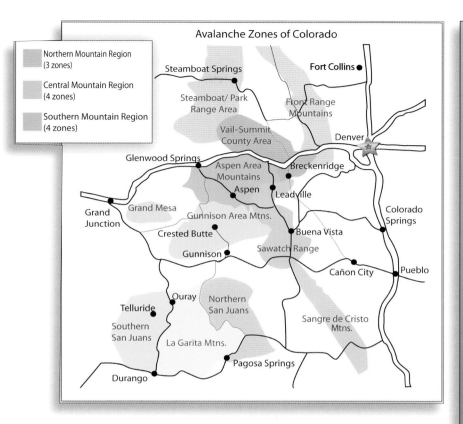

Avalanche Zones of Colorado

Northern Mountain Region (3 zones)

Central Mountain Region (4 zones)

Southern Mountain Region (4 zones)

Steamboat Springs

Fort Collins

Steamboat/ Park Range Area

Front Range Mountains

Vail-Summit County Area

Denver

Glenwood Springs

Aspen Area Mountains

Breckenridge

Aspen

Leadville

Grand Junction

Grand Mesa

Gunnison Area Mtns.

Colorado Springs

Crested Butte

Buena Vista

Gunnison

Sawatch Range

Cañon City

Pueblo

Ouray

Northern San Juans

Telluride

Southern San Juans

La Garita Mtns.

Sangre de Cristo Mtns.

Pagosa Springs

Durango

Avalanche Information

Avalanche forecasts are issued at 5 p.m. daily between November and May and are valid for twenty-four hours.

Every morning, the CAIC updates recorded phone messages throughout Colorado.

The Summit County and Buena Vista phone lines are updated Monday, Wednesday, Friday, and Saturday by forecasters in the CAIC Summit County office. Those numbers are:

Denver/Boulder
303-275-5360

Fort Collins
970-482-0457

Colorado Springs
719-520-0020

Summit County
970-668-0600

Buena Vista
719-395-4994

Durango
970-247-8187

Visit the Colorado Avalanche Information Center's website at http://avalanche.state.co.us/ to learn more.

snowslides as they can quickly clear thousands of trees from the mountainside. In fact, the Loveland Ski Area got a brand new expert run a few years ago as a slide roared right into the parking lot. It took out a few cars and some heavy equipment, but it also cleared the trees for a new run. The massive March storm in 2003 dropped 5 to 7 feet of snow just east of the continental divide in Clear Creek and Gilpin Counties. The heavy, wet snow caused several avalanches that kept I-70 closed for several days near Silver Plume. It had been many decades since such a heavy volume of snow had fallen in that area, and many of the forests around Georgetown and Silver Plume had matured without experiencing an avalanche. The snowslides that roared down over the interstate were choked with large trees that had been ripped from the roots by the power of the avalanche. Look carefully along I-70 just above Silver Plume and you can still see the paths of these slides, marked by the lack of trees.

Avalanches are one of biggest threats to outdoor sports during the winter season. Every year backcountry skiers are trapped in snowslides, and every year there are fatalities. The series of heavy storms in January 2007 resulted in a huge avalanche on Berthoud Pass that closed Highway 40 and engulfed half a dozen vehicles. The Colorado Department of Transportation (CDOT) works extremely hard during the winter months to ensure that the major mountain roadways remain safe for travel, but despite their best efforts, nature can still get the upper hand. Our highways are frequently closed by heavy snow and avalanche threats. CDOT workers use a combination of plows, snow throwers, and explosives to help bring down and clear away the threat of major snowslides. The explosives can be shot at a suspicious slab of snow using a howitzer or dropped from a helicopter. At the ski resorts, ski patrol members will carefully trek close to a worrisome snowfield and toss a small dynamite charge onto the snow. The resultant explosion cracks the weak bonds in the snow and produces a smaller avalanche in a more or less controlled fashion. Setting off numerous small slides along our mountain roads or at the ski resorts is much more desirable than waiting for a massive, destructive, and perhaps deadly avalanche to occur.

Snowslide on Star Mountain on the east side of Independence Pass. Total run of moving snow was about 1 mile with a vertical fall of 3,000 feet.

(top) "CDOT avalauncher" uses compressed nitrogen to fire an explosive projectile. It can fire a 2-pound explosive charge up to a mile.
(bottom) The "Battleship" avalanche chute along Highway 550 on the south side of Red Mountain Pass. Avalanche zone is about 1 mile long with a vertical fall of about 4,000 feet.

The snow that an avalanche packs can have the weight and consistency of wet cement. A skier caught under even a foot of snow may not be able to move at all. This is especially true of the so called "slab" avalanches that occur when old compacted snow breaks off in large chunks or slabs and comes crashing down the mountainside. Skiing in the backcountry can be a beautiful, serene experience, but it can also be a deadly one for those unfamiliar with avalanche-prone areas and avalanche safety. Be sure you know what you are doing before risking your life or those who may have to rescue you.

If you are planning to play in the backcountry, it is strongly recommended that you first become a member of the Friends of the Colorado Avalanche Information Center (CAIC). This group of highly skilled forecasters does an excellent job of predicting and warning of avalanche conditions. The CAIC has a terrific website and offers seminars to teach people about how to recognize avalanche danger, as well as proper backcountry equipment and safety tips.

Blizzards

The only kind of avalanche in Denver is found in the hockey arena, but we still can get plenty of snowy excitement from the good old high plains blizzards. The true definition of a blizzard has more to do with wind and visibility than snow. Winds of 35 mph or higher are accompanied by falling or blowing snow that drops visibility to a quarter-mile or less. The sky above can be clear, but blowing snow at ground level can produce blizzard conditions. A severe blizzard is a really bad time: winds over 50 mph, with visibility near zero due to blowing or falling snow. Certainly the pioneers of 150 years ago saw some very scary winter storms; in fact, the term blizzard comes from the German word blitzen, or "lightning." The lightning-fast changes in the weather caught many an unfortunate covered wagon in the days of old, but even today strong winter storms can bring peril to travelers. The wide-open eastern plains of Colorado offer no resistance to the wind and can allow howling storms to swirl snow into drifts 5 to 10 feet high during the worst blizzards. The big storm of October 1997 and the one-two punch storms of December 2006 brought much of eastern Colorado to a standstill for several days.

The December blizzards of 2006 brought much of eastern Colorado to a standstill—during one of the biggest travel times of the year.

(left) Planes stuck at DIA at the height of the holiday travel season during December 2006 storm. (below) Stranded motorists on I-70 near Watkins during December 2006 storm.

Blizzards on the high plains are major worries for ranchers as they suffer terrible losses from cattle being frozen to death or weakened by the combination of wind and heavy snow. Even Denver's "weatherproof" airport has a rough time with heavy snow and wind; the airport runways and taxiways are hard enough to keep open, but the roads to DIA can be slammed shut by heavy snow and multiple accidents. If the pilots and crews cannot get to the planes, it does not matter if the runways are operational.

If you drive along the road to DIA or many other highways in open country, you may notice the long lines of fences lining Peña Boulevard. These large wooden structures are "snow fences" that help to keep the roads free of blowing and drifting snow. The snow fence works by causing the wind to blow up and over the wooden structure. When this happens, the speed of the wind drops slightly. This reduces the amounts of snow that can be carried by the wind and allows the snow to fall out of the air and pile up near the snow fence. Careful placement of these fences keeps the big drifts off the roads— or so we hope.

Late Winter Storms

The cold weather season in Colorado is a long one. The calendar might say March, but in Colorado, spring could not care less. While other parts of the country are shaking off the winter doldrums, being in the month of March means little to the atmosphere over Colorado. Other states to the south and east are enjoying the first green shoots of the leaves and the yellow flowers of the daffodil, but Colorado still has weeks of winter weather to contend with.

The biggest snowstorms of the year frequently occur around the beginning of spring. In fact, the all-time twenty-four-hour snowfall record for the state was 76 inches on April 14–15, 1921, at Silver Lake, in Boulder County. This record was the North American mark until just a few years ago, when a town in New York State beat the total by about an inch. The storms of spring are such serious snowmakers because of the increasing moisture that feeds into our state in March and April. As the temperatures warm over the southern states, moist air from the Gulf of Mexico begins to head north with more vigor. The severe weather season gets off to a thunderous start over Texas and Oklahoma, but in Colorado, thanks to the combination of higher latitude and altitude, our temperatures are still chilly. Thus, moist air from the south clashes with the clinging cold over Colorado and serves to create big storm systems.

Several factors combine to produce powerful storms: warmth from the south, lingering cold to the north, and strong jet stream winds from the west. Major spring storms can draw power from all three of these as they come together over Colorado. The jet stream remains quite powerful over the central part of the nation in the late winter and early spring. As earlier stated, the jet stream tends to be the most intense over places where the surface temperatures have large fluctuations over small areas. With the building warmth from the south meeting the stubborn cold over the northern plains, the winds aloft can get revved up to speeds of 150 miles per hour or more. As these winds blast across the country, the turbulence they

The National Ice Core Lab

Climate change, forgive the pun, is a hot topic, and Colorado is playing a role in helping scientists decipher Earth's climatic history. The National Ice Core Laboratory (NICL), located in Lakewood, is a library housing ancient ice, preserving more than 15,000 meters (more than ten miles) of ice cores in a storage room kept at -33° F. Todd Hinkley is the laboratory manager.

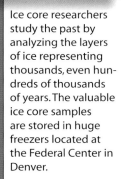

Q: Why study ice cores?
A: Ice cores are the only continuous reliable record we have of what the earth's atmosphere used to be like. Bubbles in the ice, which are descendents of the air spaces in the snow, hold old-time air. No matter how deeply the layer of snow is buried, it turns into ice. Even if it is up to a million years old, we can get that old-time air out and analyze it, telling us what the atmosphere was like back in those days. The reason we are interested in the composition of the atmosphere of the past, including greenhouse gases, and in the earth's old-time climate in general, is that we think that what the earth did, what the earth was like, must have something to do with what it will be like in the future.

Ice core researchers study the past by analyzing the layers of ice representing thousands, even hundreds of thousands of years. The valuable ice core samples are stored in huge freezers located at the Federal Center in Denver.

Q: Please describe the process of collecting an ice core sample.
A: The samples come from the present-day ice shields in Greenland and Antarctica, and from mountain valley glaciers in more temperate latitudes. We're looking for ice that is the least "scrambled" for good samples, which means we are looking for well-layered samples. Each layer equals one year, which can go up to one million years. In Greenland you can get a good record for 100,000 years. Otherwise, the bottom ice gets too beat up. In Antarctica in the last couple of years we've discovered that you can go to a million years, though most ice cores date to around 400,000 years ago.

Q: Are there any surprises in the research?
A: The most surprising discovery is how rapidly the climate can change, even within a couple of years. Earth's climate is tremendously unstable. One possible explanation is that huge sheets of ice during those unstable periods just got so thick that they broke off huge icebergs, releasing large flotillas of icebergs that disrupted the ocean current circulation. The Little Ice Age is the most recent event.

Q: How important is the information that researchers are gathering from the ice?
A: Ice cores are one of the most important tools used in painting a picture of past climates. We now know the various concentrations of greenhouse gases in previous climates. Our oldest ice core is 400,000 years old. It's from Vostok, the Russian site in Antarctica. They drilled into an underground lake, which sparked an interest from the science community about the possible existence of bacteria. If that's the case, then it raises questions about possible similarities with other planets.

create helps to foster developing storm systems. These storms have it all—strong winds aloft, moisture and heat from the south, and plenty of cold air. March is the snowiest month of the year in Denver, and April is not far behind. The foothills west of Denver get their biggest snows at this time of year, as the storms swing moisture across the eastern plains and push it up against the mountains. The storm systems earlier in the winter season often race across the state, dropping most of the moisture along and west of the divide. Springtime storms tend to deepen over southeastern Colorado and are slower to swirl onto the Great Plains. As a result, these storms bring much longer periods of easterly "upslope" flow to areas along and east of the divide.

(top) Digging out from the March 2003 blizzard in southwest Denver. (bottom) Ruts nearly two feet deep in a neighborhood in southwest Denver.

The Blizzard of 2003

The most recent example of a super-soggy spring storm was in March 2003. A strong jet stream blew down from the Pacific Northwest around the middle of the month, carving out a deep trough over Arizona. Ahead of this developing pattern, the weather was warm and pleasant over Colorado—an early taste of spring,

High temperatures soared into the mid-70s in Denver on March 13 and 14, and the upper 60s on March 15. At the same time, colder air was marching down the Canadian Rockies and marshaling just north of Montana, where temperatures were in the teens. On the morning of the March 16, Denver was still mild, and temperatures rose to 60 degrees by lunchtime, offering downtown office workers a delightful chance to enjoy a meal outdoors. Folks munching on the mall might not have noticed the thin cirrus clouds filtering the skies over the mountains, but these clouds were the feathery forerunners of a storm that would make new marks in the record books.

By the next morning, those thin clouds had begun to thicken and lower as the storm system swooped down on the central Rockies. The jet stream had bottomed out over the southwestern deserts and had made a turn toward the northeast, bringing strong winds aloft to Colorado. At the surface, a cold front was driving rapidly southward across Wyoming. Over eastern Colorado, the winds continued to blow from the southeast, and temperatures were still in the 50s. Midday brought low clouds and developing showers to the plains, while light snow fell in the mountains. By mid-afternoon, the stage was set; the cold front had pushed into northern Colorado and was arcing down from Fort Collins to near DIA. Thunderstorms developed rapidly along the cold front around 3:00 p.m., producing rain, hail, and even a brief tornado just east of the airport. Once the cold front moved south of Denver, it was not long before the wet turned to white. By evening, most of the metro area was already gripped by a major winter storm. Four to six inches of snow had fallen between 6:00 p.m. and midnight, and that was only the beginning.

The blizzard of 2003 was not as widespread as the October 1997 storm, but for Denver and the foothills it was even more intense.

The system was evolving into a "perfect storm" for producing prodigious piles of precipitation. A strong low pressure system developed over the southeastern corner of Colorado, feeding off the contrast of the cold air coming in from the north and the mild, humid air that remained over extreme southern Colorado and Kansas. The powerful jet stream was curling across the southern Rockies and forming into a deep upper-level whirlwind that would only slowly spin away to the east. The counterclockwise rotation from the surface to 30,000 feet is known as a "closed low," a feature that is so deep in the atmosphere that it basically affects levels from the surface to 6 miles high with its spinning motion. Closed lows are enormous eddies in the air that move quite slowly, often stalling in the same spot for a day or more.

Now eastern Colorado was in the front row, the best seat in the house for a major snow event. Unlike the October 1997 storm, the blizzard of 2003 was not as widespread, but for Denver and the foothills to the west, it was even more intense.

Lyons Hole

The March 2003 blizzard paralyzed the Front Range of the Rockies with several feet of snow. It put a huge dent in a multiyear drought, but also caused millions of dollars in losses to the economy.

Local weather patterns created a persistent north flow of winds parallel to the foothills for several hours between March 16 and 20, 2003, enhancing the precipitation. This small-scale wind feature is called a barrier jet, and it acts much like the jet stream passing overhead. As the barrier jet blew along the Front Range, it lifted the atmosphere as it interacted with the terrain below, squeezing out copious amounts of moisture flowing into the state from as far away as the Gulf of Mexico.

In the days after the storm, meteorologists and climatologists began researching and mapping the snowfall patterns, as they do after most large weather events. It was one of the first widespread storms to hit the Front Range since a major expansion of CoCoRaHS in the early 2000s, and the group's data were of high value.

As researchers combed over the storm reports, nearly every station from the foothills to the I-25 Urban Corridor reported several feet of snow from the storm. However, a few reports from the small town of Lyons were barely half a foot.

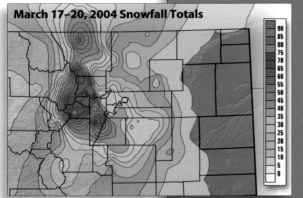

March 17–20, 2004 Snowfall Totals

Was the Lyons data faulty? Could the observers have made a data-entry error on their reports? As the research continued, and scientists contacted the citizens of Lyons to question the data, they learned that the information reported was not an error. Local weather observers noted that much of the precipitation fell in the form of rain, or of snow that melted on contact.

After recreating the blizzard with high-resolution computer models, scientists determined that the slightly higher terrain north of Lyons resulted in a small-scale, downslope wind over the town, as the persistent flow of north winds in the barrier jet blew parallel to the Front Range. A wind blowing down the slope of a mountain compresses the air, drying it out and warming it up. Due to the dynamics and intensity of this storm, the drying and warming was not dramatic, but it was enough that the town picked up less total precipitation and stayed a few degrees warmer than surrounding areas. The result was that most of the precipitation fell either as rain, or snow that melted on contact.

After the storm cleared, a visible satellite clearly showed this scenario in the town of Lyons. Researchers on this project nicknamed the outcome of this small-scale event Lyons Hole. There are likely hundreds of more local weather patterns along the Front Range and around Colorado that we have yet to discover, simply because there are no weather observations. If you have an interest in watching the weather, consider joining CoCoRaHS. Even is someone near you is already an observer, Lyons Hole shows how numerous observations within close proximity help reveal storm patterns in more detail.

Much of the far eastern plains only received a cold rain—albeit a heavy one. Southeastern Colorado was right under the low and had enough mild and fairly dry air spinning in from New Mexico to miss most of the precipitation. The western half of the state had some snow, but not a lot, as this system did not really develop until it was past the western mountains. The brunt of the March 2003 storm was from Douglas and Elbert Counties to Aurora and west to the Continental Divide. Satellite images at the time clearly showed moisture streaming from the Gulf of Mexico across the southern plains and right up I-70 as if it were coming through a pipeline.

As the moist air rose, it cooled, condensed, and dumped heavy, wet snow at a rate of 2 to 3 inches per hour throughout the night and day of March 18. This did not end until the next afternoon. The biggest snow totals hit the southwestern and western sides of Denver, with 3 to 4 feet of snow. In the foothills between 6,000 and 9,000 feet, amazing amounts of snow were reported. Many areas tallied totals of 6 feet, and a few spots in Clear Creek and Gilpin Counties recorded over 7 feet of snow. Dawn on March 20, the first day of spring, was a winter wonderland. The weight of the snow caused many roofs to collapse, not only in the mountains but also in the Fort Collins and Denver Metro areas.

After major snowstorms, meteorologists often receive many questions about the weight of snow. One of the main things to analyze to determine how much snow will fall is the ratio between inches of snow and the actual amount of liquid water. The higher the ratio, the lighter and fluffier the snow. The typical ratio is 10:1—meaning that 10 inches of snow is produced from 1 inch of liquid precipitation. The "champagne powder" that ski resorts like to brag about is sometimes a 20:1 ratio, really dry and fluffy. In the Midwest and the East, the warm, wet snowstorms can bring a slushy 6:1 ratio, the stuff that really gives a shoveler a sore back.

In the big storm of March 18–20, 2003, the official Denver total, measured by the National Weather Service at a site near the old Stapleton Airport, was 31.8 inches of snow. Many other

The gray skies of the blizzard of 2003 did have a silver lining. The ample moisture from that storm almost single-handedly wiped out a significant part of the drought along the Front Range.

spots around the city had much more—up to nearly double that total in the foothills between 6,500 and 8,500 feet. The melted total for the storm was 2.80 inches for Denver, a little closer to an 11:1 ratio from this storm.

An inch of rain on an acre of land equals 27,000 gallons of water. The storm total of 2.80 inches means that the 31.8 inches of snow equaled 76,500 gallons of water on an acre. Since a gallon of water weighs about 8.33 pounds, that snowfall would weigh approximately 638,000 pounds, or 320 tons, per acre. That is for about 32 inches of snow, so for an average 10:1 or 11:1 snow:water ratio, the snow weighs about 10 tons per inch per acre. That might explain why those roof collapses occurred, as well as the tree damage and, of course, the sore backs from shoveling.

The tremendous weight of the heavy, wet snow collapsed the roofs of these Lakewood gas stations, damaging several vehicles below.

The storm was one of the biggest in Denver history, but it still came up short of setting the all-time record for the city for a single storm. That title is still held by that amazing storm back in December 1913. That system was similar to the 2003 storm, a slow-moving low over southeastern Colorado, but it stalled for even longer and dumped much more snow on Denver and the Front Range. Denver tallied 46 inches from that storm system, while Georgetown had about 80 inches of snow.

The gray skies of the blizzard of 2003 did have a silver lining in them, for the ample amount of moisture from that storm almost single-handedly wiped out a significant part of the drought along the Front Range. The previous year had been dangerously dry and wildfires filled the skies with smoke during the spring and summer of 2002. Reservoirs were terribly low. Lake Dillon was at its lowest level in history, and it appeared that water shortages were a certainty for most of the metropolitan areas of eastern Colorado. The water content of the snow from the March storm was anywhere from 3 to 8 inches over the Denver area and the mountains. By the end of the spring melt, Lake Dillon was nearly brimming with water, as were many of the smaller impoundments in the area. Fire

(top) The Dillon Reservoir during the drought previous to the 2003 March storm. (below) Dillon Reservoir after the March 2003 storm melt.

danger was much lower in the foothills throughout the spring and farmers had the water they needed for irrigation. The March 2003 storm had wonderful benefits that lasted months and even years after the snow piles melted away.

We are fortunate in Colorado. Although the cold season easily covers half the year on the plains and perhaps nine months of the year in the high country, our winter snows offer a wealth of recreational activities to keep us busy through the extra-long winter. In addition, thanks to our mostly dry and sunny climate, we are seldom faced with the shorter but very dreary winters in the Midwest or the Northeast. The periods of cold and snow are often broken up by lovely stretches of mild and clear weather, providing a pleasant break in what would otherwise be a monotonous season of wind, white, and woolies.

And before too long, just when we've had enough, the snows begin to melt away and the cycle of the seasons begins anew over Colorado.

Average Precipitation/Snow by City and Month

	OCTOBER			NOVEMBER			DECEMBER		
	Avg. Precip.	Avg. Snow	Avg. Snow Depth	Avg. Precip.	Avg. Snow	Avg. Snow Depth	Avg. Precip.	Avg. Snow	Avg. Snow Depth
Akron	0.88	1.1	0	0.65	5.9	1	0.40	5.0	2
Alamosa	0.65	2.9	0	0.38	3.9	0	0.33	5.1	1
Allenspark	1.24	9.5	0	1.28	16.7	2	1.22	16.2	3
Altenbern	1.58	1.3	0	1.32	7.5	0	1.19	14.2	3
Antero Res.	0.71	5.0	0	0.34	5.9	1	0.27	6.0	2
Aspen	1.48	7.2	0	1.55	18.4	3	1.87	24.1	11
Bailey	1.10	6.2	0	0.73	10.1	2	0.52	8.6	5
Berthoud Pass	2.36	28.0	3	3.36	49.1	14	3.63	51.4	29
Bonny Lake	1.00	1.3	0	0.60	2.1	0	0.31	3.0	1
Boulder	1.30	5.0	0	1.21	13.3	1	0.67	10.2	1
Brighton	0.85	2.1	0	0.82	7.2	1	0.47	5.7	1
Buena Vista	0.84	2.7	0	0.53	5.2	1	0.39	4.7	1
Burlington	1.04	0.8	0	0.50	3.0	0	0.37	4.1	0
Byers	0.85	2.9	0	0.66	5.8	1	0.38	5.1	1
Campo	1.16	1.3	0	0.49	1.9	0	0.31	3.6	0
Cañon City	0.82	1.8	0	0.67	4.7	0	0.43	6.2	1
Castle Rock	1.01	4.2	0	0.85	7.9	0	0.60	8.7	2
Cheesman	1.01	3.7	0	0.78	8.1	1	0.54	7.1	1
Cherry Creek Dam	1.07	3.1	0	0.99	8.0	1	0.53	6.7	1
Cheyenne Wells	0.94	1.1	0	0.46	3.0	0	0.28	3.2	0
Climax	1.37	17.8	2	1.90	33.2	10	1.99	37.3	22
Coal Creek Canyon	1.52	14.3	1	1.11	17.2	2	0.79	15.4	4
Collbran	1.45	1.8	0	1.11	6.6	1	0.99	12.1	2
Colo. National Monument	1.14	0.7	0	0.93	3.6	0	0.78	7.3	1
Colorado Springs	0.80	3.1	0	0.47	5.2	0	0.32	5.1	0
Cortez	1.44	0.3	0	0.95	2.8	0	0.99	7.6	1
Craig	1.19	2.3	0	1.01	9.5	1	1.22	18.9	5
Crested Butte	1.52	7.8	0	1.74	24.3	4	2.23	33.6	14
Crestone	1.02	3.4	0	0.69	8.0	1	0.46	7.3	3
Del Norte	0.83	3.3	0	0.56	5.9	0	0.47	7.1	1
Delta	0.95	0.2	0	0.55	1.5	0	0.45	3.7	0
Denver — Stapleton	0.99	4.1	0	0.98	10.7	1	0.63	8.7	1

Western Regional Climate Center. Compiled by Chris Spears

	JANUARY			FEBRUARY			MARCH			APRIL		
	Avg. Precip.	Avg. Snow	Avg. Snow Depth	Avg. Precip.	Avg. Snow	Avg. Snow Depth	Avg. Precip.	Avg. Snow	Avg. Snow Depth	Avg. Precip.	Avg. Snow	Avg. Snow Depth
Akron	0.34	4.1	2	0.34	3.9	1	0.92	5.5	0	1.59	4.4	0
Alamosa	0.26	4.3	1	0.26	4.1	1	0.41	5.6	0	0.51	4.0	0
Allenspark	1.12	19.1	3	0.96	14.8	3	1.81	27.2	4	2.35	22.4	3
Altenbern	1.31	16.3	7	1.22	10.5	6	1.46	8.3	2	1.44	3.0	0
Antero Res.	0.20	4.0	2	0.27	5.3	2	0.49	8.4	2	0.64	8.0	1
Aspen	1.81	25.0	20	1.55	21.1	23	1.89	23.3	18	1.64	12.7	3
Bailey	0.40	7.1	6	0.53	9.0	7	1.25	16.6	5	1.79	14.9	2
Berthoud Pass	3.49	49.8	42	2.90	42.4	52	4.11	57.9	63	4.43	54.6	67
Bonny Lake	0.37	4.1	1	0.38	4.0	1	0.95	4.9	1	1.57	2.3	0
Boulder	0.69	10.7	1	0.77	10.9	1	1.76	17.8	1	2.43	11.6	0
Brighton	0.44	5.8	1	0.39	4.3	0	1.18	7.8	0	1.71	5.2	0
Buena Vista	0.35	4.9	1	0.42	5.6	1	0.65	7.4	0	0.91	5.4	0
Burlington	0.32	4.0	0	0.39	3.9	0	0.85	4.9	0	1.50	2.8	0
Byers	0.43	6.6	2	0.38	5.1	1	1.05	9.9	1	1.44	5.5	0
Campo	0.29	4.0	0	0.32	2.8	0	0.88	3.8	0	1.26	0.7	0
Cañon City	0.45	5.3	0	0.43	6.3	0	0.96	7.5	0	1.43	4.1	0
Castle Rock	0.57	6.5	1	0.58	7.1	1	1.50	12.4	1	1.80	9.7	0
Cheesman	0.44	6.0	1	0.59	7.3	1	1.29	12.7	1	1.65	9.9	0
Cherry Creek Dam	0.46	6.3	1	0.54	7.2	1	1.22	10.9	1	1.81	7.2	0
Cheyenne Wells	0.28	3.4	0	0.34	3.7	0	0.78	4.8	0	1.30	2.8	0
Climax	2.14	39.9	32	1.81	35.1	41	2.26	39.9	49	2.47	39.4	48
Coal Creek Canyon	0.96	16.1	4	0.98	16.4	5	2.62	37.1	6	4.24	46.1	7
Collbran	1.05	15.4	5	1.02	12.1	5	1.51	11.2	2	1.59	5.2	0
Colo. National Monument	0.84	9.3	3	0.68	4.7	2	1.03	4.7	0	0.93	1.3	0
Colorado Springs	0.30	5.1	0	0.32	4.7	0	0.90	8.7	0	1.36	6.4	0
Cortez	1.01	9.3	2	1.00	6.3	1	1.18	5.1	0	0.94	1.8	0
Craig	1.01	18.4	8	0.82	13.0	8	0.89	10.8	2	1.23	8.1	0
Crested Butte	2.69	40.0	26	2.32	34.3	35	2.34	32.0	34	1.78	17.3	13
Crestone	0.59	10.5	5	0.45	7.1	6	1.02	13.3	3	1.06	9.0	0
Del Norte	0.34	5.4	2	0.35	5.7	1	0.71	7.8	0	0.73	4.8	0
Delta	0.47	4.5	1	0.40	2.5	0	0.56	2.0	0	0.63	0.5	0
Denver —Stapleton	0.51	7.7	1	0.49	6.3	1	1.28	11.7	1	1.93	9.1	0

	OCTOBER			NOVEMBER			DECEMBER		
	Avg. Precip.	Avg. Snow	Avg. Snow Depth	Avg. Precip.	Avg. Snow	Avg. Snow Depth	Avg. Precip.	Avg. Snow	Avg. Snow Depth
Denver — Downtown	0.78	3.5	0	0.58	6.7	0	0.41	5.9	0
Dillon 1 E	0.80	6.3	1	0.88	15.2	4	0.90	15.8	6
Dinosaur Nat. Monument	1.46	1.6	0	0.80	4.7	0	0.62	8.3	2
Durango	1.87	1.0	0	1.34	5.3	0	1.78	15.4	3
Eads	0.94	0.4	0	0.55	3.2	0	0.32	2.6	0
Eagle	0.94	2.2	0	0.73	6.2	0	0.89	10.3	3
Eleven Mile Reservoir	0.71	5.0	0	0.42	6.6	1	0.35	7.5	2
Estes Park	0.82	1.0	0	0.61	3.7	0	0.48	5.5	1
Evergreen	1.22	6.7	0	0.97	12.6	1	0.66	8.5	1
Flagler	0.83	2.1	0	0.55	4.6	0	0.31	3.8	0
Florissant Fossil Beds	0.72	4.0	0	0.54	6.7	1	0.25	5.4	3
Fort Collins	1.11	2.9	0	0.60	6.7	1	0.46	6.1	1
Fort Morgan	0.80	1.0	0	0.43	3.0	0	0.25	3.5	0
Fraser	1.27	9.3	1	1.21	16.8	3	1.46	20.0	9
Fruita	0.91	0.1	0	0.73	1.2	0	0.62	3.2	1
Genoa	0.68	2.4	0	0.48	4.9	0	0.27	3.1	0
Georgetown	1.27	10.4	1	1.13	16.8	3	0.75	13.1	5
Glenwood Springs	1.46	1.1	0	1.16	5.3	0	1.30	15.3	3
Grand Junction	0.90	0.4	0	0.64	2.4	0	0.57	4.9	1
Grand Lake	1.26	5.8	0	1.36	19.5	3	1.64	26.9	11
Grant	1.02	8.3	1	0.81	12.5	3	0.65	11.8	7
Great Sand Dunes	0.86	2.6	0	0.49	4.7	0	0.36	5.6	2
Greeley	0.93	1.8	0	0.60	4.5	1	0.31	3.6	1
Green Mountain Dam	1.07	2.4	0	1.09	9.8	2	1.04	13.1	6
Gunnison	0.73	1.3	0	0.58	5.3	0	0.78	10.3	3
Hayden	1.52	4.5	0	1.45	15.8	2	1.58	24.7	7
Holly	1.07	0.4	0	0.51	2.3	0	0.33	3.7	0
Holyoke	0.97	1.6	0	0.59	5.0	1	0.34	4.5	1
Idaho Springs	0.79	6.5	0	0.66	9.2	0	0.48	8.9	1
Independence Pass 5 SW	1.69	19.7	2	2.79	43.8	12	3.11	52.5	27

	JANUARY			FEBRUARY			MARCH			APRIL		
	Avg. Precip.	Avg. Snow	Avg. Snow Depth	Avg. Precip.	Avg. Snow	Avg. Snow Depth	Avg. Precip.	Avg. Snow	Avg. Snow Depth	Avg. Precip.	Avg. Snow	Avg. Snow Depth
Denver Downtown	0.48	7.4	1	0.54	8.1	1	0.94	11.8	1	1.44	7.8	0
Dillon 1 E	0.80	14.7	6	0.90	14.8	7	1.11	17.9	9	1.19	14.7	7
Dinosaur Nat. Monument	0.64	9.2	5	0.56	6.6	6	0.88	5.9	2	1.17	3.4	0
Durango	1.64	17.6	7	1.47	15.0	5	1.71	10.5	2	1.41	3.5	0
Eads	0.30	3.6	0	0.35	3.2	0	0.81	4.0	0	1.26	1.5	0
Eagle	0.83	10.5	6	0.60	6.2	5	0.80	6.8	2	0.81	3.7	0
Eleven Mile Reservoir	0.28	5.6	2	0.30	6.4	2	0.70	12.6	2	0.91	10.9	1
Estes Park	0.37	3.8	1	0.45	6.3	1	0.87	8.6	1	1.29	4.0	0
Evergreen	0.54	8.3	1	0.68	9.6	1	1.66	18.5	1	2.14	13.9	1
Flagler	0.29	4.0	1	0.33	3.4	0	0.82	5.7	0	1.29	3.8	0
Florissant Fossil Beds	0.41	7.5	3	0.34	6.2	3	1.10	13.3	2	1.15	10.7	0
Fort Collins	0.37	6.2	1	0.49	6.8	1	1.20	10.4	1	1.99	6.5	0
Fort Morgan	0.26	4.3	0	0.21	2.4	0	0.69	4.9	0	1.21	2.2	0
Fraser	1.61	23.4	15	1.55	22.9	20	1.67	21.6	18	1.99	20.6	8
Fruita	0.69	5.0	1	0.56	2.0	1	0.85	1.3	0	0.71	0.2	0
Genoa	0.32	4.0	1	0.33	2.8	0	0.83	7.0	0	1.29	4.8	0
Georgetown	0.68	13.1	6	0.81	13.9	5	1.69	26.8	5	2.33	24.8	4
Glenwood Springs	1.47	18.1	5	1.26	11.3	3	1.43	6.7	0	1.64	1.9	0
Grand Junction	0.60	6.0	1	0.57	3.8	1	0.83	3.0	0	0.78	0.9	0
Grand Lake	1.70	29.7	19	1.38	21.1	24	1.53	19.3	25	1.78	16.1	11
Grant	0.49	9.1	9	0.55	10.6	10	1.15	18.4	9	1.39	15.5	5
Great Sand Dunes	0.44	6.8	3	0.37	5.3	2	0.77	8.3	1	0.88	5.6	0
Greeley	0.39	4.6	2	0.30	3.0	1	0.92	6.5	0	1.51	4.0	0
Green Mountain Dam	1.04	13.5	9	0.93	11.4	12	1.30	13.2	9	1.40	6.9	2
Gunnison	0.82	12.0	7	0.75	10.2	8	0.66	6.9	3	0.69	3.5	0
Hayden	1.55	25.9	14	1.22	18.6	16	1.26	14.2	7	1.62	7.9	0
Holly	0.36	4.0	1	0.37	3.4	1	0.82	4.0	0	1.27	1.1	0
Holyoke	0.40	5.7	1	0.40	4.9	1	1.08	7.9	0	1.58	3.4	0
Idaho Springs	0.42	6.9	1	0.54	8.9	1	0.93	12.7	1	1.60	16.4	1
Independence Pass 5 SW	3.51	50.1	39	2.46	38.6	48	3.97	58.8	56	3.48	45.1	55

	OCTOBER			NOVEMBER			DECEMBER		
	Avg. Precip.	Avg. Snow	Avg. Snow Depth	Avg. Precip.	Avg. Snow	Avg. Snow Depth	Avg. Precip.	Avg. Snow	Avg. Snow Depth
Joes	0.98	2.4	0	0.65	5.0	1	0.28	3.2	1
John Martin Dam	0.75	0.2	0	0.40	1.6	0	0.26	1.2	0
Julesburg	0.97	1.0	0	0.56	3.8	0	0.35	4.4	1
Karval	0.78	0.9	0	0.44	2.7	0	0.27	2.6	0
Kim	1.03	3.3	0	0.82	5.8	0	0.40	4.9	1
Kit Carson	0.80	0.6	0	0.48	3.0	0	0.25	2.7	0
Kremmling	0.85	2.2	0	0.77	7.3	1	0.74	9.0	3
La Junta	0.69	1.0	0	0.51	3.5	0	0.27	3.9	0
Lake City	1.26	5.1	0	1.03	12.9	2	0.96	13.7	6
Lakewood	1.01	3.5	0	0.97	8.2	1	0.50	6.7	1
Lamar	0.89	0.9	0	0.59	4.0	0	0.40	4.6	0
Las Animas	0.77	0.8	0	0.45	2.6	0	0.30	3.3	0
Leadville	0.97	7.4	1	1.03	12.5	3	1.50	23.2	9
Limon	0.74	2.7	0	0.52	4.8	1	0.35	3.7	1
Little Hills	1.24	2.4	0	0.97	5.9	1	0.95	10.5	3
Littleton	1.23	3.0	0	1.14	12.2	2	0.64	12.7	3
Longmont	0.84	1.4	0	0.69	5.1	0	0.45	5.7	1
Loveland	1.12	2.3	0	0.75	6.8	1	0.40	5.2	1
Manassa	0.75	2.0	0	0.41	3.3	0	0.31	4.6	0
Mancos	1.60	0.6	0	1.28	4.1	0	1.25	7.8	1
Maybell	1.21	1.7	0	1.15	9.9	1	0.87	12.1	3
Meeker	1.47	2.6	0	1.18	9.2	1	1.13	13.0	3
Mesa Verde National Park	1.70	1.6	0	1.43	7.8	1	1.51	15.3	4
Monte Vista	0.67	1.4	0	0.42	3.6	0	0.30	3.8	1
Montrose	1.02	0.6	0	0.65	2.6	0	0.62	6.4	1
Monument	1.34	9.1	0	1.41	15.9	1	0.81	12.8	1
Nederland	1.02	9.3	1	1.12	19.9	2	0.73	16.1	2
New Raymer	0.83	2.8	0	0.45	5.8	1	0.23	4.7	1
Northglenn	0.92	2.3	0	0.78	7.9	1	0.42	5.6	1
Nunn	0.85	1.7	0	0.56	7.0	1	0.22	4.8	1
Ordway	0.62	0.4	0	0.41	2.2	0	0.30	3.3	0
Ouray	2.15	5.8	0	2.06	20.4	3	1.62	21.9	8
Pagosa Sprgs	2.29	3.2	0	1.39	10.0	1	1.78	21.2	5
Palisade	1.09	0.0	0	0.86	1.2	0	0.54	2.8	0
Paonia	1.36	0.5	0	1.08	5.5	0	1.32	10.8	2

	JANUARY			FEBRUARY			MARCH			APRIL		
	Avg. Precip.	Avg. Snow	Avg. Snow Depth	Avg. Precip.	Avg. Snow	Avg. Snow Depth	Avg. Precip.	Avg. Snow	Avg. Snow Depth	Avg. Precip.	Avg. Snow	Avg. Snow Depth
Joes	0.48	5.6	1	0.42	3.2	1	0.99	4.1	0	1.47	3.7	0
John Martin Dam	0.24	2.2	1	0.26	1.4	0	0.61	2.3	0	1.02	0.2	0
Julesburg	0.37	4.4	1	0.35	3.5	0	0.95	5.6	0	1.72	2.5	0
Karval	0.28	3.3	1	0.25	1.9	0	0.69	3.7	0	1.12	1.9	0
Kim	0.56	6.9	1	0.47	5.0	0	1.31	8.0	0	1.58	5.5	0
Kit Carson	0.26	3.0	0	0.28	2.4	0	0.68	3.3	0	1.01	2.0	0
Kremmling	0.76	10.7	7	0.52	8.4	6	0.67	7.3	2	0.86	4.0	0
La Junta	0.32	4.7	1	0.31	4.2	1	0.74	5.8	0	1.16	2.5	0
Lake City	0.82	12.4	11	0.73	10.6	11	0.97	13.8	6	1.03	9.7	2
Lakewood	0.50	7.0	1	0.49	7.2	1	1.42	11.2	1	1.95	7.7	1
Lamar	0.43	5.1	1	0.42	4.5	0	0.89	5.3	0	1.28	1.7	0
Las Animas	0.37	4.0	1	0.34	3.3	0	0.72	3.9	0	1.15	1.1	0
Leadville	1.41	16.8	15	1.17	13.1	17	1.38	16.9	14	1.33	14.7	6
Limon	0.35	4.2	1	0.32	3.5	1	0.85	7.3	1	1.15	3.6	0
Little Hills	0.74	10.8	7	0.79	9.2	6	1.24	11.5	2	1.44	5.1	0
Littleton	0.36	8.9	3	0.47	7.8	1	1.44	11.9	1	1.50	7.8	0
Longmont	0.40	5.7	1	0.39	4.4	1	1.13	7.2	0	1.73	4.0	0
Loveland	0.47	6.3	1	0.52	5.5	1	1.31	7.9	1	1.88	5.0	0
Manassa	0.27	4.0	1	0.23	3.7	1	0.35	4.2	0	0.48	2.5	0
Mancos	1.45	14.7	4	1.21	10.2	4	1.55	7.7	1	1.22	1.6	0
Maybell	0.82	12.2	5	0.85	10.3	5	1.04	8.4	2	1.35	4.3	0
Meeker	1.10	14.9	5	1.02	11.8	4	1.35	11.4	1	1.73	5.5	0
Mesa Verde National Park	1.84	20.0	8	1.51	15.0	8	1.67	14.3	3	1.26	5.6	0
Monte Vista	0.29	3.6	2	0.25	3.4	1	0.50	4.4	0	0.51	2.3	0
Montrose	0.57	6.5	1	0.48	4.2	0	0.70	3.5	0	0.86	1.8	0
Monument	0.83	13.5	3	0.56	10.0	0	2.30	22.3	1	3.09	22.4	1
Nederland	0.54	13.3	2	0.59	13.1	1	1.29	23.9	2	2.18	24.3	2
New Raymer	0.26	5.0	2	0.22	3.7	1	0.77	6.7	0	1.34	4.4	0
Northglenn	0.37	6.4	1	0.39	5.3	0	1.13	6.6	0	1.87	5.9	0
Nunn	0.36	5.9	1	0.26	5.1	1	0.91	7.9	0	1.30	4.2	0
Ordway	0.30	3.5	0	0.25	2.7	0	0.69	3.7	0	1.13	1.3	0
Ouray	1.72	24.7	13	1.73	22.8	15	2.25	25.5	12	2.05	13.0	3
Pagosa Sprgs	1.97	26.4	11	1.42	18.9	10	1.60	15.1	4	1.36	5.5	0
Palisade	0.56	3.9	1	0.60	1.9	0	0.95	1.7	0	1.01	0.2	0
Paonia	1.33	13.7	2	1.30	11.3	1	1.13	7.6	0	1.56	3.2	0

	OCTOBER			NOVEMBER			DECEMBER		
	Avg. Precip.	Avg. Snow	Avg. Snow Depth	Avg. Precip.	Avg. Snow	Avg. Snow Depth	Avg. Precip.	Avg. Snow	Avg. Snow Depth
Pueblo WSO AP	0.75	1.4	0	0.50	3.8	0	0.34	4.7	0
Ralston Reservoir	1.16	2.8	0	1.14	11.7	1	0.66	9.8	1
Rangely 1 E	1.14	0.2	0	0.70	2.6	0	0.54	6.0	1
Red Feather Lakes	0.85	5.9	0	0.88	11.4	1	0.63	10.6	2
Rico	2.13	7.6	1	2.01	21.5	4	2.27	26.2	11
Ridgway	1.58	3.5	0	1.44	13.7	1	0.80	13.9	3
Rifle	1.20	0.5	0	0.89	3.8	0	0.93	11.1	2
Rocky Ford	0.78	0.8	0	0.48	3.6	0	0.30	4.3	0
Rye	1.38	3.9	0	1.30	8.1	1	1.02	7.3	2
Saguache	0.72	1.5	0	0.42	3.1	0	0.29	4.4	1
Salida	1.10	5.5	0	0.51	7.6	1	0.38	5.5	1
Sedgwick	1.13	0.7	0	0.54	5.4	0	0.25	3.7	1
Silverton	2.34	8.5	1	1.49	20.0	4	1.73	24.0	12
Springfield 7 WSW	0.92	1.6	0	0.66	4.3	0	0.38	4.4	0
Steamboat Springs	1.91	6.8	0	1.98	20.2	3	2.41	32.9	12
Sterling	0.92	0.2	0	0.50	3.3	0	0.29	3.5	1
Taylor Park	1.21	2.9	0	1.34	13.1	3	1.37	21.1	11
Telluride	1.94	9.1	0	1.56	20.9	3	1.55	24.6	8
Trinidad	0.97	1.3	0	0.79	5.7	0	0.45	7.1	1
Vail	1.59	7.5	0	2.03	31.1	7	1.39	26.6	15
Vallecito Dam	2.58	2.6	0	2.14	12.4	1	2.23	22.4	4
Walden	0.82	4.0	0	0.73	9.1	1	0.60	8.8	4
Walsenburg	1.05	5.1	0	1.08	11.7	1	0.81	13.1	1
Westcliffe	1.08	8.4	0	0.85	12.3	1	0.58	10.5	2
Wetmore	1.27	3.1	0	0.98	6.1	1	0.88	6.4	1
Williams Fork Dam	1.22	4.1	0	1.19	12.6	2	0.70	9.7	5
Winter Park	1.70	11.3	1	2.25	31.1	8	2.31	34.9	19
Wolf Creek Pass 1 E	4.50	26.2	4	4.16	54.5	16	4.30	78.7	30
Wray	0.99	1.2	0	0.60	3.7	0	0.36	3.7	0
Yampa	1.17	7.1	0	1.23	18.0	3	1.21	19.9	8
Yuma	1.04	2.1	0	0.56	4.0	0	0.29	3.3	0

	JANUARY			FEBRUARY			MARCH			APRIL		
	Avg. Precip.	Avg. Snow	Avg. Snow Depth	Avg. Precip.	Avg. Snow	Avg. Snow Depth	Avg. Precip.	Avg. Snow	Avg. Snow Depth	Avg. Precip.	Avg. Snow	Avg. Snow Depth
Pueblo WSO AP	0.32	5.4	1	0.29	3.9	0	0.83	5.9	0	1.19	3.5	0
Ralston Reservoir	0.56	8.5	1	0.65	8.3	1	1.88	13.5	1	2.38	10.4	1
Rangely 1 E	0.56	6.6	4	0.59	6.2	4	0.84	3.2	1	1.00	1.4	0
Red Feather Lakes	0.57	8.4	3	0.66	9.4	3	1.32	18.4	3	1.79	16.0	2
Rico	2.48	32.1	22	2.15	26.5	26	2.44	30.8	26	1.81	18.5	13
Ridgway	0.84	12.3	4	0.85	12.5	4	1.46	16.0	2	1.41	7.2	0
Rifle	0.86	11.1	4	0.77	7.7	3	0.95	3.7	0	1.02	0.8	0
Rocky Ford	0.31	4.2	1	0.28	3.3	0	0.72	4.3	0	1.22	2.2	0
Rye	0.96	8.9	3	1.13	10.8	3	1.91	15.1	2	2.30	8.8	0
Saguache	0.28	4.4	1	0.24	3.7	1	0.40	4.8	0	0.60	3.3	0
Salida	0.29	4.8	1	0.38	5.8	1	0.69	8.4	0	0.93	6.7	0
Sedgwick	0.26	3.7	0	0.42	4.6	1	1.04	6.7	0	1.79	3.8	0
Silverton	1.68	25.8	21	1.75	25.3	27	2.30	28.4	26	1.72	17.3	11
Springfield 7 WSW	0.45	4.9	1	0.44	4.4	0	0.99	7.2	0	1.39	3.3	0
Steamboat Springs	2.47	35.5	23	2.23	29.6	28	2.11	23.8	20	2.28	13.2	3
Sterling	0.30	3.9	1	0.28	3.0	0	0.85	4.3	0	1.21	1.9	0
Taylor Park	1.37	24.7	21	1.29	16.5	26	1.37	16.8	25	1.36	10.6	13
Telluride	1.63	27.4	14	1.69	25.3	16	2.20	31.9	12	2.20	21.8	3
Trinidad	0.47	7.0	1	0.50	7.0	1	0.99	8.3	0	1.19	5.6	0
Vail	1.76	33.6	25	2.08	34.1	31	1.82	24.7	26	2.20	21.2	10
Vallecito Dam	2.47	27.8	10	1.95	21.1	10	2.21	20.7	4	1.72	8.1	1
Walden	0.57	8.4	6	0.53	6.8	6	0.67	7.8	2	0.89	7.1	0
Walsenburg	0.70	11.2	1	0.85	11.8	1	1.59	17.2	1	1.87	12.3	0
Westcliffe	0.48	8.7	1	0.56	10.4	1	1.16	18.0	1	1.40	14.6	0
Wetmore	0.59	5.3	1	0.98	6.6	1	1.54	10.5	1	2.25	5.7	1
Williams Fork Dam	0.80	11.4	10	0.87	12.4	13	0.98	10.0	9	1.31	9.0	1
Winter Park	2.35	36.3	29	2.05	31.1	36	2.65	36.1	39	3.03	31.6	27
Wolf Creek Pass 1 E	3.71	73.4	46	4.02	66.4	54	4.97	77.8	67	3.37	41.5	50
Wray	0.39	4.9	1	0.39	4.0	0	0.90	6.2	0	1.81	2.7	0
Yampa	1.21	20.8	13	1.05	16.9	15	1.27	17.9	12	1.39	13.4	2
Yuma	0.40	5.1	1	0.41	3.7	0	0.97	6.3	0	1.50	2.8	0

CHAPTER THREE

WARM SEASON WEATHER

The long cold weather season in Colorado finally draws to a close in early May as the big soggy spring snowstorms begin to turn into rain. Along the Front Range, the average monthly snowfall for Denver drops from over 9 inches in April to just over an inch in May. At the same time, May is the wettest month of the year in Denver, averaging 2.32 inches of liquid. Snow still falls across the mountains, but the ski resorts pretty well pack it in for another season by mid-April. Arapahoe Basin, Loveland, and Silverton Mountain hang on longer, with A-Basin often making it to June and occasionally even July in a good snow year.

3

Thunderstorm Season

7 Driest Denver Mays (1872–2006)	
Inches	Year
0.06	1974
0.09	1886
0.15	1899
0.22	1919
0.34	1966, 1977
0.43	1925
0.49	1972

7 Wettest Denver Mays (1872–2006)	
Inches	Year
8.57	1876
7.31	1957
6.12	1969
5.06	1973
4.95	1935
4.88	1898, 1938
4.77	1967

Inevitably, the warmth of springtime brings an end to the snow season and a start to the thunderstorm season. The season's first round of severe thunderstorms usually arrives in late April or early May. A low pressure system moving across Colorado will still bring heavy snows to the mountains, but the warm air drawn into southern Colorado ahead of the storm will typically fire up severe thunderstorms on the plains. In early spring, the upper levels of the atmosphere are cold, and warmer air at the surface will create very unstable conditions in the skies over Colorado. The warm air easily rises up through the cold air aloft, much as a hot air balloon rises. As this air bubbles through the atmosphere, powerful thunderstorms can develop. The cold temperatures aloft allow for the formation of hail, sometimes reaching the size of baseballs or larger. The eastern plains of Colorado and southern Wyoming are among the hail capitals of the world, thanks in part to the higher elevation that puts the area closer to the chilly air aloft, and to the mountains to the west, which help inspire the development of thunderstorms that rumble onto the plains. It is not uncommon for a high plains thunderstorm to dump hail the size of golf balls, but even softball-sized hail is usually reported every year somewhere on the eastern plains. The largest hailstone on record fell on Aurora—Nebraska, not Colorado—in June 2003. It weighed nearly 2 pounds.

Hail Threat

Hail can be one of the most destructive aspects of severe weather. It annually causes millions of dollars in damage to agriculture, and it darkens the day for many a car dealer. It is not easy to predict, but there have been some attempts at hail suppression. Two methods have been primarily used, not only across the high plains of the United States, but also in Russia and China. In the first, researchers have attempted to seed

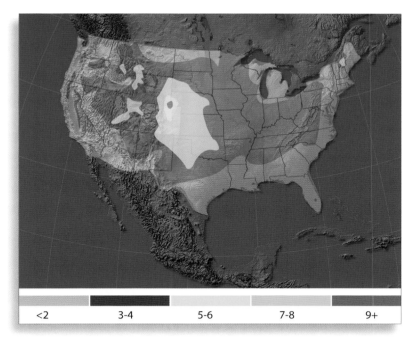

Average number of days per year in which hail is reported. Eastern Colorado and Wyoming are the "hail capitals" of the nation.

| <2 | 3-4 | 5-6 | 7-8 | 9+ |

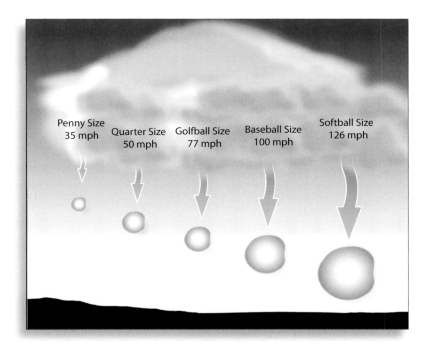

Penny Size 35 mph Quarter Size 50 mph Golfball Size 77 mph Baseball Size 100 mph Softball Size 126 mph

Speed at which various sizes of hail will fall to earth.

The majority of hail in Colorado is the size of a penny. Occasionally, baseball- to softball-size hail storms cause significant damage.

storm clouds with tiny silver iodide crystals by dropping them into the clouds or sending them up with small rockets from the ground. In theory, the minute particles will act as additional nuclei on which rain and hail can form, creating many smaller hailstones rather than fewer large and destructive ones. The science behind cloud seeding is basically sound, but in practice it has not proved to be very feasible. Hailstorms are generally intense over relatively small areas—a few hundred yards wide and several miles long—and the storms are short-lived events. Getting an aircraft to the right spot or having enough small rockets ready to launch is generally impractical.

A second, more exotic hail suppression method does not fire a projectile, but rather sends a sonic impulse into the sky using an unusual device called a hail cannon, which looks like

Hailstones undergo a series of melting and refreezing processes in the thundercloud. They arrive at the surface in a variety of shapes and sizes.

(above) Hailstorms are most common on Colorado's eastern plains, where farms and ranches dominate the landscape. (below) A hail cannon in the San Luis Valley of Colorado in theory helps protect valuable crops from potentially damaging hail.

a big metal stadium horn perched atop a small building. The cannon creates a periodic deep booming noise that travels upward. The theory is that somehow these booms will break up the hail-producing structure of the thunderstorm and prevent large hail from forming. Hail cannons are scattered across a few key agricultural areas of Colorado, including some in Weld County and in the San Luis Valley. Meteorologists question their efficacy, but farmers in hail-prone areas feel that by firing the cannons they are at least doing something to keep their valuable crops from being destroyed by hail.

Tornado Alley

One of the biggest severe weather threats in Colorado is the tornado. Colorado sits on the western edge of "tornado alley," the Great Plains, which hold the dubious honor of having more tornadoes than any other place on the planet. So many tornadoes occur over the central United States because the basic topography brings together all of the necessary components for severe weather. A rolling plain extends from northern Canada all the way to the Gulf of Mexico, rimmed on both sides by mountains, the Rockies to the west and the Appalachians to the east. Cool, dry air can easily flow southward, while warm, moisture-laden air moves north from the Gulf Coast. The stage is set for thunderstorm development as these different air masses glide and flow in a constant atmospheric dance.

Late winter and early spring, when there are strong temperature contrasts from north to south, are particularly active times. The average thunderstorm is a common result of the contrast of air masses, but for tornado-producing storms to develop there needs to be an additional factor: the atmosphere needs to be held back somehow from allowing weaker thunderstorms to develop earlier in the day. There needs to be a governor on the throttle of convection, in other words, to keep storms from popping until later in the afternoon, when the peak heating of the day occurs. If storms form too early, they will block additional sunlight from heating the ground and there will not be enough energy to fuel the truly massive thunderstorm clouds that can spawn tornadoes. Here again, the unique terrain of the western United States comes into play. The high mountains and plateaus help to warm the middle levels of the atmosphere, about 15,000 to 20,000 feet. This is due in part to sunshine warming the ground and in part to the effect of the air warming as it flows over and down the rugged terrain, which creates a layer of warm and stable air about 3 miles above the ground. This stable air is what keeps a lid on thunderstorm development, since rising columns of warm air lose their buoyancy as soon as they reach a level where the air is the same temperature or warmer. Meteorologists call this a "cap" in the atmosphere.

When the atmosphere is capped, thunderstorms will not develop until the surface temperature increases enough that any bubble or parcel of air that rises from the surface is warm enough to break the cap and then keep rising. Above the cap, the air at higher altitudes is usually much colder, so once the caps breaks, thunderstorms will suddenly explode upward and develop with great quickness and violence. It is the rapid development of thunderstorms that typically provides enough

Mid-Level Cap

Warmer Air

Mid-Level Cap Broken

(left) Data from the morning weather balloon launch helps meteorologists determine the presence of a mid-level cap. (right) If and when the cap breaks, thunderstorm development can occur within minutes. (below) Once the cap is broken, thunderstorms will build very rapidly and often become severe, producing large hail and tornadoes.

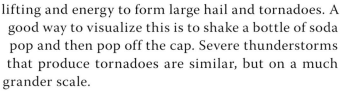

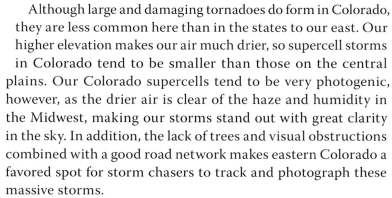

lifting and energy to form large hail and tornadoes. A good way to visualize this is to shake a bottle of soda pop and then pop off the cap. Severe thunderstorms that produce tornadoes are similar, but on a much grander scale.

The normal season for tornadoes in Colorado is from late May through June. Twisters are the most likely to occur during this time thanks to the combination of strong temperature contrasts, the mid-atmospheric cap, and strong jet stream winds aloft. The jet stream is what helps to turn average thunderstorms into whirling monsters called supercells. The supercell thunderstorm features a large-scale counterclockwise spinning motion that helps to inspire the smaller, but vastly more intense rotation of the tornado. Supercell thunderstorms may form near the Denver area, but they are more common farther to the east, where the flat terrain allows the wind currents to form a large rotating system. The supercells that develop in the relatively dry air of Colorado rumble off to the east and cause trouble for folks in more humid Kansas, Oklahoma, and Nebraska.

Although large and damaging tornadoes do form in Colorado, they are less common here than in the states to our east. Our higher elevation makes our air much drier, so supercell storms in Colorado tend to be smaller than those on the central plains. Our Colorado supercells tend to be very photogenic, however, as the drier air is clear of the haze and humidity in the Midwest, making our storms stand out with great clarity in the sky. In addition, the lack of trees and visual obstructions combined with a good road network makes eastern Colorado a favored spot for storm chasers to track and photograph these massive storms.

The Tornado Dance has been a longtime Colorado favorite, performed before thousands of school children, as well as adult service and social clubs each year. The jetstream winds blowing past a thunderstorm create a slow rotation in the storm—this spinning storm is called a supercell. If conditions are right, the rotation in the storm cloud becomes smaller and faster, much like a figure skater pulling in her arms and spinning faster. This intense spinning motion eventually drops to the ground to form a tornado.

This might come as a surprise, but Weld County can boast of being the "tornado capital of America." Over the past fifty years, no other county in the nation has had more tornadoes. It's a big county, with lots of room for tornadoes, and a lot of thunderstorms develop and rumble across it. Thanks to the varied terrain that can help create rotation in the atmosphere, many mostly small tornadoes develop in northeastern Colorado, especially Weld, Washington, and Yuma Counties.

Most Colorado tornadoes are small and short-lived, often lasting only five to ten minutes. The vast majority of our tornadoes have winds of 100 mph or less. A few, such as the one that hit Limon in 1990, can reach wind speeds of over 200

(top) As precipitation increases in a thunderstorm cloud, sunlight reflecting and refracting off the moisture can make for some ominous scenes. (above) No state is exempt from tornadoes, but the majority of those documented each year are recorded in tornado alley.

(top) Supercell thunderstorms often take on a spaceship-like appearance. (bottom) Storm chaser Tony Laubach enjoys a front-row seat within a mile of this large, dusty tornado packing winds over 150 mph.

mph. The biggest tornadoes in Colorado tend to occur where our population is the smallest, on the far eastern plains. That may be a comfort if you live close to I-25, but not so for folks in Haxtun, Holyoke, or Holly. The tragic tornado of March 29, 2007, claimed two lives in the small southeastern town of Holly. Those fatalities were the first tornado-related deaths in Colorado in almost 50 years. Prior to the Holly Tornado, the last tornado

death in the state was on June 27, 1960, in Sedgwick County. The long gap in between tornado victims can be attributed to luck, wide open spaces, and better storm warnings. Just the same, with our rapidly increasing population, those open spaces are being filled with homes and neighborhoods. It is important to know what to do and where to go in the event of a tornado.

(left) August 29, 2002: dusty debris cloud from a tornado in southeastern Aurora, near E-470 and Gartrell. (right) Supercell thunderstorm over Morgan County on July 21, 2000.

Tornado Safety

Many rules about tornado safety have been around for years. Some of the rules are still accurate and worthwhile to follow; others are not. The best way to ensure your safety during a tornado is to simply "get low and protect your head." This simple rule is easy for even a child to remember, and it could save a life. Getting as low as possible, no matter where you are, will decrease the odds that you will be hit by flying debris—the greatest hazard from a tornado. Covering your head and eyes will protect you from injury in the event there is something whipping around in the strong winds. Getting low may mean going to the basement or the lowest floor, or, in open country, perhaps, into a ditch. Protect your head by getting under something sturdy such as a bench or heavy table.

Other rules of tornado safety, such as opening various windows, have now been largely abandoned. In the past it was thought that opening the windows would help to equalize the pressure difference created by the extremely low atmospheric pressure of the tornado. By equalizing the pressure, the house would not explode outward as the tornado passed by. Research has shown that most houses are leaky enough that the air escapes anyway, and that nearly all of the damage from the tornado is caused by the violent winds, not the pressure difference. Opening the windows does little to protect your property, but it may put you in harm's way by wasting valuable time worrying about the windows instead of seeking shelter.

Another outdated bit of advice about tornadoes is to hide in the southwestern corner of the basement. The logic here is that most tornadoes come from the southwest and move toward the northeast, so by going to the southwestern corner

To escape a tornado, drive at a right angle, or 90 degrees from its movement.

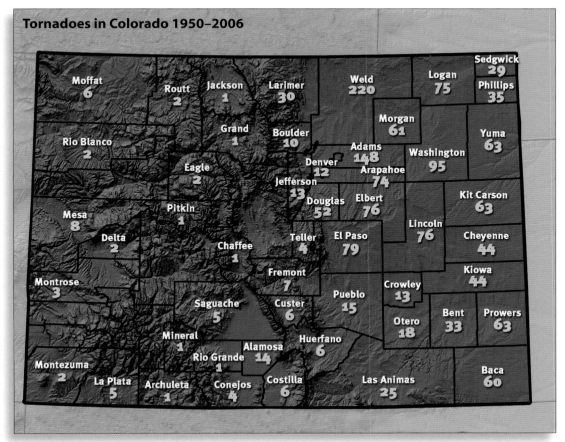

Tornadoes in Colorado 1950–2006

County	Count
Sedgwick	29
Moffat	6
Routt	2
Jackson	1
Larimer	30
Weld	220
Logan	75
Phillips	35
Grand	1
Boulder	10
Morgan	61
Yuma	63
Rio Blanco	2
Eagle	2
Denver	12
Adams	148
Washington	95
Jefferson	13
Arapahoe	74
Pitkin	1
Douglas	52
Elbert	76
Kit Carson	63
Mesa	8
Lincoln	76
Delta	2
Teller	4
El Paso	79
Cheyenne	44
Chaffee	1
Fremont	7
Kiowa	44
Montrose	3
Crowley	13
Saguache	5
Custer	6
Pueblo	15
Mineral	1
Otero	18
Bent	33
Prowers	63
Montezuma	2
Alamosa	14
Huerfano	6
Rio Grande	1
La Plata	5
Archuleta	1
Conejos	4
Costilla	6
Las Animas	25
Baca	60

Counties that are not labeled have never officially reported a tornado.

of the basement, the person hiding would be left unharmed as the house was lifted up and dropped on the northeastern corner. This sounds good in theory, but in practice this scenario seldom occurs. Besides, some tornadoes come from the west or northwest. Another point to consider is that every house does not have the same construction design or quality. If your house is a split level with a walkout basement on the southwestern side, that certainly would not be the best place to seek shelter.

The best advice is to survey your home carefully and try to locate the sturdiest part of your house. It might be under the stairs, or under a workbench in the middle of the basement, or

(left) Damage near Fleming, Colorado, from an F3 tornado on July 5, 2000. (right) Damage from a severe tornado near Lamar, Colorado, on May 29, 2001.

perhaps in an interior bathroom (the pipes add extra strength to the walls). Find the strongest part of your home and go there when a tornado threatens. Practice a family tornado drill in the same way you would make a fire safety plan, especially if you have small children.

Tornadoes seem to be happening more frequently from the Denver area to the Kansas border. But is this more perception than reality? Many longtime residents claim that there were not nearly as many tornadoes in our state forty or fifty years ago. Although our climate is changing and as temperatures warm we may indeed have more energy available for severe storms and tornadoes, any increase in the number of twister sightings is probably due much more to a better system of tracking tornado-producing thunderstorms. Fifty years ago, there were no Doppler radars, weather satellites, or high-speed computers to track short-term weather patterns. Today, the eastern plains of Colorado bristle with the latest weather technology, allowing meteorologists and storm chasers all the information they need to follow and intercept thunderstorms that may drop a tornado. In addition, the vast increase in population east of Denver and the I-25 corridor has placed many more witnesses out on the high plains, where tornadoes have roamed for centuries.

Spring Flooding

The weather by late May and early June can bring days that are filled with warmth and thunder on the plains and still cold and snow in the mountains. Sometimes all this occurs in a single afternoon! But much of springtime into early summer in Colorado is very enjoyable, with warm temperatures and bright sunshine, at least through early afternoon.

This clement weather can be a source of concern, though, since by the end of April and the start of May, deep snows have piled up in the mountains. Too rapid a warm-up will quickly melt that snow and fill rivers and streams with an icy cold surge of water. During late April through mid-June, the major concern in mountain areas is snowmelt flooding. The worst scenario for flooding is a very snowy winter followed by an early spell of sunny, hot weather. The snowpack can diminish at a rate of several inches per day, and all that frigid water fills mountain streams and reservoirs quickly. A series of warm days, followed by a soggy spring storm that brings heavy rain, can create a serious threat.

Fast waters along 10 Mile Creek as the winter snowmelt begins.

Spring melt causes high waters on Boulder Creek.

117

In addition to the threat of damage to property, our mountain rivers are cold, high, and dangerous in May and early June. The fast, frigid water poses a great risk to anyone venturing into the current. Fishermen are anxious to wade into the brisk waters, especially during the early spring caddis fly hatches. Anglers need to be extremely careful when working their way into water much deeper than knee level.

The high, fast waters also attract those seeking the adrenalin rush of rafting the whitewater. Rafting is a wonderful sport, and a major part of the local economies in the mountains. If you are anxious to get into a raft or kayak in the high water season but are not experienced in the sport, be sure to contact one of the professional rafting companies. The rough and rapid water is no place for a novice. Those who are new to the sport may be much happier waiting until July to hit the rivers, especially those prone to falling out of the raft.

Springtime Gardening

Longtime weather forecaster Bill Kuster planted his famous Kuster Garden for many years in Denver, giving gardeners very sound advice. "Do not," he insisted, "plant your spring garden before Mother's Day." It is so tempting during those warm weekends in late April, especially when the rose bushes and the tomato plants are in the garden centers, but do not be fooled. The average last date of freezing temperatures in the Denver area is May 7. Snow is still possible in Denver until about the middle of May, sometimes with flurries into early June. Many a beautiful late-April garden has had to be replanted in mid-May after a cold snap. It is best to use those warm weekends in April and early May to prepare the ground or work on the lawn, but wait to plant until the latter part of May. If you live at elevations above 6,000 feet, you may want to wait even longer, until early June. The foothills frequently are hit by late, soggy snowstorms even up to Memorial Day.

> *"Do not plant your garden before Mother's Day."*
> — **Bill Kuster**

Newly planted flowers are flocked by a late spring snow in Castle Rock.

Under Some Thunder

As the days grow longer, the sun grows stronger. By early June, Colorado finally gets into a summer pattern. The summer season is a busy one for forecasters in Colorado. Through June, the upper levels of the atmosphere are still pretty chilly, but the ground is warm—and that means conditions are right for thunderstorms to form almost every day. A typical June day in eastern Colorado starts bright and clear, with a lovely view of the snow-covered peaks to the west. The temperatures quickly rise from the early morning 50s into the 80s by lunchtime. By late morning, you may notice the first rising turrets of developing cumulus clouds to the west. These "castles in the sky," officially known as altocumulus castellanus, are signs of some instability in the atmosphere. Somewhere between 2:00 and 4:00 in the afternoon, those clouds grow together into a dark gray mass. Lightning begins to flicker in the distance and thunder rumbles across the plains. On many days, the storm

Average Last Day of Frost/Freeze

Location	32°	28°	Location	32°	28°
Akron	5/11	4/29	Denver — Downtown	4/29	4/13
Alamosa	6/10	5/27	Dillon 1 E	7/18	6/25
Allenspark	6/10	5/25	Dinosaur Nat. Monument	5/19	5/5
Altenbern	5/26	5/13	Durango	6/2	5/13
Antero Reservoir	7/2	6/15	Eads	5/2	4/20
Aspen	6/16	5/28	Eagle	6/12	5/27
Bailey	6/20	6/1	Eleven Mile Reservoir	6/10	5/24
Berthoud Pass	6/29	6/20	Estes Park	6/3	5/17
Bonny Lake	5/4	4/22	Evergreen	6/6	5/16
Boulder	5/2	4/21	Flagler	5/13	5/1
Brighton	5/3	4/27	Florissant Fossil Beds	6/25	6/3
Buena Vista	6/2	5/13	Fort Collins	5/9	4/27
Burlington	5/7	4/23	Fort Morgan	5/1	4/22
Byers	5/13	5/1	Fraser	7/27	7/9
Campo	4/27	4/16	Fruita	5/12	4/27
Canon City	5/2	4/18	Genoa	4/30	4/15
Castle Rock	5/22	5/7	Georgetown	6/19	6/10
Cheesman	5/31	5/17	Glenwood Springs	5/19	5/1
Cherry Creek Dam	5/13	5/2	Grand Junction	4/23	4/6
Cheyenne Wells	5/5	4/27	Grand Lake	7/15	6/25
Climax	7/4	6/18	Grant	6/21	6/1
Coal Creek Canyon	6/11	5/23	Great Sand Dunes NP	5/26	5/14
Collbran	5/29	5/8	Greeley	5/7	4/23
Colo. National Monument	5/4	4/23	Green Mountain Dam	6/12	5/23
Colorado Springs	5/6	4/27	Gunnison	6/27	6/10
Cortez	5/25	5/9	Hayden	6/3	5/22
Craig	6/2	5/19	Holly	5/2	4/18
Crested Butte	7/9	6/17	Holyoke	5/6	4/27
Crestone	5/27	5/10	Idaho Springs	6/10	5/27
Del Norte	5/30	5/15	Independence Pass 5 SW	7/27	6/27
Delta	5/11	4/28	Joes	5/7	4/29
Denver – Stapleton	5/2	4/23	John Martin Dam	5/1	4/13

Location	32°	28°
Julesburg	5/9	4/27
Karval	5/8	4/28
Kim	5/3	4/24
Kit Carson	5/11	4/28
Kremmling	6/18	5/30
La Junta	4/26	4/12
Lake City	6/18	6/7
Lakewood	5/10	5/1
Lamar	4/30	4/15
Las Animas	4/29	4/16
Leadville	6/21	6/10
Limon	5/13	5/3
Littleton	5/3	4/25
Longmont	5/4	4/28
Loveland	5/8	4/29
Manassa	6/8	5/23
Mancos	6/5	5/12
Maybell	6/12	5/22
Meeker	6/12	5/25
Mesa Verde National Park	5/16	5/2
Monte Vista	6/8	5/20
Montrose	5/11	4/27
Monument	5/17	5/4
Nederland	6/24	6/7
New Raymer	5/14	5/2
Northglenn	5/7	4/21
Nunn	5/11	5/1
Ordway	5/3	4/28
Ouray	5/29	5/10
Pagosa Springs	6/27	6/14
Palisade	4/20	4/4
Paonia	5/23	4/30

Location	32°	28°
Pueblo WSO AP	5/1	4/18
Ralston Reservoir	5/13	4/25
Rangely 1 E	5/15	5/1
Red Feather Lakes	6/20	6/4
Rico	7/1	6/15
Ridgway	6/21	5/31
Rifle	5/19	5/8
Rocky Ford	5/1	4/18
Rye	5/24	5/13
Saguache	6/4	5/16
Salida	5/29	5/14
Sedgwick	4/30	4/24
Silverton	7/12	6/25
Springfield 7 WSW	5/3	4/23
Steamboat Springs	7/3	6/12
Sterling	5/7	4/25
Taylor Park	6/24	6/8
Telluride	6/28	6/16
Trinidad	5/11	4/27
Vail	6/26	6/7
Vallecito Dam	6/9	5/26
Walden	7/5	6/12
Walsenburg	5/11	4/29
Westcliffe	6/14	5/30
Wetmore	5/14	4/30
Williams Fork Dam	6/25	6/7
Winter Park	6/25	6/7
Wolf Creek Pass 1 E	6/18	6/11
Wray	5/10	4/27
Yampa	6/20	6/4
Yuma	5/7	4/23

may build beyond the "garden variety" and become severe, producing heavy rain, large hail, and possibly tornadoes.

Storms that develop close to I-25 tend to grow especially mean as they roll across the vast flat prairie of eastern Colorado. Veteran storm chasers often drive long distances on the smaller roads and highways that crisscross eastern Colorado, searching for powerful storms to photograph. This stormy sequence is not an occasional occurrence over our state; it is pretty much a daily routine in June and July along the Front Range and out across the plains.

Once again, the mountains hold the key to weather conditions that we experience during the warm weather months. Think of the mountain peaks as giant heating elements at an altitude of 12,000 to 14,000 feet. The sun's energy does not warm our air directly to any great extent. Instead, the solar energy—meteorologists call it short-wave radiation— that reaches the top of the atmosphere goes through a series of events before actually heating the air. Some of the sun's rays are reflected back into space directly by clouds, snow cover, and dust in the air. Another portion of the energy is absorbed by lakes and oceans and heats the water. Some of the incoming energy evaporates water and is stored as latent heat, to be released later when the water vapor condenses

A mix of low-level cumulus clouds and upper-level cirro-cumulus clouds on a summer morning in eastern Colorado. This mix of clouds often is a sign of unstable air that may lead to strong thunderstorms later in the day.

back into liquid. Finally, some of the sunlight directly heats rocks and sand, grass, fields, and forests. The heat from the ocean surface and the land masses is the primary source of energy for the atmosphere. The warmth radiates from the land and sea and heats the air just above it, similar to the way a stove burner heats a pan. The warmer air becomes less dense because the molecules have more energy and move farther apart, and the air rises, just like a hot air balloon. This rising air is called convection, the key to most of our summertime stormy weather.

Convection from typical daytime heating causes the majority of our thunderstorms in Colorado. By early afternoon, the sun has heated the ground for many hours and temperatures at the surface have reached a peak. The warm ground heats the air just above it, causing rising columns of air, called thermals, to bubble up all over the place. Thermals are what glider pilots and soaring birds love to find, since they provide lift. As the air rises, there is less pressure above the earth's surface, and the bubble of air expands. This expansion causes

Convection

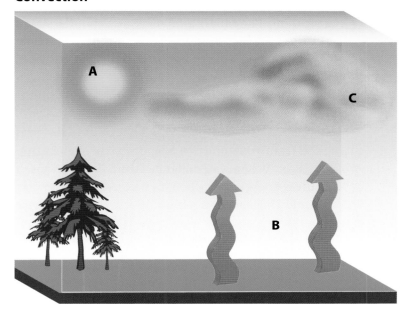

A. Energy from the sun heats the earth's surface and the air above it.

B. Molecules in the air above the surface move faster and farther apart as it heats up. As this happens, the air becomes less dense and begins to rise like a hot air balloon.

C. As the warm air rises, it cools, allowing moisture to condense, creating clouds. The point at which the water vapor condenses into liquid water may occur rather suddenly, giving the bottom of the cloud a flat appearance. This is known as the lifted condensation level, (LCL).

Late Morning

Early Afternoon

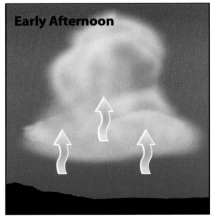

Late Afternoon

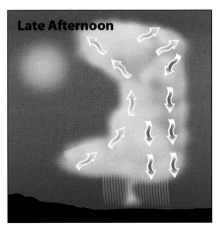

As the surface is warmed by the sun, rising columns of air called thermals develop. The rising air forms cumulus clouds that begin to build higher into the sky in the early afternoon. By late afternoon, these clouds form into thunderstorms. The rain cools the air, forming descending air currents and gusty winds.

the air bubble, also called an air parcel, to cool at a rate of about 5.4 degrees Fahrenheit per 1,000 feet of ascent (the dry adiabatic lapse rate). Cooler air cannot hold as much water vapor as warm air, so moisture begins to condense in the form of clouds. Often the condensation occurs rather abruptly at a certain altitude and temperature, which explains why the puffy clouds of a summer sky may develop a flat bottom. That flat bottom marks the exact height where the moisture in the air parcel began to condense from water vapor back into liquid water, a height meteorologists call the lifted condensation level (LCL).

In all of this, mountains provide an elevated platform for the initial heating of the air. Rather than an air parcel being heated at sea level and having to rise thousands of feet to reach the LCL, the mountains put that heating element much higher into the atmosphere. Clouds form very quickly over the mountains during a summer morning, and then those clouds can drift off over the plains by mid-afternoon. The mountains serve as a thunderstorm factory, because once condensation occurs, some chain reaction events begin. Simply put, it takes energy to evaporate water, but that energy is given back when the water condenses back into liquid. When you step out of the shower, think of the chill you feel before you towel off. That chill is the heat taken from your body to evaporate the water from your skin. When water changes from liquid to gas, it requires energy, and when it changes back from gas to liquid, that energy is released. So, in the atmosphere, water vapor condensing into a cloud actually gives off heat. That warming makes the bubble or parcel of air buoyant once again, so that it continues to rise higher into the sky. As it rises there is less pressure and therefore more expansion, and thus the parcel cools and additional water vapor condenses to form more clouds. This of course means more latent heat is released, warming the parcel again, it rises farther, creating more clouds, and so on high into the sky—an atmospheric chain reaction. The amount of heat released by condensation is considerable, since the moist adiabatic lapse rate is about 3.2 degrees Fahrenheit per 1,000 feet of ascent. Thus moist rising air will cool at a much slower rate.

As the moist air rises, some of the water vapor condenses into droplets of water, but much of it skips that phase and forms tiny ice crystals. By the time you reach an altitude of 16,000 to 18,000 feet, temperatures generally stay below freezing even in the middle of summer. The tiny droplets of water and crystals of ice swirl around inside the cloud like an immense atmospheric traffic jam. As in a traffic jam, collisions occur, and the droplets and ice crystals lock together like so many car bumpers in a fender-bender. As more and more tiny bits of water crash into each other, raindrops and snowflakes form and grow. Thus even on the hottest summer day, a tremendous blizzard can be swirling around just 3 or 4 miles over our heads.

Once evaporated, a water molecule spends 10 days in the air.

Eventually, the raindrops and snowflakes become large enough that they can no longer float, and they fall to earth. It is rarely a direct flight, as updrafts may keep the rain and snow suspended in the clouds. As time passes, the drops and flakes go up and down and swirl around until they finally land. It is this up-and-down motion that helps to create lightning, hail, and strong winds.

Flash Facts

A 1996 study found that 1 in every 52 lightning strikes in the Denver area results in an insurance claim. The national average is 1 in 57.

Lightning is caused by the violent motions inside the cloud. As the tiny drops of rain and crystals of snow swirl around, electrons are torn away from their surface, creating huge amounts of static electricity. A good analogy to consider is shuffling your feet across a carpet. The warmth that you feel on the bottom of your feet is caused by friction. The friction creates static electricity that you see as a spark that jumps when you touch the light switch.

In the thunderstorm cloud, the static charge grows until it is so strong that it overcomes any resistance in the air, and a giant spark of lightning is created. But does the lightning move down from the cloud, or up from the ground? The answer is both. If you look at a battery, you know that electricity has both positive and negative charges. Just as the adage has it for people, opposites are attracted to one another. As the turbulence in a thunderstorm strips off the negatively charged electrons, they tend to collect at the base of the thunderstorm, giving it a net negative charge. This negative charge attracts (or induces) a

Lightning Safety

In Colorado one is more likely to be injured or killed by lightning than any other weather phenomenon, and Colorado ranks third nationally in lightning-related fatalities. Even non-severe thunderstorms are capable of producing deadly lightning. For the sake of public safety, lightning experts have developed simple rules for people to follow whenever thunderstorms are threatening.

Indoors

- Stay inside. Stay away from windows, doors, and porches.
- Don't use corded telephones or cell phones.
- Avoid contact with electrical equipment or cords. Unplug equipment that is not absolutely necessary.
- Avoid contact with plumbing. Do not wash your hands, do not take a shower, do not wash dishes, and do not do laundry.

Outdoors

- Seek shelter indoors or inside a metal-roofed car immediately if the time between the lightning flash and its subsequent thunder is 30 seconds or less. Wait 30 minutes after hearing the last thunder before venturing from your protective shelter.
- Do NOT seek shelter under tall isolated trees. Standing under a tall tree significantly increases your chance of being struck by lightning.
- Do NOT seek shelter under partially enclosed buildings, such as picnic shelters.
- Know the weather forecast and watch the weather develop through the day. If there is a high chance of thunderstorms, end your outdoor activities earlier in the day.
- Avoid camping in open fields, on exposed ridges, or above timberline. Keep your campsite away from tall isolated trees or other tall objects. Set up camp in a low area, but avoid floodplains. Tents will not protect you from lighting.
- Stay away from metal objects, such as fences, poles, and backpacks. The electrical current from the lightning can travel long distances and find such conductors.

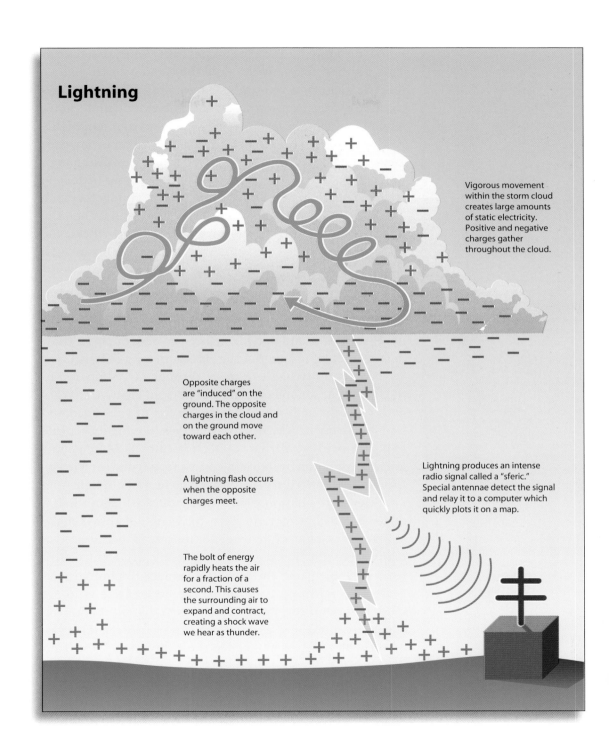

Lightning

Vigorous movement within the storm cloud creates large amounts of static electricity. Positive and negative charges gather throughout the cloud.

Opposite charges are "induced" on the ground. The opposite charges in the cloud and on the ground move toward each other.

A lightning flash occurs when the opposite charges meet.

Lightning produces an intense radio signal called a "sferic." Special antennae detect the signal and relay it to a computer which quickly plots it on a map.

The bolt of energy rapidly heats the air for a fraction of a second. This causes the surrounding air to expand and contract, creating a shock wave we hear as thunder.

Lightning and iPods

Lightning doesn't discriminate. If you can hear thunder, then you are at risk of being hit by lightning.

In July 2006, Jason Bunch was mowing the lawn and listening to his iPod at his home in Castle Rock when he was struck by lightning. "I woke up and blood was coming out my ears," Bunch said. The teenager has large scars on his feet and smaller burn marks on his hands. "From where the iPod was, it damaged my hearing and it ruptured my eardrums. Where the cord was, it burned me all down my body," said Bunch. "We need to shave my head because my hair is like dreadlocks.... I'm just extremely blessed to be alive."

Writing in a British medical journal, a team of London doctors warns of the dangers of listening to an iPod or using a cell phone during a thunderstorm. Having such devices near your head when you are hit by lightning can result in even more severe injuries; the metallic devices and wires can act as a conductor, causing potentially lethal internal injuries.

When a person is hit by lightning, the high resistance of human skin usually results in lightning being conducted over the skin rather than through the body—a process known as flashover. But one of the doctors notes that conductive materials in direct contact with skin, such as metallic objects, disrupt the flashover and result in internal injury with a greater risk of dying.

continued ▶

positive charge on the ground beneath the thunderstorm. This positive charge will follow the thunderstorm like an electric shadow. Eventually the amount of negative and positive charge grows so great that the two begin to move closer together. The negatively charged electrons move fairly easily down from the cloud base in a thin, virtually invisible zigzagging path called a stepped leader. The positive charges do not flow as easily as electrons, so they need a little help to move, traveling best over some type of conductor, such as a tall metal tower, tree, golf club—or person. When the positive charge and the negative charge finally meet, the brilliant flash called the return stroke actually occurs. All the action described in this paragraph takes just a few millionths of a second to occur.

The big danger with lightning is in becoming the pathway that allows the charges to connect and flow. That is why you never want to stand outside in an open area during a thunderstorm. It turns out that the air is a pretty good insulator, so the charges struggle to move through air, compared to moving along an object, such as a person. Positive charges can travel through your body to the top of your head and flag down any nearby negative charges looking for a place to go. Unfortunately, that connection can kill. More people are fatally injured by lightning on average each year than by tornadoes or hurricanes. The average number of lightning fatalities in the nation each year is 100, with about half a dozen deaths in Colorado. The stories do not always make as big a news item as hurricanes or tornadoes, because there really is not much to see after a lightning strike: the victim is rarely shown, and there is little damage to photograph.

During lightning conditions, the best advice is to get indoors, even if the storm clouds seem distant. Lightning can easily travel several miles and can strike even if the sky directly above is clear—hence the expression "bolt from the blue."

Lightning may travel up and down the jagged path of the stepped leader several times, back and forth like water sloshing in a tub. The flashes are so very quick that our eyes cannot discern the individual flashes and instead we see a flicker of lightning over and over. Just as a movie is actually a series of individual images fooling our eyes into a sense of continuous motion, the speed of the individual flashes is so quick we see them as one flash that flickers. Studies have shown that lightning does indeed strike twice—in fact, that flicker may actually be as many as a dozen multiple flashes in the same lightning channel, all in the course of a split second.

Lightning is also extraordinarily hot, about 50,000 degrees Fahrenheit—or five times the temperature of the surface of the sun. As this arc of energy races through the air, it rapidly heats the air for a fraction of a second. This heating causes the surrounding air to expand rapidly and then contract as the heat source quickly disappears and the air rapidly cools. The very quick heating and cooling of the molecules of air creates a sound wave. Thunder can be scary, but is not dangerous—though the family dog might disagree. In fact, thunder can be useful. The sound waves take about five seconds to travel 1 mile, while the lightning is seen instantaneously. So when you see the lightning, begin to count slowly until you hear the thunder. When you hear the thunder, divide the number of seconds counted by five to get the approximate distance from you to the lightning. As an example, let's say that you see flash of lightning. You count to fifteen before hearing

The moral: leave the electronics for inside use when lightning looms.

The 30/30 Rule

A good rule to learn is the 30/30 lightning safety rule. This simply states if the time between seeing a lightning flash and hearing the thunder is 30 seconds or less, seek shelter immediately. Then stay in that safe place until 30 minutes after the last sound of thunder.

Colorado typically experiences more than half a million cloud-to-ground lightning strikes each year. Most lightning casualties in the United States occur between 12:00 p.m. and 4:00 p.m. local time.

(top) It is estimated that lightning causes over $330 million in damage in the United States each year. (middle) A dramatic flash of light illuminates the skies over Wheat Ridge on a summer's night. (bottom) A large bolt fires from the skies over Lakewood in late June of 2006.

Photographing Lightning

When thunder rumbles, the hunt is on for Colorado lightning photographer Ken Langford.

The object of his lens is a powerful combination of beauty and danger, and pursuing the perfect picture is not for the faint of heart. With each lightning strike there is the promise of catching the fiery beast on film, or the threat of death. In Langford's own words, his chases are "precarious, because lightning is capricious. I tend to be cautious."

A weather aficionado since his childhood days in Connecticut, Langford is a member of Colorado's Lightning Data Center, whose mission is to better understand lightning for the sake of public safety. He is also a widely published photographer, and his first advice to anyone wanting to photograph lightning is simple: stay safe. "If you always shoot from inside a car with the windows rolled up," he says, "then that is the safest thing that you can do."

Langford's next tip: be prepared to shoot with the first rumble of thunder. "The first time you hear thunder you need to leave to go shoot lightning, because the average life of a non-severe thunderstorm is only about twenty minutes. You can get perfectly good lightning out of a non-severe storm. If you drag your heels for ten minutes getting your equipment together, then the storm is dissipating by the time you go out to shoot."

When thunderstorms do bubble up along the Front Range, Langford already knows where to go to get the best shots. "I have dozens of spots around the city picked out. If I look up and see a storm, then I can just go to one of my spots and start shooting the storm, ideally within five to ten minutes."

Lightning strikes over Sloan's Lake and St. Anthony's Hospital in Denver.

Langford generally uses a 24mm lens for close storms, and 50 or 60mm for less close stuff. Beyond 200mm, he says, an atmospheric attenuation factor colors the lightning and diminishes its spectacular qualities. He prefers to photograph lightning on film rather than using digital technology, because film is better suited to shooting at night without producing visual noise and to capturing the contrast ratio of lightning.

If the rumble of thunder sends you scrambling for your camera, Langford offers these pointers:

1. Know how to use the manual settings of your camera.
2. Shoot at night.
3. Use a tripod.
4. Use the widest aperture setting.
5. Use a slow film such as Kodachrome 64.
6. Focus to infinity.
7. Shoot using the bulb setting.

Lightning Injuries/Deaths by County and Month (1980–2006)

	April Injuries	April Death	May Injuries	May Death	June Injuries	June Death	July Injuries	July Death
Adams	1	1	1	1	6	1		
Alamosa								
Arapahoe	2		12	1			1	1
Archuleta	1						2	
Baca								
Bent								
Boulder					12	2	9	1
Broomfield								
Chaffee					2		2	1
Cheyenne								
Clear Creek							4	
Conejos								
Costilla								
Crowley								
Custer								
Delta								
Denver			3	1	12	1	3	1
Dolores								
Douglas			1		2	1	6	
Eagle					14	1		
El Paso			12	2	11		11	5
Elbert						1		
Fremont						1		
Garfield								2
Gilpin								
Grand					19		1	
Gunnison							8	
Hinsdale								
Huerfano							5	
Jackson								
Jefferson			13	1	7	2	12	4
Kiowa								

	August		September		October		Total	
	Injuries	Death	Injuries	Death	Injuries	Death	Injuries	Death
Adams	4						12	3
Alamosa	2						2	
Arapahoe	5		2	1			22	3
Archuleta							3	
Baca								
Bent								
Boulder	6	1					27	4
Broomfield								
Chaffee				1			4	2
Cheyenne								
Clear Creek	2						6	
Conejos								
Costilla			1				1	
Crowley								
Custer								
Delta								
Denver	2		2				22	3
Dolores								
Douglas	2		1				12	1
Eagle		1	3				17	2
El Paso	16	2	1				51	9
Elbert								1
Fremont								1
Garfield								2
Gilpin								
Grand							20	
Gunnison			2				10	
Hinsdale								
Huerfano	6						11	
Jackson								
Jefferson	1		2				35	7
Kiowa								

	April		May		June		July	
	Injuries	Death	Injuries	Death	Injuries	Death	Injuries	Death
Kit Carson								
La Plata							4	
Lake							2	
Larimer			2	1	10	1	15	1
Las Animas								
Lincoln			1					
Logan							1	
Mesa		1			2			
Mineral								
Moffat								1
Montezuma				1				
Montrose				1	1			
Morgan							2	
Otero								
Ouray						1		
Park					1		1	1
Phillips								
Pitkin	2	1					1	2
Prowers								
Pueblo					5	1	1	
Rio Blanco								
Rio Grande					1	3		
Routt							3	2
Saguache							1	1
San Juan							1	1
San Miguel					2			
Segwick								
Summit	2	1			2		7	
Teller							2	2
Washington								
Weld			1		4			
Yuma								

	August		September		October		Total	
	Injuries	Death	Injuries	Death	Injuries	Death	Injuries	Death
Kit Carson	2						2	
La Plata	1	1					5	1
Lake							2	
Larimer	18	2	1		5		51	5
Las Animas								
Lincoln							1	
Logan							1	
Mesa			1				3	1
Mineral								
Moffat								1
Montezuma	3						3	1
Montrose				2			1	3
Morgan	1		1	1			4	1
Otero				2				2
Ouray								1
Park	2	3					4	4
Phillips								
Pitkin							3	3
Prowers			3	1			3	1
Pueblo			1				7	1
Rio Blanco	1	1					1	1
Rio Grande							1	3
Routt			1	1			4	3
Saguache							1	1
San Juan	4						5	1
San Miguel	1						3	
Segwick								
Summit	2	1					13	2
Teller	2	2					4	4
Washington								
Weld	2		1				8	
Yuma								

U. S. Cloud-to-Ground Lightning Flash Density per Square Mile

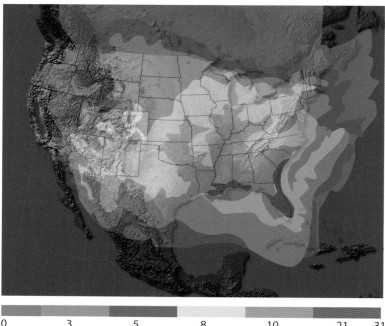

0   3   5   8   10   21   31

the thunder. Fifteen divided by five is three, so the lightning strike was 3 miles away. This can be a life-saving tool, because if the amount of time between the flash and the thunder is growing smaller, it may be a good idea to stop what you are doing and get inside.

It is possible to track lightning and use it as a forecasting and warning tool. Each cloud-to-ground lightning strike creates a brief but intense radio signal called a sferic. This signal is the crackling sound that you hear when listening to an AM radio station during a thunderstorm. The sferic has a unique signature for a cloud-to-ground lightning strike. Special antennae have been set up all over the United States to detect this special radio signal. When a lightning strike occurs, the sferic is detected by many of these antennae at virtually the same time, since the signal travels at the speed of light. By triangulating between each of the antennae, one can pinpoint the location of the lightning. The calculations are all done

Colorado Cloud-to-Ground Lightning Flash Density per Square Mile

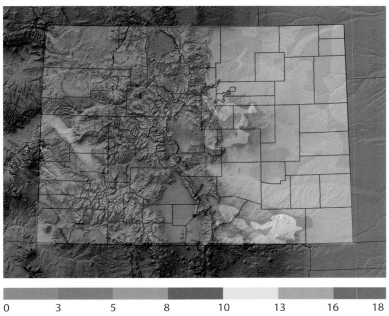

0	3	5	8	10	13	16	18

by computer. The system is so fast that meteorologists and researchers have often reported seeing the lightning out the window, then seeing the strike displayed on a computer screen, and finally hearing the thunder.

Some research links sudden increases and decreases in lightning frequency with the development of tornadoes. Thunderstorms are immense electrical systems with many complex spinning motions. There seems to be some correlation to a peak in cloud-to-ground lightning activity about fifteen to twenty minutes before a tornado forms, followed by a sudden slowing of lightning activity at the time of the touchdown of the tornado. This relationship is not clearly understood at present, but further research could lead to additional methods to help detect and warn of tornado conditions.

It is common for Colorado to receive 10,000 to 15,000 lightning strikes on a single stormy day. The lightning-strike detection systems are used by area TV stations and are important in the detection of lightning-caused forest fires. Forest rangers can refer to the lightning-strike map and send aircraft out to look for signs of smoke in areas where lightning has been intense. The system is also used by National Aeronautics and Space Administration (NASA) and is considered a "launch critical" device—in other words, if lightning is detected near the Kennedy Space Center, a rocket launch will be delayed.

You are generally safe in your car during a lightning storm, provided that it is not a convertible. It is another "atmospheric legend" that the car is safe due to the rubber tires. If static charges can move through a mile or two of air, they will have no problem skipping over 6 inches of automobile tire. The reason that cars (and airplanes) are generally safe during thunderstorms is that if lightning strikes, the electric charges tend to flow over the outer surface of the vehicle rather than inside.

Hail Tales

Hail is another result of the extreme turbulence inside a thunderstorm. Inside the storm cloud is a swirling combination of snowflakes, raindrops, and something called supercooled water. Under certain conditions, water may stay in liquid form even at temperatures well below freezing. This supercooled

Hail as big as baseballs can cause massive property damage.

water really wants to become ice, but it needs something to attach itself to. A bit of dust or a tiny crystal of ice usually does the trick nicely. In a thunderstorm, the wild wind motions throw tiny ice crystals and bits of dust around, and these bump into the supercooled water to form tiny little nuggets of ice. These nuggets are further tossed about, bumping into more ice crystals and more supercooled water, and they gradually grow to become small hailstones. The upward motion of the hail is supported by the thunderstorm updraft, while the downward motion is, of course from gravity. The hail will go up and down and all around inside the thunderstorm as it encounters all the turbulent motions inside the cloud.

Think of the flight of the hailstone as a giant juggling act in the sky. Each trip around the inside of the thunderstorm adds layer after layer of ice, and the hailstone grows larger. Eventually the hail gets so big and heavy that it cannot stay suspended in the cloud any longer, and it comes crashing down to earth. It is estimated that a hailstone the size of a baseball needs to have an updraft of at least 100 mph to stay aloft. When such large hail comes down, some of it melts before hitting the ground, but much of the stone remains intact all the way to earth. The result can be devastating, for large hail causes millions of dollars in damage each year to crops, cars, and rooftops across Colorado, especially from the Front Range to the Kansas border.

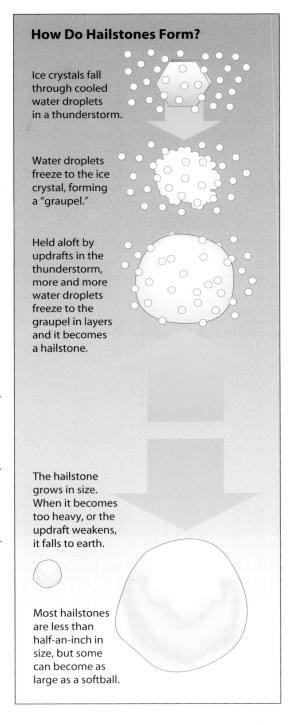

How Do Hailstones Form?

Ice crystals fall through cooled water droplets in a thunderstorm.

Water droplets freeze to the ice crystal, forming a "graupel."

Held aloft by updrafts in the thunderstorm, more and more water droplets freeze to the graupel in layers and it becomes a hailstone.

The hailstone grows in size. When it becomes too heavy, or the updraft weakens, it falls to earth.

Most hailstones are less than half-an-inch in size, but some can become as large as a softball.

Strong Straight-line Winds

Another dangerous type of weather associated with thunderstorms is the downburst, a strong straight-line wind that differs from a tornado in formation, but produces results that can be just as damaging. Downburst winds are created by the downward rush of rain-cooled air from the base of the thunderstorm. As the rain and hail fall from the storm, evaporation and cooling occur. This cooling makes the air heavier, and it sinks rapidly toward the ground. When the air hits the ground, it fans out in all directions, swirling away from the thunderstorm base like water spraying down from a garden hose. This swirling air has a horizontal axis of rotation, as opposed to the vertical one of a tornado. Nonetheless, the winds of a downburst can reach speeds of hurricane strength (75 mph) and may even exceed 100 mph. These winds can do great damage and even cause death. Just a few years ago a man was killed in a trailer home in Washington County by a blast of downburst winds.

Downburst

A downburst is created when rain-cooled air drops rapidly to the ground and fans out in all directions. Downbursts often reach speeds of 60–75 mph and can exceed 100 mph.

Scientists can study wind-damage patterns and determine if a storm was a downburst or a tornado. In the tornado, the debris will be patterned into a series of swirling curls along a distance of hundreds of yards or even miles. In a downburst, the debris will fan out from a central point, much as if you blew a breath of air over a layer of sand. Downbursts tend to create wider damage fields than tornadoes, but usually are not as strong. A major downburst might have winds of 125 mph, while a powerful tornado will have winds exceeding 200 mph, even approaching 275 mph. Winds of just 100 mph will do significant damage to trees and buildings.

Recent studies show that strong downburst wind events may actually get some of their momentum from the jet stream. Satellite photos indicate that just before a powerful downburst, the top of the thunderstorm cloud may actually sink several thousand feet. It is almost as if the storm is taking a deep breath and exhaling out a big blast of wind. Research shows that a portion of the jet stream momentum may actually travel down through the thunderstorm and race out from the bottom of the storm. This gives the thunderstorm winds an extra boost of power. Large-scale damaging downburst events are called derechos, from the Spanish word meaning "straight ahead," and are often associated with this impulse of jet stream winds that traverse through the thunderstorm. Derechos often have a very distinct pattern on radar as the middle part of a line of thunderstorms will bow out ahead of the rest of the line. One could imagine that the powerful straight-ahead wind flow is blowing the heart of the storm cell out ahead of its flanks. In meteorology, this type of radar report is simply called a bow echo. Strong, large-scale downburst wind events can occur over eastern Colorado, but they are much more common in the Midwest. Our drier climate limits the formation of most long squall-line thunderstorms, which are much more likely to feature derecho events, since they have longer life cycles and thus time for all of the atmospheric elements to come together.

Large scale damaging downburst events are called "derechos" from the Spanish word meaning "straight ahead."

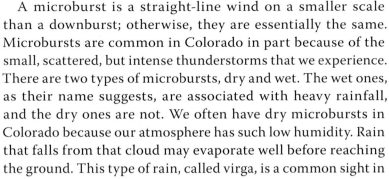

A microburst is a straight-line wind on a smaller scale than a downburst; otherwise, they are essentially the same. Microbursts are common in Colorado in part because of the small, scattered, but intense thunderstorms that we experience. There are two types of microbursts, dry and wet. The wet ones, as their name suggests, are associated with heavy rainfall, and the dry ones are not. We often have dry microbursts in Colorado because our atmosphere has such low humidity. Rain that falls from that cloud may evaporate well before reaching the ground. This type of rain, called virga, is a common sight in our summertime sky. Virga is that tattered cloud edge or the ragged look to the bottom of a thunderstorm. When the rain evaporates, it cools the surrounding air, making the air denser and causing the air parcel to drop quickly to the ground. The air then hits the surface and fans out in all directions.

Virga is precipitation that evaporates before reaching the ground and locally strong winds can often develop below areas where virga is observed.

Forecasters sometimes refer to microbursts as out-flow boundaries. Often these strong, gusty winds of 50 to 75 mph will whip through, blowing over lawn furniture, patio umbrellas, and such items but bringing not a drop of rain. Wet microbursts, on the other hand, have enough moisture to produce strong winds and heavy rainfall; they are sometimes mis-taken for tornadoes because the rain obscures visibility so much that no one can tell if there was a funnel or not. The outflow boundaries are important for meteorologists to keep an eye on, since several small thunderstorms scattered over the plains may produce microburst outflows that can eventually collide. When these outflow boundaries run into each other, the air is forced to rise and can form into a new thunderstorm. Sometimes small tornadoes will develop along these colliding boundaries as the surface wind patterns swirl around and are drawn into the updraft of the developing thunderstorm.

Microbursts are major hazards to aviation and have caused several airline accidents. Pilots always try to take off and land into the wind. By flying into the wind, there is a greater amount of air flowing over the wing surfaces to create lift. This is very important on landing, too, when speed and engine power are reduced. If a microburst occurs near the airport, it can suddenly cause the wind to shift to the opposite direction. A plane landing into the wind will quickly have a tailwind instead of a headwind. The plane loses lift and begins to fall too fast, ending up short of the runway. If there is time, the pilot can increase engine power to gain more lift, but it takes jet engines a few seconds to increase thrust, and those few seconds are not available when the plane is already close to the ground. Major airports, including Denver International Airport, have sophisticated wind-measuring equipment that can identify developing microburst conditions and warn pilots ahead of time. With that warning, a pilot might elect to circle until the microburst conditions are over, or even go to a different airport.

Approaching and departing aircraft rely upon twenty-nine wind speed and direction sensors that provide crucial wind-shear information to a central computer that reports to air traffic controllers at Denver International Airport.

Heavy Rains and Flooding

As the lazy days of summer roll on, the main threat from thunderstorms switches from the June worries of hail, microbursts, and tornadoes to heavy rain and flash flooding. By July, the jet stream winds typically become much lighter over the United States, and the strongest winds aloft tend to be found over Canada. The lack of strong winds at 25,000 to 30,000 feet means that thunderstorms do not have much in the way of steering currents. Storms that develop tend to move at only 5 to 15 mph and therefore can dump a tremendous amount of rain over any one particular area. It is not uncommon during the middle and late summer for a thunderstorm to produce 3 to 6 inches of rain in just a few hours' time. This kind of downpour cannot completely soak into the soil, so it runs off into ditches, dry washes, and low-lying areas. Slow-moving thunderstorms and flash flooding are the main weather hazards in Colorado from mid-July through early September.

Up to a foot of rain fell in just four hours on Big Thompson Canyon.

Urban Flooding

With the rapidly increasing population along the Front Range metropolitan area and the reshaping of the area's topography by urban and suburban development, the risks associated with flooding are greater than ever.

The cities most at risk are along Colorado's Front Range. Boulder, Fort Collins, Golden, and Colorado Springs top the list, mainly because of their proximity to the foothills. Heavy rain in the adjacent canyons could inundate these communities simply because these cities reside in drainage basins. Floodwaters will cascade downstream right into the homes and businesses nestled against the foothills of the Rocky Mountains.

A more likely threat—one that threatens every community in Colorado—is torrential rain from a stationary thunderstorm located over an urban area, according to flood expert Matt Kelsch, a hydrometeorologist with the University Corporation for Atmospheric Research in Boulder. As little as 1 inch of rain during a fifteen-minute storm could create dangerous flood conditions within a city. Timely flash-flood warnings may be unlikely in such a short-lived storm, and the resulting flooding could create potentially life-threatening hazards.

City streams and waterways overflow their banks during urban floods. Hazardous materials may contaminate the flood waters. Fires and explosions occur as gas lines rupture and electrical lines spark. Flooded roads become rivers. Even large SUVs become buoyant in water as shallow as 2 feet deep. Once a car begins to float the driver no longer controls it, and the vehicle will travel toward the faster and deeper water.

The first step in making this deadly mistake can be as simple as attempting to drive through a water-covered road. "Drivers often find themselves in trouble long before they know it," Kelsch points out. "SUVs have a higher center of gravity, so when they do float they have a tendency to flip over.

City planners are reacting to the inevitability of flooding by developing better mitigation techniques, especially in newer developments. Bike paths meander along floodplains, underpasses along natural waterways are wider and reinforced to withstand the force of floodwaters, and developers are using parks and greenbelts to retain more natural ground cover within the urban environment. Flooding will still occur, but the intent is to allow the water to flow through the drainage basin as naturally—and with as little obstruction—as possible.

Flood-Safety

1. Avoid getting caught in a flood. Stay aware of the weather forecast and observe the weather as it changes through the day.
2. Do not drive through water-covered roads. If you can't see through to the bottom of the road, then the depth of the water is unknown.
3. Climb to safety. If you are in a canyon or any location where the water is rising, then climb to the highest point.
4. Avoid staying, or camping, in low-lying areas, especially during the thunderstorm season.
5. Have an escape plan and a place to meet other family members in case you get separated. If family members do get separated, have everyone call a friend or relative living outside your immediate area.

The combination of light winds aloft and our rugged terrain can create intense downpours with tragic consequences. The Big Thompson Flood of 1976 remains one of the worst weather disasters in state history. The weather situation on that day was a combination tailor-made to produce incredible localized rainfall amounts. The winds aloft were very light, only 5 to 10 mph at 20,000 feet. At the surface, a weak cold front had pushed into northeastern Colorado and had stalled up against the foothills. Behind the front, moisture-laden winds swirled into northeastern Colorado from the east. This weather pattern created a thunderstorm that stalled for hours between Estes Park and Loveland. The easterly winds served as a moisture transport that fed the humid air into the mountains and foothills. The rugged terrain forced that air to rise, fueling the intense thunderstorm. This is not an unusual development, but in this particular case, the light winds aloft could not blow the storm away from the mountains.

In the summer of 1997, a similar event on a slightly smaller scale hit on the southwestern side of Fort Collins. This intense, nearly stationary storm developed under conditions much the same as those twenty-one years earlier and dropped 14 inches of rain over just a few acres of land. The resultant runoff created

The Big Thompson Flood

- Weak upper level winds allowed the storm to remain stationary over the steep narrow cliffs of Big Thompson Canyon.

- The storm gained strength from low level easterly winds bringing in a steady stream of humid moist air.

- 10 to 12 inches of rain poured into the canyon, with 8 inches falling in less than 2 hours. The steep, rocky canyon walls channeled the rainwater, and the river quickly overflowed its banks and became a flash flood.

WARM MOIST AIR

Notable Colorado Floods		
Date	**Major Stream or Location**	**Deaths**
May 1864	Cherry Creek at Denver	N/A
July 1896	Bear Creek at Morrison	27
Oct. 1911	San Juan River near Pagosa Springs	2
July 1912	Cherry Creek at Denver	2
June 1921	Arkansas River at Pueblo	78
May 1935	Monument Creek at Colorado Springs	18
May 1935	Kiowa Creek near Kiowa	9
May 1942	South Platte River Basin	N/A
May 1955	Purgatoire River at Trinidad	2
June 1957	Western Colorado	N/A
June 1965	South Platte River at Denver	8
June 1965	Arkansas River Basin	16
May 1969	South Platte River Basin	0
Sept. 1970	Southwest Colorado	0
May 1973	South Platte River at Denver	10
July 1976	Big Thompson River in Larimer County	144
July 1982	Fall River at Estes Park	3
June 1983	North Central Counties	10
May–June 1984	Western and Northwestern Counties	2
May–June 1993	Western Slope	0
July 1997	Fort Collins and 13 Eastern Counties	6
May–June 1999	Colorado Springs and 12 Eastern Counties	0

Source: Kistner and Associates, 1999. Flood Hazard Mitigation found at
http://www.assessment.ucar.edu/flood/flood_table.html.

a lake full of water that pooled behind a railroad embankment. Eventually the waters broke through an overwhelmed drainage culvert and poured into a mobile home park. It was an eerie scene as rescuers fought raging waters while dodging flames from ruptured propane tanks in their attempt to save the residents. Despite their courageous efforts, six people lost their lives.

The very next day another flash flood occurred in northeastern Colorado near Sterling. Once again, sluggish thunderstorms dropped several inches of rain over a small area. The flat terrain allowed the water to spread out over a larger area, but many roads and fields were flooded by the storm.

A few safety tips are worth mentioning in the event of flash floods. First, know your area and understand the risk, if any, of flash flooding. If you live in or are camping in an area that is liable to flood, have an emergency plan already in place and discuss it with your family—even the youngest members. Be on the lookout during the middle to late summer for any sign of thunderstorms in the area. If the storms are slow to move away, there may be a potential for flash floods. Remember that in mountainous areas, rain upstream from you, not directly overhead, creates a flash flood. If you have access to TV or radio, try to stay up on the latest weather information. In the

In the Big Thompson Flood, 144 lives were lost, and floodwaters destroyed 418 homes and 52 businesses. Damage from the flood was estimated at $40 million.

Fort Collins, July 28, 1997. Floodwaters rose 5.5 feet in three minutes along Spring Creek. (below) During the storm event, 14.5 inches of rain were measured over Quail Hollow in southwest Fort Collins.

Fort Collins, July 28, 1997. In a mobile home park along Spring Creek, a rescuer struggles through flood waters, with fire from ruptured propane tanks nearby.

event of a flash flood, move very quickly to higher ground. If you are in your car, do not attempt to drive through a flooded area of unknown depth. Many deaths have been caused by drivers trying to ford flooded spots and instead being swept away by raging water. At the very least, your car may be completely flooded and be totaled by water damage.

Summer Monsoon

The late summer monsoon is a wet weather pattern that develops each year across Colorado and the southwestern United States. The term monsoon is defined as a seasonal shift of the wind. Most people think of a monsoon as the rainy season in tropical regions. In Colorado, weather forecasters speak of the monsoon as the annual flow of moist winds across Mexico, Arizona, and New Mexico. The official beginning of the monsoon is defined by forecasters as the time when the dew point temperature in Phoenix, Arizona, reaches at least 55 degrees for three consecutive days. This humid air then moves farther north and helps to fuel an almost daily dose of soggy, slow-moving thunderstorms that can drop several inches of rain in just an hour. Satellite images clearly show that the monsoon moisture moves from the Pacific Ocean and flows across Mexico into the desert Southwest and Colorado.

On occasion, moisture from a dying hurricane in the Gulf of Mexico will join forces with the Pacific moisture and produce extremely heavy rains over Colorado and adjacent states. The summer monsoon tends to begin in late July, reaches its peak in August, and diminishes just after Labor Day.

Heavy rain over Schaefer Draw in northeastern Colorado flowed through Weldona and Atwood and into Sterling on July 29, 1997.

Wildfire

Colorado's warm season weather problem is often not rain. Dry years offer another major weather concern: grass and forest fires. If weather conditions are moist in the spring, there is enough moisture to produce a great deal of growth of grass and underbrush. When the weather dries out, so does all the lush growth, and that dead vegetation becomes excellent tinder for fires. Dry years can still feature thunderstorms, but they often produce lots of lightning and little rain. Lightning is a major cause of fires not just in Colorado, but over most of the Rocky

151

Mountains and the western United States. In recent years, forestry officials have adopted new policies about letting some of these natural fires burn, if they pose little threat to people or property. The idea is to allow small fires to burn away some of the fuels on the forest floor to minimize the chance of a catastrophic fire at a later time. This marked a big switch from the old "Smokey the Bear" policy of putting out all fires. It is a wise policy, but it still offers the risk of a fire getting out of hand. Unfortunately, the explosive population growth along the Front Range has put too many homes into forested areas, making it impossible to let a fire burn in many places.

On October 29, 2003, fire near Jamestown was started by a downed power line during a windstorm.

Both caused by humans, the Buffalo Creek Fire in 1996 and the enormous Hayman Fire of June 2002 were frightening examples of what may happen in the future. Both fires were quickly spread by hot, dry winds and fueled by tinder-dry and plentiful ground vegetation. From small beginnings, each fire blew up into a raging conflagration. The heat from the flames was unusually intense and burned hot enough to sterilize the soil. Seeds that normally are activated by a medium-size fire were rendered lifeless. Heavy rains followed the fires a few weeks later, causing severe erosion. The dirty, ash-laden water poured into Strontia Springs Reservoir after the Buffalo Creek Fire and into Cheesman Reservoir following the Hayman burn, causing tremendous pollution to two of Denver Water's primary impoundments. The water sources had to be shut down for several weeks in order for the smoky silt to clear.

Helicopter makes a water drop on the Missionary Ridge fire in 2002.

In the years since the fires, each area has been notoriously susceptible to flash flooding anytime there is a moderate to heavy rainstorm nearby. The areas will struggle for decades to get plants to regenerate.

That both fires occurred in some of the few relatively un-populated areas along the Front Range is remarkable. Had either fire been just a few miles farther to the northwest, Evergreen and Conifer could have had real tragedies on the order of some of the catastrophic fires in southern California. In the burned-out areas around Hayman (137,000 acres) and Buffalo Creek (nearly 12,000 acres), grasses and small plants are reestablished, but very few large few trees survived. It will be centuries before the area has a mature forest again.

The Missionary Ridge Fire burned 70,000 acres outside Durango in 2002, including portions of the watersheds of Vallecito Reservoir, Lemon Reservoir, and the Animas River. These water bodies make up part of the water supply for the city of Durango, the city of Bayfield, and the Southern Ute Indian tribe. The fire started on June 9 and eventually involved nearly 3,000 personnel in fighting the blaze. Despite their efforts, the fire consumed fifty-six homes and twenty-six outbuildings and cost nearly $31 million to fight.

Forecasting Fire Weather

On June 8, 2002, Colorado's largest wildfire in recorded history erupted southwest of Denver. The Hayman Fire eventually burned more than 137,000 acres and caused almost $40 million in damage. The fire was sparked during a time of severe drought across the Front Range, and the fuels—vegetation such as trees, brush and grasses—were extremely dry. Conditions were so ripe for wildfire that on June 17 the fire spread half a mile in four minutes.

Prevailing weather conditions, such as wind, humidity, and temperature, are important elements for firefighters, who depend on weather forecasts as they develop strategies for battling wildfires. Fire weather forecasters play a crucial role during the wildfire season.

Meteorologist Dan Leszcynski is the Fire Weather Program Manager for the National Weather Service office in Boulder, Colorado.

Q: What is fire weather forecasting?
A: Fire weather forecasting is geared specifically toward forecasting fire situations. The fire weather forecasters are especially concerned with relative humidity and wind. They have to be very adept in their knowledge of the local terrain and how the local terrain can affect winds.

Q: Do fire weather forecasters work on fire weather forecasts every day, or is your job more events-driven?
A: We routinely issue fire weather planning forecasts starting on April 1 through October 31.

Q: How does fire weather forecasting differ from regular forecasting?
A: Fire weather forecasters really focus on forecasting relative humidity for the fire community, and in giving more detail in the wind forecast. Also, pinpointing forecast information that could be critical to a land manager, such as thunderstorms that put out dry lightning, gusty winds, that type of thing. We look at how fuels may be susceptible to fire starts, and there are some critical weather patterns.

Q: What are some of those patterns?
A: Mainly, thunderstorms that put out lightning but very little rainfall. Another one is strong and gusty winds, which may have an impact on a fire.

Q: Are there computer forecasting models that are specifically geared toward fire weather forecasting?
A: Right now there is not a computer model that's specific toward fire weather forecasting. The forecasters will look at all the existing computer model information and in the back of their minds they'll think about what forecast information might have the biggest impact on the fire situation.

Q: You mentioned that wind is one of the primary forecasting elements that you are looking at. You're not just looking at surface winds, but winds at different levels of the atmosphere.

A slurry bomber fights a fire along Colorado's Front Range.

A: That's correct. The winds aloft, even near 30,000 feet, will have an impact on what is happening at the surface, which will have an impact on the fire. The forecasters will go through each level of the atmosphere to get a forecast for the winds to determine how the winds near the surface might impact the fire.

Q: How does topography influence your forecasts, and fire behavior?
A: We issue a couple of different forecast products. One is the routine daily fire weather forecast, similar to the public zone forecasts, and that information is averaged for the entire zone. There's another forecast that is more site-specific, and it is issued at the request of the land managers. If they are concerned about a particular point, then they will ask us for a forecast that is specifically designed for that point. They will give the latitude and longitude and we will give them a site-specific forecast for that point. The topography has a significant impact on the weather and winds at that location. We have to base the wind forecast on the topography.

Q: How much of the forecast is intuitive?
A: Actually, in a sense, it is a little intuitive. The forecaster needs to know how the winds will interact with the topography, the lay of the land. Right now, there is not a forecast model that can do a great job on the local terrain, so the forecaster takes the information from the model and looks at the local topography. We have to look at the aspect (angle of the mountain slope), because if it is a south aspect it will tend to be warmer and drier than along the north side. In other words, the forecasters will adjust the winds based on the topography.

The Hayman Fire burns near Florissant in 2002.

Q: Do you have mobile weather stations that you can set up near a fire so that you can get more specific weather information?
A: Yes. There are certified incident meteorologists who are specially trained to go out and work with the fire team. They need a forecaster right there working with them. When the meteorologist gets to the fire, they can order as many of these weather stations as they need. What they end up doing is putting them up in strategic locations so they can get weather data. It's very helpful to have the additional information so they can adjust the forecast.

Q: Some of these fires get big enough to actually create their own weather.
A: The process is similar to how thunderstorms develop.

Q: What's your biggest challenge as a fire weather forecaster?
A: Trying to forecast local winds. You're looking at the model data and trying to come up with a forecast for a particular location and what the winds are going to do at that spot without actually being at the location. We do the best we can, but something can always come up.

Charred remains of an old stone foundation following a spring, 2006, wildfire in Boulder County.

The recent invasion by pine bark beetles has devastated many of our lodgepole pine forests across Colorado, and now there are huge tracts of dead and dying trees drying out in our mountain and foothill forests. This dead timber is prime fuel for wildfires and may provide an ominous portent of massive wildfires in the future. The infestation of the pine bark beetles may be nature's way, but humankind has aided the problem with earnest but misguided forestry practices in the past century. The efforts to extinguish virtually all fires has left dense old-growth forest where allowing more frequent smaller fires would have thinned the woods and allowed fresh growth. As we learn more about how to better handle leaving certain fires to burn, the forests should come back into balance for coming generations. The problem for people is that the time frame is long compared to a human life, and with the increased development of housing in forested areas, there are many areas in which forest fires simply cannot be allowed to burn naturally.

Because so many Coloradoans choose to live among the tall trees, here are some basic fire safety rules to consider. During fire weather, stay tuned to TV and radio for updates and information about existing fires. If you live in an area that has a threat of fire, have a plan of action ready for your family and evacuate quickly when necessary. Consider getting a fireproof box or safe to keep important documents or family items. Clear away trees and brush from close to your house and make sure that your access road is in as good a shape as possible for fire crews. Above all, please be extremely cautious with outdoor burning. Human activity caused both the Buffalo Creek Fire in 1996 and the Hayman Fire in 2002. In both cases the fire was thought to be out, and therefore left unattended. We cannot prevent lightning-caused fires, but Smokey the Bear was right about the kind we make: "Only you can prevent forest fires."

Dry Heat

Although the dry weather makes forest fires a threat, it is the low humidity that makes summertime in Colorado so appealing. Unlike our neighbors to the east, we actually can go outdoors in relative comfort even on a really hot summer day. Our dry climate is a result of both altitude and—as stated in Chapter 1—location, location, location. Because we are about as far away from the ocean as one can get in the United States, any moist air has a long way to travel to get here. Our high elevation serves to block many of the moisture-laden storms from getting here, or weakens them and dries them out before they do. The result is summertime comfort.

Let's revisit another point from Chapter 1, namely the dew point, the temperature at which the air would be saturated with moisture and the relative humidity would be 100 percent. If the air temperature were 80 degrees and the dew point 60 degrees, the air would have to cool to 60 in order for it to become saturated. Once the air is saturated, clouds, rain, snow, fog, or dew may occur. It is called the dew point because on a clear night, when the air cools down to it, dew gathers on the grass. If conditions are below freezing, not a common occurrence in summer, we can call the dew point the frost point, but usually we just stick with dew point to keep it simple.

Hottest Highs

Bennett 118°*
July 11, 1888
(*Unofficial)

Sedgwick 114°
July 11, 1954

Las Animas 114°
July 1, 1933

Denver 105°
August 8, 1878
July 20, 2005

In Colorado, our dew points in the summer are usually in the 30s and 40s. That is why we do not usually have morning dew like our neighbors in the Midwest and East. Sometimes dew points drop way down to the teens or even single digits. This occurs when we have a strong southwesterly wind that comes from the desert. The air is already quite dry, but it dries out even further as it rides up and over the mountains. When the air is that dry, it is almost too dry and can make your eyes, skin, and nose dry out to the point of being very uncomfortable.

Most of the time, our low dew point makes it very pleasant to be outdoors. In contrast to Colorado dew points in the 40s, the Midwest and East usually sweat through dew points in the 60s and 70s all summer long. The old saying, "It's not the heat but the humidity," seldom applies in Colorado. In fact, dew points above 65 are rarely reported except way out on the eastern plains. When we get dew points in the 50s in Denver, we usually have heavy rains from thunderstorms.

Although ours tends to be a dry heat—the same can be said about an oven—we still get our share of sweltering days in Colorado. The all-time hottest day in Denver was August 8, 1878, when the thermometer soared to 105 degrees. That mark stood alone for well over a century, until the sizzling summer of 2005, when Denver again hit 105 degrees on July 20. That heat wave in 2005 was a memorable one as triple-digit highs were recorded in Denver on seven different days, and most of the state sweltered under a relentless, hazy summer sun.

In some older climate references, you may find the record high for the entire state listed as 118 degrees, recorded at Bennett on July 11, 1888. There is controversy about the accuracy of this reading, and now weather experts say that the thermometer was not set up properly. The next warmest reading for the state that day was only about 105 degrees. So, depending on which reference you check, you might also find the state record high listed at 114 degrees, set on July 11th, 1954, at the town of Sedgwick, and at Las Animas on July 1, 1933. According to the Colorado Climate Center, these are the accurate readings.

When it's that hot, people tend to get cranky. But the good news about Colorado is that you can always head for the high country to cool off. The all-time record highs for Aspen and Vail are only 93 and 95 degrees, respectively. In addition, one of the benefits of our dry heat is that our nighttime temperatures tend to cool off considerably, more than in the Midwest or the East. The temperature tends to fall much more easily on a dry, clear night, when the heat from the day can escape easily into space. Forecasters often look to the dew point as a gauge as to how cold temperatures may fall overnight. In the Midwest and the East, that means that nighttime temperatures may not drop much below the 60s in the summertime. In Colorado, our summer dew points are often in the 40s, so even after a very hot day, our nighttime temperatures can dive down into the 50s and even the upper 40s. Air conditioners run all summer long in St. Louis and Chicago, but in Colorado many folks can get by either without an air conditioner at all, or by using one just during the day.

> *When it's hot, people tend to get cranky—the good news about Colorado is that you can always head for the high country to cool off.*

The drier air also gives rise to a home appliance you will not see in the Midwest and East, the swamp cooler. This device is simply an evaporative cooler that takes advantage of our low summer humidity. Swamp coolers run water in front of a fan. The water evaporates, cooling the air, and the fan blows the cool air inside. Because our air is so dry, the slight increase in humidity is not unpleasant, and the cooling is most welcome. Swamp coolers do not work efficiently in areas with dew points much above 55 degrees, since there is already quite a bit of moisture in the air.

Overall, the warm season in Colorado brings us just about every type of weather, sometimes violent, but much of the time delightful. By mid- to late-August, the often lazy, sometimes crazy days of summer begin to ease. The last of the red-hot forecasts are issued, and the nighttime lows begin to dip enough that a light jacket or sweater becomes necessary. Once again the change in seasons draws near as the warm weather season fades and thoughts turn to autumn, and then winter.

CHAPTER FOUR

STORM CHASING

There are many ways to get your thrills—skydiving, whitewater rafting, extreme skiing, perhaps running with the bulls in Pamplona. For a select group, the thrill is in the challenge and the danger of driving into the heart of some of the most severe storms on Earth. Each spring, thousands of storm chasers seek out the core of severe thunderstorms in the hopes of catching a fleeting glimpse of the gold standard of severe weather—the tornado.

Like the gold prospectors of the nineteenth century, most tornado chasers come up empty-handed many more times than they strike pay dirt. It rarely works as it does in *The Wizard of Oz*, where the tornado came to Dorothy, or *Twister*, when the chasers witnessed more than a half-dozen tornadoes in one twenty-four-hour period. Instead, tornadoes are pretty hard to come by. There are about 100,000 thunderstorms every year in the United States. Of those, about 10,000 are classified as "severe": winds of at least 58 mph, hail of three-quarters of an inch or larger, and/or very heavy rainfall. Of the 10,000 severe storms, only about 1,000 tornadoes are produced each year. Thus, 1 percent of all thunderstorms actually produce a tornado.

The average life span of a tornado is about ten minutes, and the average path length is but a mile or two. Tornado chasing really is the meteorological equivalent of panning for a golden nugget.

Most experienced tornado chasers will tell you that the biggest risk from driving all over the countryside is not getting hit by a tornado, but rather fighting boredom through the miles of driving and avoiding a condition called "square butt" from sitting in the car so long. There are other risks involved in this endeavor: car trouble, falling asleep at the wheel, hydroplaning in heavy rain, collisions with other vehicles, severe hail damage, and getting struck by lightning. If this still sounds like fun to you, here are some guidelines to basic storm chasing.

The growth in interest in storm chasing can be traced back to the movie *Twister* as well as through storm chasing documentaries on the Weather Channel and the Discovery Channel. It is a fascinating endeavor, but one that probably appears more glamorous than it turns out most of the time. Much like casting for a trophy fish, the actual amount of time you'll spend reeling in that catch is tiny compared to the time spent preparing, traveling, and waiting for the prize.

Storm Chasing Basics

According to experts in tracking tornadoes, there are some basic things that are very important to successful storm chasing. First, be sure that you have a dependable vehicle. Colorado and western Kansas are vast open areas, and there is a tremendous amount of territory with no service station or towing company nearby. It is extremely important to make sure that you are prepared in case of an automotive breakdown. Check overall aspects of your car's health, but also be ready to handle minor road repairs—possibly in the dark or the rain. And make sure that the spare really has air!

Second, have an excellent set of maps—the higher the detail the better. Go to a good map store and buy the latest book of state and county roads available. You will need to know all the little side roads and the condition of those roads, since tornadoes rarely follow the interstate. Many roads that appear just fine on a map are quite different when you drive on them. The clay soils of eastern Colorado can quickly turn into "goo" when hit by heavy rain. In addition, check out some of the new Global Positioning System (GPS) mapping software, which is getting to be very detailed and can provide a quick escape route when conditions are changing fast.

Radio contact is extremely important for safe and successful storm chasing. Storm chasers will equip their vehicles with CB radio at a minimum and most often ham radio equipment as a way to stay in touch with other chasers in the area. There is training and licensing required to become a ham radio operator. Classes are available in the Denver area and at many areas across the state. A Web search will find many options.

Many of the most successful tornado trackers also have built specialized mobile weather centers in their vehicles. These units may include satellite radio hookups that enable the chasers to receive up-to-the minute satellite, radar, and weather conditions, as well as the latest advisories from the National Weather Service. When tracking a severe thunderstorm, do

Many storm chasers add a touch of personality to their vehicles. Tony Laubach calls his van "White Lightning." It sports his "WX Nerd" license plates as he covers tens of thousands of miles each season.

A sedan loaded with weather gadgets and communications gear hauls storm chasers around the country.

not be surprised by the array of weather gadgets you may see on the roof of a passing car—satellite dishes, windvanes, and other prognosticating paraphernalia.

Severe-Storm Meteorology

The most important thing to know about storm chasing is the meteorology of severe weather events. You must be savvy about the general weather pattern in order to determine when and where a severe storm will erupt. It is even more important to understand storm structure in order to know where the tornado will most likely form from a severe thunderstorm. This last point is not only critical for successful storm chasing, but it also might save your life! Tornado chasing can be a dangerous hobby, it is not a pastime to be taken lightly. If you want to get a taste for it in a safer and probably more successful fashion, it is recommended that you ride along with a professionally guided storm tour. One very good local company is Silver Lining Tours. Roger Hill is the owner of this company and a witness to nearly 400 tornadoes in his chase career. For a fee, Roger and his chase partner will take you in their radar-equipped tour van and get you to the heart of the storm. For more details on Silver Lining Tours, check its website, www.silverliningtours.com.

7News Meteorologist Mike Nelson sits with storm chasers from around the country at their annual convention.

An annual event held in the Denver area each February, the National Storm Chaser Convention is attended by most of the top storm chasers in the world. There they spend three days showing off the results of their summer trophy hunts. The convention is sponsored in part by the 24/7 Weather Center and is a great place to get pointers. For more information about the convention, visit its website at www.chaserconvention.com.

Supercell Thunderstorms

As we have already noted, the usual thunderstorm does not spawn a tornado. The average summer thunderstorm tends to develop, mature, and die away in a matter of an hour or so and will do little more than bring rumbles of thunder, some hard rainshowers, and maybe a bit of hail. To get a tornado, a much larger storm complex is generally required. Most tornadoes develop from massive churning thunderstorms called supercells. These huge thunderstorms form with a combination of strong temperature and humidity gradients near the surface and increasing wind shear as you go higher in the atmosphere. The low-level temperature and humidity help to spark the initial thunderstorm, and the vertical wind shear helps to create a slowly rotating thunderstorm that may last for several hours. The best time for these storms to bloom is in the spring and early summer. At that time of year, there is

(left) A classic "elephant trunk" tornado kicking up reddish dust on the plains of eastern Colorado. (right) A bell-shaped supercell thunderstorm. This type of storm shows strong rotation and often produces large hail and tornadoes.

still a large temperature contrast from north to south across the nation. As the increasing warmth of the air over the Gulf of Mexico pushes northward, it clashes with the leftover chill of winter. The result of this meeting of the air masses is seldom quiet, and big thunderstorms are the result. In addition, the jet stream winds tend to be quite strong in the spring and early summer, and those powerful winds aloft create the vertical wind shear that gets everything spinning.

The counterclockwise rotation of the supercell is what turns a garden-variety thunderstorm into a tornado producer. This large-scale rotation is what eventually intensifies into the rapidly spinning vortex that drops from the heavens as a tornado.

Types of Supercells

There are actually several varieties of supercell thunderstorms. The classic supercell features the rotating structure of the storm and produces heavy rain and hail just to the northeast of the main updraft. This is the most common type of supercell and is often seen over the eastern plains of Colorado. The "low precipitation," or LP, supercell is similar to a classic supercell—except that it produces very little rain. The updraft is so powerful in an LP storm that it literally keeps the raindrops suspended in the clouds, not allowing them to fall to the ground. On radar, an LP super cell will show up with an intense radar echo, since the clouds are literally chock-full of rain and hail. Low precipitation supercells can produce tornadoes, but often bring very little rainfall. The biggest threat, besides lightning and the tornado itself, is from very large hail. LP supercells may not drop much moisture in the form of rain, but they can dump huge hailstones of tennis ball to softball size. Such large hail will surely break most of the windows in your car and cause severe damage to the auto body as well, not to mention that very large hail can kill a person. Although LP supercells are dangerous, they also can be extremely photogenic.

Storm chaser Tony Laubach watches a high precipitation supercell over eastern Colorado, June 2006, keeping an escape route open.

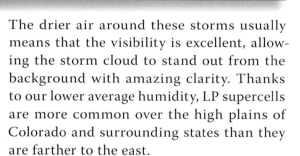

(right) A maturing supercell thunderstorm near Burlington, Colorado, during June 2006. (bottom) Low precipitation supercell thunderstorm at sunset near Goodland, Kansas.

The drier air around these storms usually means that the visibility is excellent, allowing the storm cloud to stand out from the background with amazing clarity. Thanks to our lower average humidity, LP supercells are more common over the high plains of Colorado and surrounding states than they are farther to the east.

The last type is the "heavy precipitation," or HP, supercell. HP supercells obviously dump very heavy rainfall and hail. These storms can occur elsewhere in Colorado, but they are more common in the far eastern part of the state as well as in Kansas and Nebraska. High precipitation supercells are a dangerous breed as they can bring flash flooding, complicating a storm escape route. In addition, HP supercells may produce so much heavy rain that they obscure the view of a developing tornado. When visibility is poor, you are in a vulnerable position, especially if the storm is occurring late in the day. When storm chasing, be alert to what other storm chasers may be saying on their mobile radios and listen to the National Weather Service radio for updates on the status and type of supercell storms in the area.

Tornado Season

Prime time for storm chasers begins in early April and lasts until about the end of June. Storm chasing season first starts in Texas and slowly works its way to the north and west. Oklahoma and Kansas enter into the picture in April and early May. By the middle of May, Colorado has warmed sufficiently and is set to enter the severe thunderstorm season. Although we get tornado-producing storms in May, the real mean season for Colorado is early June.

By early June, the atmosphere has warmed enough to fire off severe thunderstorms, hailstorms, and tornadoes on just about any day over eastern Colorado. Throw in a weather front or a strong current of jet stream winds, and the odds increase dramatically. Keep an eye on weather forecasts on 7News or check the Weather Channel to know when a particularly stormy day may be on the way. This will allow you to plan a storm chasing trip a day or so ahead of time.

We strongly recommend, too, that before heading out to chase tornadoes you take the time to read as much as possible about severe storms and tornadoes and attend a SkyWarn meeting supported by ham radio operators and the National Weather Service. This program is set up to train storm spot-

A large "cone" tornado churning over farmland during an intense early-season thunderstorm.

ters what to look for and how to stay out of extreme danger during severe weather events. SkyWarn spotters are often ham radio enthusiasts who use their radio skills to relay valuable information to the National Weather Service. The truth is, the true storm chasers would probably prefer not to see a bunch of wannabes with videocameras out on the roads, since it greatly increases the risk of a collision. Nonetheless, if you are properly trained in storm chase protocol and where to look, you can be of some value. For more information about SkyWarn meetings, call your local National Weather Service office or go to www.skywarn.org.

How Tornadoes Form

Now, if you are still interested in seeking out one of nature's rarest sights, here are some basic tips about where to look and what to look for. Most tornadoes form on the southwestern side of a supercell thunderstorm because of its rotating structure.

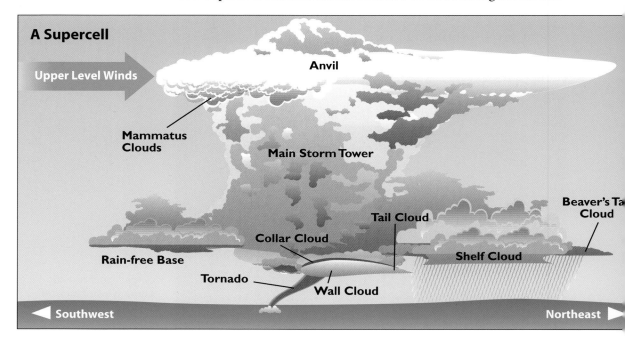

A Supercell

Upper Level Winds

Anvil

Mammatus Clouds

Main Storm Tower

Beaver's Ta Cloud

Tail Cloud

Collar Cloud

Shelf Cloud

Rain-free Base

Tornado

Wall Cloud

Southwest

Northeast

A moist low-level inflow feeds the storm from the south or southeast, ahead of the main body of the supercell. This muggy air rises up into the heart of the severe storm and helps to form the main tower of the thunderstorm. Increasing winds aloft create a wind shear that begins to turn the storm tower toward the northeast in a slow rotation. As the tower builds into the more stable air of the stratosphere, the lifting motion stops and the top of the thunderstorm is blown off into the familiar "anvil" shape. When an anvil forms, you have a mature thunderstorm that can produce rain, wind, and hail. The heaviest precipitation tends to fall on the northeastern side of the storm, ahead of the strongest updraft. The updraft acts like a conveyor belt that carries low-level moisture up into the center of the storm and then pushes that moisture out to the east or northeast by way of the stronger upper-level winds. When the rain and hail fall down, the air is cooled and sinks toward earth. At this point, complicated circulations develop that create a swirling downdraft toward the southwestern edge of the storm. This sinking, rotating air is what helps to create the tightening vortex that becomes a tornado.

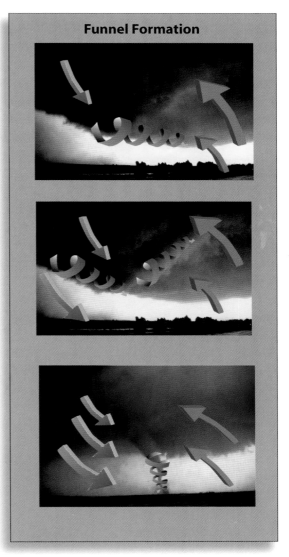

Funnel Formation

Storm Chasing Techniques

If, after this brief description, it has occurred to you that approaching the thunderstorm from the southern or southeastern side makes sense, you may be on the right track to be a successful storm chaser. If the storm is moving from west to east

A Storm Chaser's Life

Events in life that can be measured in seconds are likely to become etched in our memory for a lifetime. Ask tornado chaser Tim Samaras and he can tell you about such a moment without hesitation: 82 seconds, June 24, 2003. "The closest I came to a tornado is probably the big Manchester tornado on June 24, 2003," he recalls. "The rumble rattled the whole countryside, like a waterfall powered by a jet engine. Debris was flying overhead; telephone poles were snapped and flung three hundred yards through the air, roads ripped from the ground, and the town of Manchester, South Dakota, literally sucked into the clouds."

Unlike most storm chasers, it isn't the thrill of the chase that motivates Samaras; it's the promise of the catch. It's about science. Samaras is the designer of the latest generation of tornado probes, and he was on a mission: to put a probe in the path of this rapidly approaching vortex. It was a pulse-pounding, adrenaline-pumping, life-defining moment.

Facing a tornado with wind speeds in excess of 200 mph and a history of devastation, Samaras successfully deployed his 45-pound tornado probe in the path of the F-4 twister. It took a direct hit 82 seconds later. The probe survived, and his effort made history. Samaras holds the record for measuring the lowest barometric pressure drop of a tornado, which is 100 millibars, and his work is on the leading edge in tornado research.

The probe is called a "Hardened In-Situ Tornado Pressure Recorder," or HITPR. The pyramid-shaped device is engineered to withstand the harsh environments within the strongest tornadoes, and the overall design actually keeps the probe on the ground. The probe is able to record pressure, temperature, relative humidity, wind speed and direction, and even 360 degrees of video when properly equipped. The data the probe gathers allows engineers to design buildings that are better able to withstand ferocious tornadic winds, and will someday allow meteorologists to increase the lead time for tornado warnings.

Despite its glamorized depiction in the film Twister, the life of a tornado chaser is more accurately characterized by the countless hours spent driving seemingly endless roads. Samaras drives 35,000 miles each May and June looking for the next perfect storm. "One day we will be chasing in Oklahoma and the next day we have to be in North Dakota. We end up driving through the night to get there. I'm in a different motel room every night, and sometimes I have to look out a window to remember where I am."

But for Samaras it's not about the hours. It's about those 82 seconds.

The HITPR, also called a "turtle," is designed to withstand and to measure the forces within a tornado.

or southwest toward the northeast, as most of them do, then a southern or southeastern approach will allow you to spot the tornado from a position of good visibility. By following the southern edge of the storm, you will not be in the bands of heavy rain and hail and should be in a better location to actually see the tornado. One of the significant dangers in storm chasing is getting hit by a tornado that is wrapped in rain or obscured from your view. This is most likely to happen if you try to "punch the core" of the storm by driving into the storm cell from the north or northeast. Punching the core of a severe thunderstorm is a very good way to get all of the windows in your car blown out by large hail or getting killed by driving blindly into the path of a rain-wrapped tornado.

Thunderstorms are all unique, but most often the best and safest odds are from a southern approach. You still may face rain, large hail, and the ever-present risk of being hit by lightning, but chances are you'll see more tornadoes and live to tell about them by using that southern or southeastern rule of thumb.

Storm researcher Tim Samaras quickly deploys a HITPR (Hardened In Situ Tornado Pressure Recorder) in the path of an approaching tornado. It is dangerous work, but a direct hit will provide valuable information about the forces inside the tornado.

The greatest risk of storm chasing is actually being on the road for hundreds and even thousands of miles. Numerous chasers have been involved in accidents, from simple fender benders to rollover accidents in which injuries were sustained.

Even with good defensive driving habits, things happen. It is best to have a driver who is totally focused on the road, with the navigator as spotter. When the spotter sees something, then he or she suggests that the driver pull over, if it is safe to do so, for all to have a look.

A good set of road maps and a GPS navigation system is a very valuable asset in storm chasing. You need to be able to plan your route so as to allow yourself an escape route in the event that things get too intense. By keeping an eye on the storm and knowing that you have an alternate route, you should be able to get out of the way if necessary. Remember that thunderstorms can do strange things, and you can quickly find yourself in a dangerous spot. Keep a watchful eye on the sky all around you—including directly overhead. Never wait to abandon a spotting location if the weather is closing in fast, and avoid the temptation to get

(top) Rear-flank downdraft winds can reach speeds of over 100 mph. (bottom) With the dry climate of Colorado, a rear-flank downdraft from a supercell thunderstorm on the eastern plains can kick up quite a bit of dust and debris.

too close to the storm. The most destructive winds are very close to the tornado, but debris can fly a long way away from the funnel and be a major danger. There is also a hazard from strong straight-line winds that rocket around the backside of the supercell. These winds are called rear flank downdraft (RFD). The RFD winds can reach 75 to over 100 mph and sweep a nasty wall of dirt and rain that is quite unpleasant and very dangerous.

Severe Storm Clouds

Some cloud formations are common with tornado-producing storms. The one that is most often mentioned is the wall cloud. This is a lowering of the cloud base near the region of intense thunderstorm updraft. It is formed when the strong updraft draws rain-cooled air from the front of the thunderstorm upward. This upward motion creates a lowered cloud base as the moisture in the air condenses. The wall cloud will have a slow but steady counterclockwise rotation and may not be associated with heavy rain or hail. Often the heavy precipitation is just to the northeast, and the wall cloud is visible in what is called the "rain-free" area.

Wall clouds are often confused with shelf clouds. A shelf cloud is typically on the front of the storm, and a wall cloud develops on the backside of a supercell thunderstorm.

(top) Aerial view of a collar cloud on the inflow shelf cloud of a supercell thunderstorm. (above) At first glance, rain shafts in a thunderstorm can look like a developing tornado. Look for signs of rotation in the clouds to determine if it is a tornado.

Only a small percentage of the wall clouds observed actually spawn a tornado, so if you see one, watch it for several minutes to see what happens next. A dangerous wall cloud that is about to produce a tornado will have a strong rotation. From this rotating base, the tornado will begin to grow down toward the ground. At this point you may in fact already have a tornado on the ground, even if you cannot see it. Remember that tornadoes are just rotating columns of air and air is invisible. The classic tornadoes seen on television and in movies are made visible by clouds and debris. Look at the ground under the wall cloud and the developing funnel and check for any signs of swirling dust. It may be that the rotation of the air has already reached the ground, even if the condensation funnel has not. This is particularly important in eastern Colorado, where the air is

relatively dry. Often our tornadoes show rotation at the base of the cloud, then nothing in between until you see the swirl of dust on the ground. Even without the classic tornado shape, it is still a tornado capable of doing damage.

A collar cloud is an accessory cloud that surrounds the wall cloud. It rotates at a slower rate than the wall cloud, but a storm chaser should note it. Collar clouds will not always form with the wall cloud, but you may hear this jargon used by veteran tornado chasers.

(top) A beaver's tail indicates a large amount of moisture flowing into a thunderstorm. (bottom) Stovepipe tornado complete with wall cloud and tail cloud.

(top) Striations around a northeastern Colorado supercell. (middle) A shelf cloud associated with a severe thunderstorm near Springfield, Colorado. (bottom) A roll cloud is similar to a shelf cloud, but it is not attached to the thunderstorm base. It may rotate horizontally.

Another type of cloud often seen with a super-cell thunderstorm is the beaver's tail. This cloud enters the northeast side of the updraft portion of the storm and has the appearance of the tail of a beaver. The beaver's tail is an indication of strong low-level moisture inflow into the storm, and a good sign that the storm has the strong wind shears and sufficient moisture to foster a tornado. According to Roger Hill, "the beaver's tail points the way to the 'action area,'" that is, where the strongest lift is occurring within the storm updraft.

Sometimes confused with the beaver's tail is another cloud simply called the tail cloud, which is much smaller in scope. It is a thin tail, or needle-shaped cloud accessory to the wall cloud. It usu-ally forms on the north side of the wall cloud and looks like a tail pointing toward the area of heavi-est precipitation (usually toward the northeast). It forms at a lower level than the beaver's tail and is farther back toward the southwestern part of the thunderstorm. The tail cloud points the way to where the strongest low-level convergence and rotation are located in the storm. Once again, this type of cloud is not always seen, even with a large and violent tornado.

Striations, stripes that form on sides of the thunderstorm, are good signs of rotation. These rings that form on the clouds give an excellent indication that the storm is a strong supercell that may produce a tornado, and can give the supercell an ominous "mothership" appearance straight out of a Steven Spielberg movie. Striations occasionally form on wall clouds as well and can be very photogenic, especially in late daylight.

A shelf cloud is a common sight along the leading edge of a severe thunderstorm. This low-level cloud looks like a dark wedge attached to the front of the storm. The shelf cloud is associated with gusty straight-line winds ahead of the storm. It is caused by condensation of water vapor as warm air rises over the cool low-level outflow from the storm. This type of cloud may show signs of rotating, but it will do so along a horizontal axis, like a pencil rolling off a desk. The shelf cloud is sometimes called an arc cloud or arcus cloud. Shelf clouds are not tornadoes, although they are sometimes mistaken for them, but they are associated with straight-line winds that can cause some damage and they make for some intense-looking pictures.

Similar to the shelf cloud, the roll cloud is an ominous sight ahead of an approaching thunderstorm. The roll cloud is a low-level cloud that moves or rolls along ahead of the gusty straight-line winds of a thunderstorm. It is slightly different than a shelf cloud in that it is not attached to the rest of the thunderstorm, but simply rolls out ahead. Although they look scary, roll clouds are actually formed when the downdraft is weakening. The roll cloud breaks away from the parent thunderstorm and slowly dies away as it rolls on ahead. Although they can cause strong straight-line winds, roll clouds usually look worse than they really are.

Cumulonimbus mammatus clouds sound scary, but in fact they are no threat at all. These are the odd-looking, bubble-shaped clouds that are seen on the underside of thunderstorm anvils. They are caused by rain-cooled air that condenses on the outside of the cumulonimbus cloud. Mammatus clouds are not dangerous in themselves, nor do they produce a tornado. They are signs of strong turbulence within the parent thunderstorm, however, and are usually seen with storms that are causing severe weather. The name mammatus comes from the shape of the cloud, which resembles a breast. Mammatus clouds make for some spectacular pictures, as they are often seen bathed in a red or gold color—backlit by the setting sun as the storm moves away to the east.

Scud clouds sound frightening enough, given memories of the first Gulf War. In weather terminology, scud clouds are

(top) Scud clouds over eastern Colorado. (above) Mammatus clouds with an eerie late afternoon glow.

simply tattered scraps of low clouds that swirl around under a severe storm. They are moist leftovers from all the business up above. These cloud fragments can give a surreal appearance to things, but they are just signs of plenty of moisture and turbulence in the air. The scud clouds that form in the wake of thunderstorms along the Front Range often wisp their way around the foothills, making for a very scenic tapestry. Scud clouds are often mistaken for tornadoes or funnel clouds because of their appearance. However it is important to note that scud clouds are not tornadic. They can signal the potential for tornado conditions, but they themselves are not tornadoes. Sometimes it is hard to tell if it's a scud or really a funnel. The best way is to detect any rotation using a good set of binoculars.

Types of Tornadoes

The supercell thunderstorm is the most common source of tornadoes, but there are others. A tornado is, of course, just a rapidly rotating column of air, of which there are two other types commonly seen in Colorado: the gustnado and the landspout.

The gustnado, or gustinado, as it is sometimes called, is a slang term for a gust-front tornado. It is small and usually weak and short-lived. Gustnados form on the leading edge, or gust front, of a thunderstorm. They are caused by swirling wind motions in the local area that come together in a vertical column for a brief period of time. A good way to visualize a gustnado is to think of the swirling eddies that spin off in the water from the bow wake of a boat. These miniature tornadoes are sometimes visible only as debris clouds or dust swirls near the ground. Because gustnados form on the leading edge of the storm, they are not usually associated with classic supercell thunderstorm structure and generally are more likely to be seen with a shelf cloud instead of with a wall cloud. Recent studies have shown that gustnados can form on the edges

Tornado Cousins

Gustnado

Gustnado—swirling winds from a storm can spin into short-lived vertical columns.

Landspout

Landspout—low level winds are drawn into the updraft of a developing thunderstorm, creating rotation.

of straight-line downburst wind events. The analogy of this would be the swirling patterns that form when you pull a canoe paddle through the water. These gustnados are sometimes called bookend tornadoes, since one will form on each end of a strong straight-line wind event. They can cause some confusion for those determining whether a storm was a tornado

(left) A weak landspout churns over open country northeast of Fort Morgan. (right) Landspout tornadoes are common east of I-25, such as this one photographed near Strasburg.

or a downburst, since the resulting damage has both straight and spinning characteristics. In fact, this type of storm is a hybrid, both a downburst and a tornado.

The landspout is another form of a tornado that is often seen in Colorado. This type of non-supercell tornado is formed when colliding wind boundaries from several thunderstorms come together to create a swirling low-level circulation. This whirl of wind is then drawn into the updraft of a developing thunderstorm. As the swirling winds are drawn into the storm, the rotation tightens up—much in a way a figure skater spins faster as she pulls her arms in. These twisters are really closer to a dust devil than a tornado, and are usually wider at the bottom than at the top—sort of an "upside down" tornado. The landspout tornado is common along the Front Range because the topography tends to concentrate low-level wind circulations from small, but intense thunderstorms. When thunderstorms pop up and die away, they help to create numerous outflow boundaries that swirl all over the plains just east of Denver. Because landspouts form from the ground up, they are not associated with wall clouds or classic tornado structure. Instead, they form under a rapidly developing thunderstorm that might not even be producing rain yet.

Landspouts can last as long as 15–30 minutes and can create a fair amount of damage; they are technically tornadoes and require warning the public. Although meteorologists usually do issue warnings on TV for landspouts and gustnados, they try to mention that these are smaller than the classic supercell tornado. Nonetheless, landspout tornadoes tend to be common in the Denver area and adjacent plains, so keep an eye out for them. Even a landspout can be destructive, with winds of 75 to 125 mph. In fact, in August 2002, a small outbreak of landspout tornadoes developed near Parker Road and E-470, causing some minor damage and scaring an awful lot of people in the area. As more and more housing is built east of E-470, the odds are good that sometime soon a landspout will really tear up a neighborhood.

Because our state is semiarid, we generally do not have to worry too much about waterspouts. A waterspout is simply a tornado that forms or moves over water, which occasionally happens even as far inland as we are. In the summer of 1997, for instance, a tornado developed near Baseline Reservoir in Boulder and was even photographed over the water—technically a waterspout, but just barely. There has been some theory given that temperature and humidity contrasts between lakes or reservoirs and the adjacent land area could create conditions slightly more conducive to the formation of tornadoes or waterspouts, but there is little hard research on this matter.

One last type of tornado bears mention: the cold air funnel. This is about as distant a relative of the classic supercell tornado as you will find. Cold air funnels are small, weak twister sisters that develop from a small rainshower or thunderstorm if the air aloft is very cold and unstable. The cold air funnel rarely touches the ground and usually is seen as just a thin tail of spinning clouds. These funnels often develop after a cold front has pushed through the area and the atmosphere is still somewhat turbulent. Cold air funnels are not dangerous for all intents and purposes, and usually we will not even issue a warning for them. A special weather statement might be broadcast about the possibility of cold air funnels, though, just to keep the public from getting too excited.

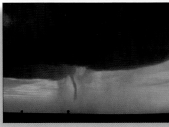

(top) A short-lived tornado near Bennett, Colorado, on August 20, 2006. (middle) A gust-front tornado, also known as a gustnado. (bottom) A trio of landspout tornadoes. Note that the bases are wider than the tops.

The Fujita Scale

Storm chasers will often discuss the success of their expedition by comparing the size and strength of the tornadoes that they witness. The most common basis of comparison is the Fujita scale (F scale). Theodore Fujita of the University of Chicago developed the Fujita scale of tornado intensity based upon the damage that the storms leave behind. Fujita had studied damage patterns caused by the atomic bombs dropped on Hiroshima and Nagasaki and wanted to create a similar means of categorizing the 700–1,000 tornadoes that strike the United States each year. Because the scale is based on wind damage to buildings and trees, there is one flaw in the formula. What happens if a very strong tornado does not hit anything? We often have powerful twisters in eastern Colorado that simply spin around in a field—what might be called natural crop rotation. In the case of a huge tornado that does not hit anything, meteorologists usually rate such a storm at a lower F scale than it might be. There is a tendency among storm chasers to say, "That would have been an F4 or F5 had it hit anything." Nonetheless, the Fujita scale has long been the standard by which tornadoes are measured. All tornadoes and most other severe local windstorms are assigned a single number from this scale, according to the damage caused by the storm. With practice, you can learn to classify a tornado

Tim Samaras has seen over 100 tornadoes in his storm chasing career. This is one of his favorites from May of 2004.

by its overall size and appearance as well as by the structure of the parent thunderstorm; a classic supercell is more likely to produce a strong or violent tornado.

Original Fujita Scale		
Weak Tornadoes		
F0	40–72 mph	light damage
F1	73–112 mph	moderate damage
Strong Tornadoes		
F2	113–157 mph	considerable
F3	158–206 mph	severe damage
Violent Tornadoes		
F4	207–260 mph	devastating damage
F5	261–318 mph	incredible damage

In the United States, 80 percent of all tornadoes are F0 or F1. About 17 percent reach the F2 to F3 classification, and only 2–3 percent become F4 or F5. However, the vast majority of tornado deaths are caused by the F2 through F5 tornadoes. It is likely that there really are a greater number of strong tornadoes, but they just do not hit anything, and are classified at a lower F scale.

The Enhanced Fujita (EF) Scale	
EF Number Three-Second Gust Estimate	
EF 0	65–85 mph
EF 1	86–110 mph
EF 2	111–135 mph
EF 3	136–165 mph
EF 4	166–200 mph
EF 5	Over 200 mph

As of 2007, the Fujita scale was being replaced by the enhanced Fujita (EF) scale, which tries to rate tornadoes more accurately. This new system will allow for rankings of tornadoes that do nothing but damage vegetation or signs. A new wind scale has also been created to complement the new scale. Before his death in 1998, Fujita mentioned that future corrections to his scale were needed. The new EF scale is now going to

Tornadoes Broken Down by Fujita Scale Rating (1950–2006)*

County	Number of Tornadoes	F0	F1	F2	F3	F4	F5	Unrated	Deaths	Injuries	Property Damage ($)	Crop Damage ($)
Adams	148	88	47	9	2	0	0	2	0	43	26.761 M	6.5 M
Alamosa	14	9	4	1	0	0	0	0	0	0	14,000	0
Arapahoe	74	46	27	1	0	0	0	0	0	1	8.92 M	0
Archuleta	1	1	0	0	0	0	0	0	0	0	1,000	0
Baca	60	38	16	2	0	1	0	3	0	4	2.969 M	0
Bent	33	18	8	3	0	0	0	4	0	8	1.416 M	0
Boulder	10	2	6	2	0	0	0	0	0	0	283,000	0
Broomfield	0	0	0	0	0	0	0	0	0	0	0	0
Chaffee	1	1	0	0	0	0	0	0	0	0	25,000	0
Cheyenne	44	26	14	3	0	0	0	1	0	5	2.526 M	3,000
Clear Creek	0	0	0	0	0	0	0	0	0	0	0	0
Conejos	4	3	0	1	0	0	0	0	0	0	25,000	0
Costilla	6	4	1	0	1	0	0	0	0	0	5,000	0
Crowley	13	6	4	2	0	0	0	1	0	0	28,000	0
Custer	6	4	1	1	0	0	0	0	0	0	5,000	0
Delta	2	1	1	0	0	0	0	0	0	0	25,000	0
Denver	12	5	3	3	1	0	0	0	0	13	32.575 M	0
Dolores	0	0	0	0	0	0	0	0	0	0	0	0
Douglas	52	27	23	2	0	0	0	0	0	6	988,000	0
Eagle	2	1	1	0	0	0	0	0	0	0	25,000	0
El Paso	79	51	17	7	2	0	0	2	0	19	9.636 M	0
Elbert	76	47	24	3	1	0	0	1	0	0	256,000	0
Fremont	7	3	4	0	0	0	0	0	0	0	54,000	0
Garfield	0	0	0	0	0	0	0	0	0	0	0	0
Gilpin	0	0	0	0	0	0	0	0	0	0	0	0
Grand	1	1	0	0	0	0	0	0	0	0	3,000	0
Gunnison	0	0	0	0	0	0	0	0	0	0	0	0
Hinsdale	0	0	0	0	0	0	0	0	0	0	0	0
Huerfano	6	4	1	1	0	0	0	0	0	2	528,000	0
Jackson	1	0	1	0	0	0	0	0	0	0	0	0
Jefferson	13	7	5	1	0	0	0	0	0	0	2.5 M	0
Kiowa	44	27	13	2	1	0	0	1	0	1	643,000	0

* Data does not include the March 2007 Holly Tornado.

Tornadoes Broken Down by Fujita Scale Rating (1950–2006) (continued)

County	Number of Tornadoes	F0	F1	F2	F3	F4	F5	Unrated	Deaths	Injuries	Property Damage ($)	Crop Damage($)
Kit Carson	63	32	23	5	0	0	0	3	0	6	319,000	0
La Plata	5	2	3	0	0	0	0	0	0	0	85,000	2,000
Lake	0	0	0	0	0	0	0	0	0	0	0	0
Larimer	30	15	11	3	0	0	0	1	0	0	65,000	0
Las Animas	25	18	5	1	0	0	0	1	0	0	290,000	0
Lincoln	76	46	20	6	2	0	0	2	0	15	29.3 M	0
Logan	75	48	20	3	2	0	0	2	0	4	3.345 M	0
Mesa	8	7	1	0	0	0	0	0	0	0	1,000	0
Mineral	1	0	0	1	0	0	0	0	0	0	10,000	0
Moffat	6	4	2	0	0	0	0	0	0	0	28,000	0
Montezuma	2	0	1	1	0	0	0	0	0	0	50,000	0
Montrose	3	0	3	0	0	0	0	0	0	1	23,000	0
Morgan	61	33	20	8	0	0	0	0	0	0	1.041 M	0
Otero	18	6	8	1	0	0	0	3	0	0	161,000	0
Ouray	0	0	0	0	0	0	0	0	0	0	0	0
Park	0	0	0	0	0	0	0	0	0	0	0	0
Phillips	35	22	6	4	0	0	0	3	0	1	828,000	0
Pitkin	1	0	0	1	0	0	0	0	0	0	25,000	0
Prowers	63	43	16	2	1	0	0	1	0	1	585,000	0
Pueblo	15	7	7	1	0	0	0	0	0	0	112,000	0
Rio Blanco	2	0	1	0	0	0	0	1	0	0	38,000	0
Rio Grande	1	1	0	0	0	0	0	0	0	0	3,000	0
Routt	2	1	1	0	0	0	0	0	0	0	3,000	0
Saguache	5	3	2	0	0	0	0	0	0	0	253,000	0
San Juan	0	0	0	0	0	0	0	0	0	0	0	0
San Miguel	0	0	0	0	0	0	0	0	0	0	0	0
Sedgwick	29	15	8	3	1	0	0	2	2	10	333,000	0
Summit	0	0	0	0	0	0	0	0	0	0	0	0
Teller	4	1	3	0	0	0	0	0	0	0	3,000	0
Washington	95	65	18	4	2	0	0	6	0	4	661,000	0
Weld	220	111	81	15	1	0	0	12	0	13	3.735 M	0
Yuma	63	32	21	7	0	0	0	3	0	14	3.364 M	0

be the official standard to measure the strength of tornadoes. It takes into account that it often requires much lower wind speeds to create F5-like damage. Using analytical models, lab testing, and real-world measurements with mobile Doppler radar and in situ tornado probes, researchers will continue to fine-tune the new EF scale.

The EF scale was developed while keeping the extensive history of F-scale rankings in mind. The idea is to improve upon the method of categorizing tornadoes without making a scale so different that the decades of ratings under the former system would suddenly become meaningless. Part of the ranking of the new EF scale will be based upon the observed damage to various structures or vehicles: for example, the damage to a mobile home versus the damage to a brick structure or the damage to a hardwood tree versus that to a softwood tree. The hope is that by adding a greater amount of detail to the damage report, each tornado incident will be better represented against other severe wind damage.

The new EF scale will take some getting used to, but during the initial severe weather seasons there will likely be many comparisons of the old with the new. Ultimately, the EF scale will become a familiar part of the weather jargon, like the old F scale and the Saffir-Simpson scale for hurricanes.

Colorado Storm Chasing

The state of Colorado truly is a favorite hunting ground for tornado chasers, even though we typically miss the truly monstrous storms that blast Kansas, Oklahoma, and Texas. As earlier mentioned, our flat plains offer great visibility, a lack of trees to block the view, and a good road system to get close to the storm. Veteran storm chasers actually avoid tracking tornadoes in certain parts of the United States, such as extreme eastern Texas, Arkansas, and northern Louisiana. Those areas are heavily forested and can be dangerous places to chase, since the hazy skies make viewing storms difficult. In storm chaser slang, this area is referred to as "the Jungle."

Denver Convergence Vorticity Zone

(top left) Warm moist winds over southeastern Colorado collide with drier west winds from the mountains resulting in prime locations for storms to develop. (top and bottom) Developing thunderstorms over western Kansas. When the outlines of clouds are crisp, it indicates a great deal of instability and a rapidly developing storm.

Some of the best staging areas in Colorado for storm chasing are not far from Denver. The Palmer Divide to the south and the Front Range to the west often serve to develop local wind patterns on stormy days that actual focus thunderstorm formation of certain areas. The Denver Convergence Vorticity Zone (DCVZ) is an area where the winds often converge during summertime afternoons. The action of westerly winds off the mountains colliding with a southeastern wind dropping down from the Palmer Divide creates a turbulence zone that typically runs from about Elizabeth to Bennett to Keenesburg. Along this line, severe thunderstorms often fire in the mid-to late afternoon and roll on toward the east. Storm chasers often can park somewhere along the DCVZ and just wait for the fireworks to begin. In addition, starting out around the Bennett area tends to provide the storm chaser with several good road choices to follow the most promising-looking clouds.

If, after all our warnings, you still have the urge to go find a tornado, please be sure that you know what you are looking for and the risk that you may be taking. Gather up your knowledge and your patience, gas up the car, pack a good lunch, and good luck!

CHAPTER FIVE

Two Centuries of
WEATHER
OBSERVING

Colorado can boast of being home to some of the finest meteorological minds in the world. With the combination of the National Center for Atmospheric Research (NCAR), the National Oceanic and Atmospheric Administration (NOAA), and the Environmental Systems Research Lab (ESRL), all in Boulder, plus many excellent local statewide National Weather Service offices, we have enough highly skilled weather experts in the area to give pause to any non-meteorologist trying to present a weather report on TV. Beyond the federal forecasters, we have the Colorado Climate Center in Fort Collins and a very highly regarded Department of Atmospheric Science at Colorado State University. Along the Front Range, both the University of Northern Colorado and Metropolitan State College in Denver offer fine undergrad programs in meteorology.

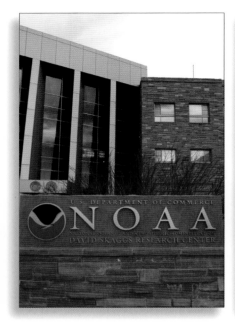

(above) The David Skaggs Research Center in Boulder is home to several agencies within the National Oceanic and Atmospheric Administration (NOAA), including the Denver/Boulder office of the National Weather Service. (top, right) The National Center for Atmospheric Research (NCAR) Mesa Laboratory in Boulder, Colorado.

One reason so many weather experts have settled in Colorado is our abundance of weather—and weather drama. We make headlines with intense windstorms, massive cold waves, and devastating droughts and fires, and we have done so for many, many years.

In Colorado, when you want to know about historical weather, you turn to Nolan Doesken, the state climatologist at CSU in Fort Collins. Visiting with Nolan is a memorable experience, for few people are more enthusiastic than he about Colorado's weather history.

Colorado Climate History

Deep in the basement of the Colorado Climate Center in Fort Collins rest all the old weather records, which date to before Colorado was even a state. Dependable weather records began to appear about 1870; the earlier weather entries about Colorado weather are in the form of traveler's diaries, journals, and letters.

According to the Colorado Climate Center Library, sometime around 1870, the Colorado Promotion and Publicity Committee came up with the statement that "Colorado has 300 days of sunshine a year." This comment was picked up by the *New York Independent* newspaper and run in its issue of September 26, 1872. The 300 days of sun has stuck in the minds of residents and visitors ever since, but it really is more legend than fact. Says Doesken, "To come up with three hundred days of sunshine a year, you have to count days that are sunny in the morning and cloudy in the afternoon as well as days when the skies are covered by clouds, but not thick clouds. This will get you into the upper 200s, unless you are in a place like Alamosa, which may legitimately be able to claim 300 days of sunshine a year."

Still, the abundant sunshine, deep blue skies, and clear, dry air made a profound impact on writers in the nineteenth century. M. L. Baggs, author of *Colorado, the Queen Jewel of the Rockies*, wrote, "If you are a stranger to Colorado, you are constantly talking as you travel along about the surprising climate, the exhilarating, bracing air, the piney smells, the turquoise sky, and the brilliant sun." After living in Colorado for seven

Hundreds of leather-bound volumes of early Colorado weather observations are stored at the Colorado Climate Center on the CSU campus.

years, G. B. Price offered this description of the winter months: "There are few spots on Earth where December, January and February are such delightful, clear, clean invigorating months as in Colorado. Scarce a cloud to break the blue serenity, or a drop of rain or a fall of snow except upon the higher mountains. Such is glorious winter in Colorado!" No wonder folks in the Midwest and East flocked to come here.

The daily recording of weather observations in Colorado began with farmers, ranchers, miners, and some business owners who kept lists of temperature, sky, and precipitation data as well as certain personal and business remarks. Most of these records did not start in earnest until after the Civil War and were certainly advanced as the railroads were built.

Early Weather Observers

Decades earlier, in the fall of 1806, an exploring party led by Colonel Zebulon Pike arrived in Colorado. His team attempted to climb the mountain that today bears his name. In his journal he recorded: "26th November, Wednesday. We had a fine, clear sky, whilst it was snowing at the bottom. . . . 27th November, Thursday. The unbounded prairie was overhung with clouds, which appeared like the ocean in a storm; wave piled on wave and foaming, whilst the sky was perfectly clear where we were. Commenced our march up the mountain, and in about one hour arrived at the summit of this chain: here we found snow middle deep; no sign of beast or bird inhabiting this region. The thermometer which stood at nine degrees above zero at the foot of the mountain, here fell to four degrees below zero."

Pike had observed an autumn upslope event on the eastern plains. Low-level winds blowing in from the east had pushed clouds over the plains, while the higher mountain areas were basking in sunshine. The mountain they were actually climbing was not the one we today call Pike's Peak. The climbing party was instead on the summit of nearby

Cheyenne Mountain and from the top could see the much higher mountain to the north.

In 1820, Major Stephen H. Long, an army engineer, led a second expedition into Colorado. Captain John Bell acted as the official journalist for the party and wrote an account that included weather references. On Wednesday, July 5, the explorers camped on the Platte River near the mouth of a creek in a grove of cottonwood trees. Bell observed, "the trees shade us from the scorching rays of the altitude of the mercury at ninety-one degrees." The creek they camped on they named Cannon Ball Creek, because of the large round stones in its bed. Today, thousands of cars and trucks race by this stream every day. We know it by its modern title, Clear Creek. Apparently Major Long, for whom Long's Peak is named, was unimpressed with the high plains of western Kansas and eastern Colorado, claiming that the land was "unfit for civilization and of course uninhabitable for a people depending upon agriculture." In addition, Major Long declared the area "a great desert" and that sending settlers there would be "out of the question."

Colorado had a minor role in helping to enlist weather observers, starting in the late 1840s. Professor Joseph Henry, the first federal meteorologist, directed a project sponsored by the Smithsonian Institution to develop a national cooperative effort to monitor and document the weather. Only a few records of Colorado's part in this project are known, with some early data from Golden, Central City, Colorado City, Fountain, Fort Morgan, and Templeton Gap in the 1860s.

John C. Frémont made four expeditions into the Rocky Mountains and kept detailed weather observations of temperature, barometric readings, wind, rain, snow, and sky cover. Part of his motivation was to provide accurate data for the construction of railroads. In the winter of 1848–1849, Frémont crossed the San Juan Mountains in order to find the best path for a railway. He wanted to see the mountains under the most adverse conditions so that the safest route could be determined for the railroad. His men faced a terrible ordeal of snow, wind, and bitter cold, and many in the party were lost.

Colonel Zebulon Pike, one of the first to document Colorado's weather.

Frémont wrote in a letter to his wife that prior to the onset of a blizzard, "the cold was extraordinary; at the warmest hours of the day (between one and two) the thermometer standing in the shade of only a tree trunk at zero (Fahrenheit); the day sunshiny with a moderate breeze."

In Colorado, several weather-observing programs were set up after 1850. Probably the very first was at Fort Massachusetts, near Blanca, in the San Luis Valley, starting in the fall of 1852. In addition, the post surgeons at some of Colorado's early forts recorded weather conditions for a few years before 1870.

Denver was destroyed twice in its infancy, by fire and flood. Native Americans warned settlers not to settle there.

With the end of the Civil War and the construction of railroads, the 1870s and 1880s opened up vast areas of the West. As Americans poured across the prairie, the need for accurate weather information grew. J. T. Gardner, a member of surveying expeditions into the Colorado Rockies, was responsible for establishing meteorological stations at four sites: Denver, Cañon City, Fairplay, and Mount Lincoln. These sites all had substantially different elevations, allowing comparisons to be made of pressure and temperature. Readings were taken three times daily at 7:00 a.m., 2:00 p.m., and 9:00 p.m. Long before there was a road, a cog rail system, or even a tourist center at the top that sold freshly made doughnuts, the brave Mr. Gardner spent two grueling days and a night on the top of Pike's Peak, writing to his wife, "It snowed and blew bitterly cold, but there were hours of wonderful clearness when I saw points 150 miles off."

Early Government Observations

The first government organization to take consistent weather observations was the U.S. Army Signal Service. On February 9, 1870, a joint resolution of Congress provided "for taking meteorological observations at the military stations in the interior of the continent and at other points in the States and

Territories of the United States, and for giving notice on the northern lakes and at the seacoast, by magnetic telegraph and marine signals, of the approach and force of storms." The U.S. Army Signal Service (later called the Signal Corps) was given the responsibility for developing and operating the telegraph network. The Signal Service was established in 1860 and had linked telegraph wire over much of the eastern United States by the beginning of the Civil War. After the war, Congress ordered the Signal Service to extend the lines westward. In 1871, a station was established in Denver, and the first daily report was issued on November 20. For the next few years, the extent of western data was very sparse, owing to a lack of stations west of the Mississippi and inadequate telegraph lines. In 1872, Congress formally extended the services throughout the nation. In the beginning, all forecasts were made from Washington, D.C. It was not until 1881 that some local forecasts were allowed and not until 1890 that the local forecast program was substantially expanded.

In the summer of 1873, the Signal Service established a weather station at the top of Pike's Peak, at an altitude of 14,100 feet, after two soldiers climbed to the top and reported that a year-round weather station was feasible. Daily reports were made from the mountaintop perch for many years; at the time, it was the highest observation point in the world and only the second mountain post—the first being Mount Washington, New Hampshire. The Pike's Peak reports were of great interest, since the wild weather events included intense storms of hail, snow, thunder, and startling electrical phenomena such as St. Elmo's fire. When the weather was quiet, the crews would sometimes relieve boredom by spinning tales of adventure on the mountains, much to the delight of readers in the eastern newspapers.

The first reports from Pike's Peak were sent by telegraph starting on November 6, 1873. The telegraph line was difficult to maintain and was knocked out frequently by weather and occasionally by wild animals, and it was abandoned in November 1882. The federal government reorganized the

The first reports from Pike's Peak were sent by telegraph starting on November 6, 1873. The telegraph line was difficult to maintain and was knocked out frequently by weather and occasionally by wild animals.

weather-gathering responsibilities in 1891, when Congress transferred such duties from military to civilian control, creating the U.S. Weather Bureau within the Department of Agriculture. The U.S. Weather Bureau allowed the Pikes Peak Station to become obsolete, and it was eventually closed.

The First Forecasts

Early forecasts from the Signal Service and the Weather Bureau used an elaborate system of flags to display the weather forecast for the next twenty-four hours. Certain colors and designs of these flags indicated storms, cold waves, heat, or calm conditions. In the April 1887 *Bulletin of the Colorado Meteorological Association* were the following instructions from the chief signal officer: "Flags should be furnished and someone engaged to the displaying of them." In the May issue, the bulletin noted that new weather flags were available at a price of $8.75 for bunting or $3.00 for cotton. The Weather Bureau used the flag system for over forty years and abandoned it only when the system was replaced by radio.

Pike's Peak, west of Colorado Springs, provided weather observations from 1873 to 1891.

The extensive cooperative observation program of volunteer weather spotters began shortly after the inception of the Weather Bureau. This network had steady growth through the early part of the twentieth century, but expanded rapidly around World War II. At the end of 1940, with a rapid shift in the economy from agriculture to transportation and manufacturing, the Weather Bureau was transferred to the U.S. Department of Commerce. By 1970, when the Weather Bureau was officially renamed the National Weather Service, more than 270 official weather stations existed in the country.

For Colorado, weather observations expanded greatly during the 1880s. In 1885, the Colorado Meteorological Association (CMA) was chartered under the motto, "Exactness, Continuity,

Thoroughness." The next year, the CMA began publishing a monthly weather bulletin containing organization news and tables of weather data from around the state. That July, the bulletin began providing daily precipitation records. In 1889, a new state weather service was established, and by 1891 the U.S. Weather Bureau had taken over the weather-gathering duties. The CMA gradually turned over its reporting responsibilities and ran its course. It did, however, serve a very valuable function in providing a publication outlet for Colorado weather data and getting Coloradoans interested in their state's weather.

From that humble start, the weather observation network has expanded dramatically over Colorado. Hundreds of observations pour into the Colorado Climate Center each day. Some of the data come from sophisticated satellites and radars, as well as automated weather stations that continuously feed in their data. In addition, many dedicated volunteers take daily weather observations from homes, schools, and businesses. Some of these weather spotters have been dutifully taking down weather data for over fifty years in the same location. This group of trained volunteers is part of the National Weather Service Cooperative Observers Program. In addition, a wonderful program called Community Collaborative Rain and Hail Study (CoCoRahs) has greatly increased the density of detailed weather data across the state. CoCoRahs is the brainchild of Nolan Doesken, who was frustrated with the scarcity of accurate rain and hail information during Colorado's heavy storm events.

The Fort Collins flood of 1997 was the catalyst. In that event, up to 14 inches of rain fell over the southwestern corner of the city, while the "official" observations closer to downtown and on the east side reported much less. In order to really pin down the intense, but small-scale rain and hail events, Doesken realized that we needed a dense network of volunteer weather watchers. CoCoRahs observers are equipped with a large and accurate rain gauge as well as a "hail pad," a square of Styrofoam covered in aluminum foil. The pad is set flat outside, and when it is pelted by hail, the depths and number of the dents enable researchers to determine the size and intensity of the hail. From a modest start with only a few volunteers in 1999, CoCoRahs has really taken off, and today there are thousands of observations being fed into the Colorado Climate Center each day via the Internet. In fact, CoCoRahs has gone national, with volunteers in states from coast to coast. For information on joining, go to www.cocorahs.org.

Automated weather stations are very important in providing large amounts of dependable data, but there is no substitute for the human touch in weather observing. Many of today's researchers and meteorologists built their first weather stations as kids. It is not a hard thing to do, and it can be a lot of fun. Beautiful home weather stations are available with very accurate solid-state instruments that feed automatically into your home computer. These weather stations are similar to the ones used by schools and ski areas and can provide vast amounts of accurate data. The new computer weather stations vary in price, but generally run between a few hundred and a couple thousand dollars. Check a good home electronics store; several excellent catalogs also offer weather stations. Many of the newest weather stations are even wireless.

A typical CoCoRahs station consists of the 4-inch-diameter rain gauge and a hailpad. During the winter, a snowboard is added for accurate snow measurement.

Whether human eyes and ears witness the weather or an automated station does, one thing is for sure: we get plenty of variety in Colorado. An old saying goes, "If you don't like the weather, wait five minutes and it will change." In Colorado, you do not even need to wait the five minutes. Our weather can go on some amazing roller-coaster rides, from warm and dry to bitter cold and snowy to everything in between.

In that light, with Nolan Doesken's help, we present some of the biggest weather stories in Colorado history.

Heavy Snows in Georgetown

According to weather historian William E. Wilson, formal weather observations began in Georgetown in 1878, when a station was established and Dr. W. R. Bradley started taking daily readings. It was common at the time for weather observers to be men in technical professions, doctors or engineers who were keen observers of natural phenomena and familiar with the use of instruments. Dr. Bradley was a homoeopath who lived and had his office at the corner of Rose and First Street (now Eighth). Thus the first weather station in Georgetown was located there. The biggest snowstorm ever reported was on December 4–5, 1913, when Georgetown was hit by 86 inches of snow.

Snow is piled up to the rooftops in Georgetown during the 1913 storm.

The *Georgetown Courier* reported that it was the "deepest snow since the glacial period," but there were numerous earlier reports of major snows that dated back to the Civil War: April 1862, "about five feet"; spring 1875, "heavy fall of snow on mountains causing landslides"; May 22, 1876, "Four feet deep. Heavy, crushed in buildings. Followed by disastrous landslides, one of which came down the gulch and extended into Taos Street"; March 6, 1881, "Heavy fall of snow delayed the train 10 hours"; January 1883, "Heavy snowfall over most of state"; April 23, 1885, "three to four feet of snow fell in one night and crushed the rink building"; May 1889, "three feet of snow in Georgetown within a week"; February 1889, "Snow was three feet deep in the park"; and May 29, 1894, "Snowstorm turned into a torrent of rain that lasted 44 hours and converted streets in lower part of town into rivers." So much for our 300 days of sunshine!

The Great Snowstorm of December 2–6, 1913

"There was a huge snowstorm in Denver. The streetcars could not run and a big trench was dug down the street so people could get to their houses. It was so deep that all we could see were people's heads above the snow banks as they walked down the street on their way to work. Men were so exhausted that folks brought them into their homes and set them down in front of big potbelly stoves and gave them coffee." So recalled Meryl Alberta Eaves Stewart of a snowstorm that hit Colorado in early December 1913. The storm was caused by a low pressure system that swirled in from the desert Southwest on November 30. At first the low was not much different from many that we get during the course of a Rocky Mountain winter. On December 1 and 2 it brought light to moderate snows as the low slowly dropped into New Mexico. However, on December 4, the low began to gradually move almost due north over the eastern plains of Colorado. This brought a tremendous easterly upslope flow to the plains and mountains east of the Continental Divide. Heavy rains soaked the far eastern plains, while amazing amounts of snow fell closer to the mountains. Of all the reporting stations, Georgetown was the winner with an incredible 86 inches of snow, 63 inches of it coming on December 4. The *Georgetown Courier* did manage to publish on December 6, but its inside pages were blank.

Bevington family, 1913 Denver snowstorm

In Denver, 46 inches of snow fell during the storm, a record that still stands for the single heaviest snowstorm for the city.

For many places along the Front Range, a similar storm would not hit again for ninety years, when the massive upslope storm of March 2003 brought snow amounts that challenged these numbers. Still, the official snow total for the 2003 storm was 31.8 inches in Denver, more than 14 inches less than the storm in 1913.

The closest runner-up could have been the one-two punch of the holiday storms in 2006. The first storm, just before Christmas, dumped over 20 inches of snow. The next system, eight days later, had the potential to drop another 2 feet of snow, but it moved just far enough to the east to drop its biggest load on the far eastern plains.

The December 1913 storm was a rarity in not only its intensity but also its timing. Huge, moist upslope storms are much more common in the months of March and April. In fact, December is rather low on the list for heavy snow in Denver, ranking fourth in average monthly snowfall behind March, November, and April, respectively. As in the storms of 2003 and 2006, travel was nearly impossible at the height of the storm and for many days after. In 1913, there were few automobiles in Colorado—only 13,624, according to the Colorado secretary of state. Trains and streetcars were the primary transit of the day, and the massive snowstorm snarled travel throughout the Front Range. The storm began with a wet slushy snow, but as temperatures fell the slush began to freeze into a rock-hard coating over the tracks. The additional snow piled up on top of that layer of ice, making it difficult to get the tracks cleared and the trains and trolleys running again. The December 5 issue of the *Rocky Mountain News* displayed a map of the Front Range pinpointing the location of all the stalled trains from Pueblo to Fort Collins and east to near Sterling; some of the trains were simply stuck in the drifts, but some had even been derailed by the ice and snow. Many passengers stayed on board and were kept relatively warm and well-fed by the staff in the dining cars, but as the hours passed, the provisions ran low. On one train stalled at Arapahoe, a conductor slogged 10 miles through deep snow

The December 1913 storm was a rarity in not only its intensity but also its timing. Huge moist upslope storms are much more common in March and April.

to reach the nearest store; he returned with cans of beans and loaves of bread, to the relief of the thankful passengers.

By Saturday, December 6, the railroad companies had brought in their big rotary plows and hundreds of men to shovel out the tracks and clear the big Denver rail yards. Progress was slow, even with the giant rotary plows affixed to steam locomotives. One rotary heading south from Cheyenne, Wyoming, encountered drifts 8 to 10 feet higher than the plow. Another snowplow working up Waterton Canyon battled thirty-two snowslides; each had to be dug out with a combination of the rotary plow and backbreaking manual labor. In Clear Creek Canyon, the plow attempting to clear the tracks between Georgetown and Silver Plume had to dig through a snow slide from Griffith Mountain. The snow was not only hard, deep, and heavy but was also littered with rock and hundreds of tree stumps ripped from the mountainside. Some of the rail crews resorted to using dynamite to help break up the concrete-like combination of snow and ice that clung to the tracks.

(top) The 1913 storm remains the heaviest five-day total snowfall in Denver's history. (bottom) Some of the most intense snow of the 1913 storm fell on December 4–5, with 37.4 inches in Denver and 63 inches in Georgetown.

The heavy snow clogged Denver's trolley lines, too. The streetcars were equipped with small plows in front of the car, but these were no match for the weight of the snow. Hundreds of men were employed at shoveling the tracks throughout the city, but the wind and snow often filled the cleared sections as fast as the men could shovel. In addition, the few automobile owners caused more trouble as some intrepid drivers attempted to get their autos through the storm, stalling over the tracks or dragging more snow into the path of the tired and frustrated shovelers. By Saturday, the Denver trolley companies had drafted an army of 4,000 men to shovel out the city's tracks. Much of the snow was loaded onto flatcars and hauled to bridges over the South Platte River, where it was dumped into the water below. Over the next week, the city of Denver employed 300 teams of men to clear the streets, paying them $2.50 per day—equivalent to about $50 today. The snow was hauled to vacant lots and piled as high as possible. At the present site of the Civic Center, the mountain of snow was so high that remnants of it lasted until the following summer. Although there is no record in either the *Post* or the *Rocky Mountain News*, there is a legend that a snow-scattering party was held on the following Fourth of July, with children bringing pails and toy shovels to spread the remnant snow and help speed the melting.

Horses, skis, and snowshoes were useful in getting around when mechanized methods of moving failed. Skiing was not yet a major sport but a social activity on the order of tobogganing. During the 1913 storm, it became more than just play. Skis and snowshoes were a vital method of transportation. In the mountains, there are numerous stories of trapped miners and citizens getting out of the deep drifts via skis and snowshoes. One incredible trek was made by A. D. Lukens and R. A. Roberts, who walked 70 miles from high in the Platte Canyon to their homes in Overland Park. Reported the *Post*, "The two men were cutting mine props above Shawnee, far up the Platte Canyon, when the snow came. Their cabin was snowed in and it was necessary to tunnel to get water. After being housed in for three weeks, the longing to spend Christmas at home overcame their fear of hardship and they started for Denver, although they had three weeks' rations in their cabin. Neither had ever used snowshoes or skies, but they made large snowshoes for the journey from Shawnee Point, at timberline, to Shawnee, and started out over eight feet of snow. The snowshoes soon became useless, and then they made skis, nine feet in length, and continued their journey. They made the first four miles in thirteen minutes, and the seventy into Denver in twenty-two hours of actual traveling."

Following the storm, local carpenters made skis in their shops and sold them for a dollar a pair. Carl Howelson, a Norwegian who imported and made skis, sold out his entire stock. He spent the winter teaching Denverites his native sport. In fact, during the Stock Show there was even a ski-jumping

> *There is a legend that a snow-scattering party was held on the following Fourth of July, with children bringing pails and toy shovels to spread the remnant snow to speed melting.*

During the 1913 storm skiing was less of a sport and more of a means of transportation.

exhibition, with Howelson making a jump of 30 feet. Later that winter, Howelson help arrange the first winter carnival in Steamboat Springs. The success of that event convinced locals of the need for a ski jump in town; it was built the next year and is still known as Howelson Hill.

A thirty-year-old named George Cranmer was among the witnesses to Howelson's skiing exhibitions and was inspired to take up the sport. Cranmer later became the manager of the Denver Park System and was the driving force behind the purchase and development of Winter Park Ski Area. So, in essence, the great storm of 1913 served as the catalyst for skiing to become the major sport it is today in Colorado.

The Silver Lake Snowstorm of 1921

Heavy April snowfalls are not uncommon along the Front Range in Colorado. In April, 1921, the Silver Lake cooperative weather station recorded a twenty-four hour snowfall total of 76 inches, a two-day accumulated snow-fall of 87 inches, and a storm total of 95 inches. Silver Lake is actually a reservoir owned by the city of Boulder; it is perched at 10,200 feet about 17 miles due west of Boulder and about 2 miles east of the Continental Divide. The average monthly snowfall for April at Silver Lake was 49 inches during the period 1911 to 1948, and monthly totals for April exceeded 70 inches eight times during that period. The weather observations at Silver Lake were taken by the reservoir caretaker, who lived at the site. Silver Lake was an official co-op observation station from 1910 until it was closed in 1996. Daily snowfall reports were taken from 1910 through 1948. According to the climate report, a daily melted precipitation report of 5.60 inches of water was published for Silver Lake, with an asterisk indicating that it was a two-day total from April 14 and 15. It was not immediately recognized as such, but in an article published in 1953 by J. H. L. Paulhus of the U.S. Weather Bureau, the Silver Lake snowfall observation became the national record. Based on the reported time the snowfall began, Paulhus prorated the 87-inch accumulated amount evenly over twenty-seven-and-a-half hours to come up with a 76-inch, twenty-four hour snowfall for the observational day (6:00 p.m. local time on April 14 to 6:00 p.m. on April 15). Paulhus performed an analysis that indicated the amount of snowfall reported was indeed physically possible given the storm conditions. The storm in 1921 held the national twenty-four hour snowfall record with 76 inches until 1997, when a monster "lake effect" snowstorm dumped 77 inches of snow in twenty-four hours on Montague, New York. The snowstorm was a classic spring upslope storm along the Front Range, but precipitation did fall statewide. Forty-six weather stations recorded at least an inch of water content, and fifteen had more than three inches of water.

Several reporting stations still give April 15, 1921, as their one-day maximum precipitation total for the month of April.

Several reporting stations still give April 15, 1921, as their one-day maximum precipitation total for the month of April. Examples include 3.97 inches at Cheesman Reservoir and 4.80 inches at Idaho Springs. The snow amounts from nearby reporting stations indicate that the 1921 storm was perhaps the biggest since 1913. Other totals in the 1921 storm included: 52 inches at Georgetown, 50 inches on Longs Peak, and 48 inches at both Grand Lake and Estes Park. These huge accumulations were very similar to the massive upslope storm that hit the Front Range in March of 2003.

During the 1921 storm, elevations below 7,000 feet had much more rain mixed in with the storm, and there were several reports of thunder during the event. Thunder is not unusual in strong springtime snowstorms and is a sign that some locales may have had much heavier amounts of precipitation than others. Just before the onset of the storm, Silver Lake reported 5.5 feet of aged winter snowpack. The next snowpack report came in at 6:00 p.m. on April 16, about nineteen hours after the snow had stopped. Thirteen feet of snow were reported on the ground at that point, which then settled to a depth of 11 feet by April 19. That storm was the last in what was a big winter for snow at Silver Lake: the 1920–1921 seasonal snowfall total was 627 inches, whereas the 1911–1948 average for the station was 268 inches.

A Rare November Tornado in 1922

The peak season for tornadoes in Colorado is from late May through early July, with the prime time for twisters being the first two weeks of June. In Colorado, statistics show that 90 percent of tornadoes occur between 1:00 p.m. and 9:00 p.m., and half of all tornadoes are reported between 3:00 p.m. and 6:00 p.m. Most Colorado tornadoes are small and short-lived, lasting only about ten minutes. Imagine the surprise, then, back in 1922 when a large and damaging tornado developed in the early morning hours of November 22. The storm rolled across Lincoln County between 5:00 a.m. and 7:00 a.m., and at times the path of the twister was a mile in width. The damage path extended for several miles, and the rare November storm left four people dead and caused $130,000 in damage.

The Wild Weather of the 1930s

While the Depression decade of the 1930s is best known for heat, drought, and dust storms, Colorado also experienced hail, tornadoes, floods, and extreme cold. The year 1934 was the hottest and driest year in Colorado's history until the drought

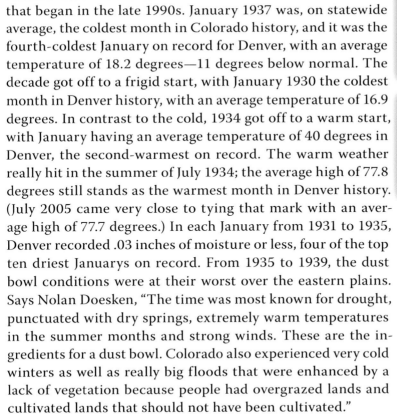

that began in the late 1990s. January 1937 was, on statewide average, the coldest month in Colorado history, and it was the fourth-coldest January on record for Denver, with an average temperature of 18.2 degrees—11 degrees below normal. The decade got off to a frigid start, with January 1930 the coldest month in Denver history, with an average temperature of 16.9 degrees. In contrast to the cold, 1934 got off to a warm start, with January having an average temperature of 40 degrees in Denver, the second-warmest on record. The warm weather really hit in the summer of July 1934; the average high of 77.8 degrees still stands as the warmest month in Denver history. (July 2005 came very close to tying that mark with an average high of 77.7 degrees.) In each January from 1931 to 1935, Denver recorded .03 inches of moisture or less, four of the top ten driest Januarys on record. From 1935 to 1939, the dust bowl conditions were at their worst over the eastern plains. Says Nolan Doesken, "The time was most known for drought, punctuated with dry springs, extremely warm temperatures in the summer months and strong winds. These are the ingredients for a dust bowl. Colorado also experienced very cold winters as well as really big floods that were enhanced by a lack of vegetation because people had overgrazed lands and cultivated lands that should not have been cultivated."

Colorado experienced extreme weather during the Dust Bowl. Both record heat and record cold were recorded.

The Eastern Plains Blizzard, November 2–6, 1946

A massive early season snowstorm enveloped the eastern plains of Colorado during the first week of November 1946. This storm began as cold rain on the eastern plains and then quickly turned to snow as a push of chilly air swept down from Canada. The low pressure center of the storm stalled on the eastern plains and produced many hours of light to moderate snow that finally tallied to several feet of snow. Many areas on the eastern plains reported at least 3 feet of snow, even well east of the Denver area. Strong northerly winds whipped the snow into huge drifts that stalled travel by air, road, or rail. In the end, thirteen people died.

Snow fell continuously for 70 hours and 46 minutes, the second-longest period of snowfall in Denver history. The storm was heralded as "the worst since 1913" by newspapers in the Denver area. One article in the *Arvada Enterprise* claimed that the "snow started on November 2nd at 4:20 a.m. and the official total was 28 inches at Stapleton Field."

The storm hit all up and down the Front Range and seemed to really sock it to Castle Rock. It was the Saturday before the general election in 1946, and the snow kept getting heavier and heavier. Radio reports claimed that the snow would begin to taper off, but by Sunday morning, it was still falling heavily. Locals recall that the "clearing by morning" forecast was still being issued as the snow piled 3 feet deep. Dairy farmers

Heavy snow during November 1946 caused numerous building and roof collapses around Denver. The great snowstorm impeded traffic for days, and many cars and buses were abandoned. Schools and businesses were closed for several days because of the heavy snow.

around Castle Rock and Parker were soon out of empty milk cans as the milk trucks were mired in the snow. Eventually, those with cream separators would use them and separate out the oldest milk, dumping the skim and keeping the cream. Every available clean container was used to store milk for several days before the roads were again passable.

The storm left much of Douglas County snowbound for over a week, including Election Day. In one local precinct, only one person made it to the schoolhouse to cast a vote—the election judge for the precinct. In the patriotic wake of World War II, the great snow of November 1946 did give Front Range residents a solid alibi for not voting.

The snow season from September 1946 to the following spring also made the record books for Denver. The first snow fell on September 22, 1946, and the last reported snow fell on June 11, 1947—an incredible 263 days from the first snow to the last.

The Great Freeze of 1951

A severe cold wave in 1951 gripped Colorado with record chill. The cold wave hit statewide, with Denver plummeting to -24 on January 31. On February 1 the temperature bottomed out at -60 at Taylor Park Dam and hit -40 in some areas along the Front Range, killing many cherry orchards. Denver began the month by dipping to -25; the all-time record for the city for February and Fort Collins hit -41. "This storm changed the landscape of the Front Range," says Doesken. "This was a large cherry orchard area before the freeze. It killed fruit orchards and scared fruit growers away for many years. Fruit and wine growers are now creeping back in." Many fruit growers shifted to the Western Slope area as the mountains do a better job of blocking the arctic air masses from flowing into the Colorado River Valley around Fruita and Grand Junction.

For many locations, the cold wave of 1951, most notably the extreme cold on the morning of February 1, is considered the coldest day in recorded history since it affected the mountains, the Front Range, and the eastern plains. Also in 1951, another deep freeze hit, but this time in June. The low in Denver hit 30 degrees on June 2, the coldest ever recorded for that month and the latest date for the last freeze until June 2007, when the low hit 31 degrees on the 8th. Snow accompanied the chill in 1951, with a third of an inch reported in the city of Denver.

Massive Mountain Storm, December 29–31, 1951

Possibly the greatest mountain snowstorm in the history of Colorado, a huge, slow-moving upper-level trough stalled over the western United States for several days at the very end of 1951. This feature combined with a surface front that became

Up to 3 feet of snow fell in the Dillon area with twice as much snow in the higher mountains nearby.

stationary over the Continental Divide and created a perfect snowmaking machine for the high country. Thirty-six inches of snow fell in Dillon—almost a quarter of the seasonal average. Dillon is a relatively dry place compared to the surrounding mountains. Perhaps twice as much snow fell in the higher terrain nearby. The snowstorm may have been a Pineapple Express event, with a several-day onslaught of Pacific moisture borne on a very strong jet stream. Large amounts of precipitation fell on the normally drier parts of western Colorado, in places such as Eagle. In addition, large amounts of precipitation spilled over the mountains and down onto the Front Range; some places east of the mountains may have gotten close to a half-inch of moisture.

The heavy amount of precipitation indicates the storm was so strong and moisture-laden that upslope was not the chief component for producing snow. Instead, the clouds had so much water to spare that they did not dump all the snow over western Colorado and along the Divide. Locations such as Estes Park that usually only get a tiny amount of precipitation from westerly spillover were hit with heavy snow.

The Snowslides of 1958

A strong southwesterly flow in the jet stream brought moisture-laden storms into southwestern Colorado, piling up deep snows in the San Juan Mountains. The huge snowpack created extreme avalanche conditions that manifest themselves in a couple of very memorable slides. Robert Duncan of Montrose was a "young buck," in his words, working on electric lines for the Western Colorado Power Company. Duncan recalls,

> We were working out of Paonia. On February 13, about midnight, we had a call to get over to Telluride to fix a 44,000-volt power line running through Ophir Canyon—it had been taken out by a snowslide. We loaded up our trucks and the crew and headed for Telluride, which was over 100 miles away. We arrived at daybreak, having followed a snowplow most of the way, it was snowing pretty hard. . . .
>
> The next morning, they sent a D7 Caterpillar and a Dodge Power Wagon for us to pull the replacement poles, wire, and other equipment to the site. It was about lunchtime when everything arrived in the town of Old Ophir. Harry Wright, a co-worker, was in the Power Wagon and had just opened his lunch bucket and poured a cup of coffee. The wind was blowing very hard and there were ice crystals in the air that felt like sand when they hit your face.
>
> All of a sudden, all Hell broke loose. Seven slides came down at about the same time. One big slide came down on the upper part of town and split just above the old jailhouse. The upper part went down to the bottom of the canyon, the other half into town; this is the one that did all the damage. It picked up the Power Wagon and threw it into a cabin, burying it with Harry still in it. This slide also knocked the old school house off its foundation, knocked a store building several feet and tore the back porch off a house, filling it with snow. As the snow settled,

Robert Duncan, who worked for the Western Colorado Power Company, documented the dangers and difficulties that winter snows posed to those maintaining the power grid in the San Juans.

we gathered at the "Cat," as that was the last place we had seen Harry. The slide had swept the truck about 500 feet away, pushing it up against the eaves of an old cabin.

The truck was completely buried in snow, but Harry managed to take a wrench and smash the door window, cutting his hand, but otherwise escaping unharmed. After Harry dug himself out, we decided we had better get out of there while we still could. We paired up and snow-shoed out two at a time, so the whole crew wouldn't be caught if more slides ran. You could hear slides breaking loose all the time as we were walking out. . . .

We went back into the canyon one week later. There were big stands of timber that had been wiped completely out. Slides had run where they had never run before, if you ever get into Ophir Canyon, you can still see the timber lying everywhere from those slides in 1958.

A Nasty Start to 1962

A major winter storm dropped 13.5 inches of snow on Denver from January 7 to 10, 1962. Most of that fell on January 8, with northeasterly winds gusting over 30 mph. Behind the snow, arctic air invaded the region. The overnight lows dropped to 24 degrees below zero on both of the next two days. The high on January 9 never climbed above zero.

January was a tough month for Denver residents, just digging out from a major snow. A cold spell settled into Denver for more than a week from January 15 to 23. Overnight lows dropped to zero or below for nine consecutive days. The cold broke briefly on January 20 thanks to Chinook winds. The afternoon high warmed to 38 degrees. But just a few hours later, a reinforcing surge of arctic air moved into Colorado. There were several deaths attributed to this tough month of winter weather, mainly from traffic accidents and overexertion. Hundreds of water systems around the metro were damaged due to frozen pipes. One woman froze to death in Morrison.

Bitter Cold of Early 1963

January 1963 was extremely cold, not only in Colorado and across the western states, but also over most of the lower forty-eight. In the records, the month is listed as the coldest in seventy-five years for the nation. Even in northern Europe, extreme cold was reported along with heavy snow. For Colorado, it was the second straight very cold January, following the arctic chill of 1962.

Temperatures across metro Denver and much of northern Colorado fell below zero for up to sixty-eight hours. Denver dropped to 25 degrees below zero on January 11 and 12. The high of -9 on January 11 was the coldest January high ever recorded in Denver. Light snow also accompanied the bitter blast. Broken water pipes caused damage all across the city.

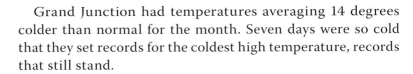

Grand Junction had temperatures averaging 14 degrees colder than normal for the month. Seven days were so cold that they set records for the coldest high temperature, records that still stand.

Big Floods of 1965

Colorado has suffered occasional catastrophic flooding ever since settlers arrived during the gold rush of 1858–1859. Much of the fledgling frontier town of Denver was wiped out by flooding on Cherry Creek in 1864. A century later, a flood left a bigger long-term legacy. The destruction it brought in a major metropolitan area prompted community leaders to do all they could to minimize the potential for such disasters in the future. June had been dry at the beginning, but that changed as heavy clouds built in the afternoon skies mid-month. Several days of extremely heavy thunderstorms across much of eastern Colorado resulted in damaging and widespread flooding on June 14–18, 1965.

The surface weather pattern consisted of a moist easterly flow that pulled humidity into the state from the Midwest. High in the atmosphere, a deep upper-level storm system over the western part of the nation made the atmosphere very unstable. Each day, another round of powerful thunderstorms developed and tracked slowly over the Front Range. Soils quickly became saturated with water and any additional rainfall simply had nowhere to go.

Several dams failed, including one near Cripple Creek. "Denver was hard hit," says Doesken. "Bridges on I-25 were washed out. It flooded all the way to downtown

Violent thunderstorms hit the Front Range with heavy cloudbursts in June 1965. Rain totals in Castle Rock were 12 inches, with 14 inches at both Palmer Lake and Larkspur. The South Platte River grew more than a half-mile wide during the flood. Denver was nearly isolated as most east–west routes into the city were closed due to the flood.

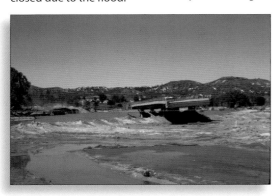

near Union Station. It flooded in many different areas of the state. There was even a flash flood on the Blue River in Breckenridge, and it is highly unusual to have flash floods that high up."

Heavy rains hit in many areas of Colorado, with the southeastern plains also hard hit. Just to the southeast of Lamar, 15.5 inches of rain fell in fourteen hours, while Holly reported 11 inches of rain in six hours.

The flooding for the Denver area was the direct result of 14 inches of torrential rain near Larkspur that sent a wall of water—20 feet high in some places—down Plum Creek and into the South Platte River. Plum Creek is typically just a tiny flow of water as it passes by Louviers; the average flow is 150 cubic feet per second (cfs). At the height of the flood, Plum Creek was flowing at 154,000 cfs, twenty times higher than the previous record. The first area near Denver to be hit hard was in Littleton, as the Columbine Country Club had its golf course and surrounding luxury homes devastated. Overland Park golf course on the northern side of Littleton suffered a similar fate. The Centennial Horse Track, which was within days of opening its racing season, had most of its track and stable areas heavily flooded, but a rescue operation by owners, trainers, and jockeys saved some 140 horses. The water supply for the city of Littleton, which consisted of a series of wells along the river, was virtually destroyed. For months after the flood, water for the city had to be provided by a network of firehoses run from the nearest Denver outlets.

As the flood continued north, it was more than just fast water roaring through the countryside. It now included a dangerous stew of debris—old cars, refrigerators, and a variety of junk that either had been dumped along the river over the years or had been pulled into the churning waters. This semi-liquid battering ram destroyed twenty-six bridges, including every one from Littleton north to the Colfax viaduct. Both Public Service Company power plants along the river were shut down, and emergency circuits became waterlogged and shorted out.

The flooding for the Denver area was the direct result of 14 inches of torrential rain near Larkspur that sent a wall of water—20 feet high in some places—down Plum Creek and into the South Platte River.

As the high waters flowed north, other streams added to the flow: Sand Creek and Clear Creek, and farther north the Bijou and Little Beaver and the Poudre River. The communities of Sterling, Fort Morgan, and Brush became isolated as the waters spread out over a quarter-million acres of farmland. There was a benefit to the water, as the region had been in the midst of a three-year dry spell.

The flooding in 1965 left twenty-four people dead, caused over a half billion dollars in damage, and resulted in the construction of the Chatfield Dam to control flooding on the South Platte. The dam had long been recommended, and was actually planned in the 1930s, but it took a disaster to finally convince state and federal officials to get it built. The project was completed in 1972, and today the dam not only serves to protect Denver but has also created lovely Chatfield Lake.

Big Thompson Flood, July 31, 1976

Perhaps the greatest weather tragedy in Colorado history, the Big Thompson Flood hit with fast and deadly force. The weekend of July 31–August 1, 1976, marked the centenary of Colorado statehood. Thousands of campers and hikers had flocked to the high country for a weekend of fun and celebration. By Sunday morning, August 1, the newspapers were not full of details of the big party, but instead of the terrible tragedy in Big Thompson Canyon. An intense but localized thunderstorm developed on the afternoon of July 31 just east of Estes Park. This storm transformed from typical to terrible due to a combination of light winds aloft and moist easterly winds at the surface. The easterly surface winds acted as a moisture conveyer system to push humid air well up into the heart of the thunderstorm.

The light winds aloft—only about 10 miles per hour from the west—provided little means of moving the storm, so it stalled over the same area for several hours. Amazing amounts of rain fell over a very small, rugged canyon filled with hundreds of un-

The Big Thompson Flood

On July 31, 1976, one of Colorado's worst natural disasters unfolded in the Big Thompson Canyon about an hour northwest of Denver. Thousands of people in the canyon were celebrating Colorado's centennial that weekend. A stationary thunderstorm developed during the afternoon that soon unleashed a foot of rain within three hours. A wall of water swept through the area, scouring the canyon free of boulders, cars, homes, and campers. In the end, 144 people died, and the flood caused more than $40 million in damage. The disaster was a shocking reminder of the dangers of flash flooding in Colorado.

Eve Gruntfest, of the University of Colorado–Colorado Springs, is an internationally recognized expert in flash flooding and natural hazard mitigation. She shares her thoughts on the disaster.

Q: Was the Big Thompson flood Colorado's worst natural disaster?
A: The Pueblo flood in 1921 was probably worse, but the details are sketchy with that flood. More people probably died in the Pueblo flood than in the Big Thompson flood. The Big Thompson wasn't even the most expensive. The blizzards of December 2006 — January 2007 will probably cost more, even if you adjust the cost of the Big Thompson to 2007 dollars. However, it was the last time until Hurricane Katrina that so many people died in a natural disaster in the United States.

Portion of US 34 destroyed by the Big Thompson flood.

Q: Is the Big Thompson the turning point in how we perceive flash flooding?
A: Absolutely. There was a worse flood in Rapid City in 1972, but the Big Thompson reminded us that it can happen again.

Q: What cities along the Front Range are you most concerned about?
A: Well, Boulder for sure, and Manitou Springs. I think Black Hawk is considered to be in an extremely dangerous location, especially the road getting there. And Colorado Springs. We haven't done nearly as much as Boulder has as far as public awareness. What I've said for years is that we have this great detection system, and right after the Big Thompson people needed to do something, so they went crazy over these stream gauge and rain gauge systems that they called warning systems. They're not; they're really detection systems. They monitor the streams, but they don't do anything to get the message to the people in a timely manner to do the right thing.

Q: So what do we need to do?
A: We need to have public education so that people know which areas are most vulnerable and they need to know that this can happen with very short notice—with or without official warning. Ideally, you would be able to tell people in advance, even days in advance, that heavy thunderstorms might be possible. I think many people are in denial about the threat, and so many people have moved to Colorado since 1976 that many people don't know about the Big Thompson. They don't understand that, yes, Colorado is a dry place, but we can have incredibly serious flash floods.

Destruction left by the raging flood waters of the Big Thompson flood. (bottom) Remains of the generator station that supplied power to the city of Loveland. The remains can be seen in the Viestenz-Smith Mountain Park today.

wary picnickers and campers. Bob Berling, manager of the Bureau of Reclamation Colorado–Big Thompson Project, estimates that at least 50 million tons of rainwater were dumped by the storm, mostly in the area between Estes Park and Drake. The heaviest rainfall near Glen Haven and Glen Comfort amounted to nearly 12 inches of rain—7 to 8 inches of that falling in just two hours during the evening of July 31. The average stream flow on the Big Thompson River before the onset of the rain was only 165 cubic feet per second. The peak flow on the Big Thompson at the mouth of the canyon was 31,200 cfs at about 9:00 p.m. The first signs of trouble came from Colorado State Patrolman Bob Miller, on duty at Estes Park. Miller was asked to drive up and check on reported rock and mudslides on Highway 34 in Big Thompson Canyon. At about 8:35 p.m., Miller radioed to Estes Park police, "We've got to start taking people out. My car's gonna be washed away. I've got a real emergency down here." Greeley State Patrol radio dispatcher Jay Lorance issued orders to Officer Timmy Littlejohn to begin stopping traffic on Highway 34 west of Loveland. Patrolman Miller radioed

Big Thompson Flood

Light winds aloft provided little push to move thunderstorms away from the Big Thompson Canyon. Moist easterly winds at the surface fed humid air into the storm, producing very heavy rainfall that stayed over the same area for several hours.

back to Estes Park, "Advise them we have a flood. The whole mountainside is gone. We have people trapped on the other side [of the river]. I'm up to my doors in water. Advise we can't get to them. There is no way. I'm going to get out of here before I drown. Got to get to a higher level."

Sergeant Hugh Purdy of the Colorado State Patrol was driving from Loveland toward Drake, trying to find the headwaters of the flood. His journey began at 8:50 p.m. when he radioed from near the mouth of the canyon, "The water will be coming down here. I'll try to pick it up as I go up. See if I can find out where it is at." At 9:00 p.m. Purdy radioed, "You better have Loveland starting to contact people along the Thompson . . . east of the Narrows. I'm about two and half [miles] east of Drake and the river is pretty good, so it's gonna be coming down better than this later. Call the power plant on the Thompson and advise them to get everybody out of the low [spot] in there." Purdy's last radio transmission was at approximately 9:15 p.m. "I'm right in the middle of it. I can't get out . . . about one-half mile east of Drake on the highway. [Tell the cars] to get out of the low area down below."

Purdy's body was found about 8 miles downstream from the site of his last radio transmission. His car was ground up beyond recognition and was identified only by a key ring inscribed Colorado State Patrol.

Rangers from Rocky Mountain National Park were aware of the unfolding tragedy and helped to aid those trapped in the flood. Actual damage to the park was small, considering that 10 inches of rain fell across the area that evening. According to Roger J. Contor, the superintendent of Rocky Mountain National Park, "We lost 3.7 miles of the Gem Lake Trail, which cost about $40,000 to rebuild."

Lieutenant Leo Baker of the Larimer County Sheriff's Office put in a call for help from the National Park Service (NPS) employees. Fifty NPS personnel responded to the call and raced to the canyon with heavy equipment, helping to push away earth and debris from the highway and trying to keep some sort of road open for escape and rescue. Tragedy did happen before the eyes of one crew, headed by Chief Ranger Dave Essex. The NPS vehicle was driving back up the canyon from the Tuckaway cabins when it was halted by a torrent washing across the road from the hillside. Some of these instant rivers were as much as 5 feet deep and falling into the Big Thompson River at tremendous speed.

The National Guard gathers in Loveland on August 1, 1976, to coordinate search-and-rescue efforts in Big Thompson Canyon.

(top) The washed out remains of the Bureau of Reclamation water siphon and Highway US 34 after the Big Thompson Flood. (bottom) Automobiles and other debris left after the deadly flash flood.

Mr. and Mrs. Fred Woodring, Tuckaway residents, were behind the rangers in a four-wheel-drive International Scout. Apparently Mr. Woodring thought his vehicle could best the waters surging across the highway in front of the Rangers. He swung around and started across. Essex and his crew watched helplessly as lightning flashes showed the Scout being hurled from the road. Headlights of the stricken vehicle shooting skyward occasionally marked its tumbling progress, showed that it had been caught in a pile of debris across the river. Mr. Woodring managed to climb to the top of the Scout, awash in the surging waters. Mrs. Woodring's body was found later, pinned underneath the vehicle. By the light of searchlights, Essex attempted to hurl a rope to Mr. Woodring, but the elderly man was carried away into the darkness before he could be saved.

At the mouth of the canyon, a surging wall of water and debris, including big propane tanks emitting an eerie whistle as they lost pressure, came smashing out onto the plains. According to Bob Berling, 1.5 million pounds of resistance would have been required to turn back the water at the Narrows. The force of the water at the mouth of the canyon was equivalent to 35,000 horsepower—enough to generate 26,000 kilowatts of electricity. A huge water siphon—part of a Bureau of Reclamation project—was broken and dislodged by the extreme force. This giant pipe weighed over 220,000 pounds and was full of another 873,000 pounds of water, bringing the total mass to over a million pounds! The siphon, deeply embedded in the mountainside, "came out like a big soda straw," said Larimer County Sheriff Bob Watson.

> *At the mouth of the canyon, a surging wall of water and debris, including big propane tanks emitting an eerie whistle as they lost pressure, came smashing out onto the plains.*

The replacement for this siphon can be seen today just above Highway 34 at the lower entrance to the canyon. Just a mile up the canyon, there is also a very interesting display of the remains of the power plant that was located along the river. The floodwaters tore away everything but the large turbines that were bolted deep into the bedrock. The cleanup from the flooding lasted for many months, with the rebuilding of Highway 34 taking nearly a year. One hundred and forty-four people died in the flooding; several bodies were never recovered. The property damage was estimated at $40 million.

Dry Winter of 1976–1977

Severe weather usually brings to mind a major storm. In the winter of 1976–1977, there simply were no major storms until it was too late. A stubborn surface high-pressure system over Utah blocked any stormy weather from moving into Colorado for most of the winter season. This high helped to push the jet stream well to the north of the state, taking away the prospect of strong winds aloft bringing much moisture to the mountains.

The resulting snow drought of 1976–1977 was a financial disaster for ski resorts as nearly all the Colorado ski areas had marginal conditions for nearly the entire season. Snow had to be trucked from the Continental Divide to the ski areas in order to create adequate cover at the bases of the mountains. As a result, most Colorado resorts began to add snowmaking capabilities, a technology formerly used only by resorts in the "snow-challenged" Midwest and New England. The pattern lasted almost all winter and did not ease until March, when a huge blizzard developed on the eastern plains, that killed nine people.

"There was no decent skiing until March and that month northeast Colorado had a big blizzard where twenty foot high drifts were commonplace and the ground blown clear in other spots," Nolan Doesken recalled.

Christmas Eve Blizzard of 1982

There are a few weather events that always bring the question, "Where were you during the big storm of —?" Perhaps no other storm in recent memory begs this query more than the massive snowstorm that buried Denver and much of eastern Colorado on Christmas Eve of 1982. The storm did not escape early detection: forecasters had been cheerily predicting a white Christmas for the Denver area for several days in advance. What came as a surprise was the intensity of the storm—most early prognostications were for a modest snowfall of about 6 inches.

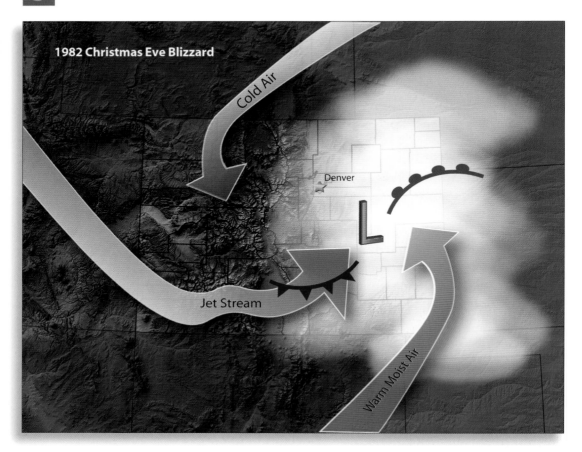

1982 Christmas Eve Blizzard

Cold Air

Denver

Jet Stream

Warm Moist Air

The set-up for the Christmas Eve Storm of 1982. Moist air flowed into eastern Colorado, while very cold air spilled down from the north. A strong upper level jet stream provided energy to help develop a massive winter storm.

That forecast began to change by late in the day on December 22. Two different weather makers were bearing down on Colorado. A powerful Pacific cold front roared onshore in California early on that day, bringing heavy rain, high surf, and hurricane-force winds to the San Francisco area. The fierce winds downed six high-voltage power lines atop Altamont Pass, one of the windiest spots in the United States. The loss of the transmission lines caused a massive power outage throughout California, Arizona, Utah, and Nevada, darkening Disneyland and knocking out some of the bright casino lights in Las Vegas. As that storm moved eastward, it dumped up to 2 feet of snow in the Wasatch Mountains around Salt Lake City and dropped 1 to 2 feet of snow in the mountains of Colorado.

At about the same time, strong jet stream winds aloft were helping to carve a large trough of low pressure over the southwestern deserts. At the surface, a new low pressure system began to form over the southeastern plains of Colorado. The counterclockwise flow around this low started to pull moisture-laden air toward Colorado from the southern plains. As the humid air mass moved toward the northwest, it cooled, the moisture condensed into clouds and precipitation, and it developed into a very large storm system. To the east of Colorado, severe thunderstorms, hail, and tornadoes raked Kansas and Oklahoma. The rain changed to snow over the far eastern plains of Colorado, but the focus for the flakes was along the Front Range. The strong easterly surface wind produced perfect upslope conditions from Longmont and Boulder, through Denver, south to the Palmer Divide.

Shortly before midnight on December 23, the storm had intensified into a full-fledged high plains blizzard. Dawn broke on Christmas Eve with the Denver Metro area stranded in a sea of white. Snow fell heavily throughout day on December 24, often at a rate of 2–3 inches per hour. Winds howled at 50 miles per hour, whipping the snow into 10-foot drifts and driving the wind chill factor to -35.

Roads, shopping centers, businesses, and airports were shut down at the height of holiday travel and preparations. For the first time in Denver history, both the *Denver Post* and the *Rocky Mountain News* were unable to publish their Saturday morning editions. Stapleton Airport closed at 9:30 a.m. on Christmas Eve and did not reopen for thirty-three hours. It took more than five days for air traffic to return to normal. Needless to say, spending Christmas at the airport was not the way thousands of stranded travelers dreamed of a white Christmas, especially as food and liquor supplies dwindled. One of the first planes to finally take off late on Christmas Day carried the Denver Broncos, who arrived in sunny, warm Los Angeles, only to be thrashed by their archrival Raiders the next day.

Christmas Blizzard 1982 Snow Totals	
Golden Gate Canyon	48″
Wheat Ridge	34″
Golden	34″
Thornton	34″
Lakewood	30″
Littleton	29″
Englewood	29″
Longmont	27″
Aurora	26″
Denver	25″
Boulder	24″
Parker	24″
Dillon	12″
Sterling	12″
Colo. Springs	7″
Fort Collins	4″
Pueblo	2″
Greeley	1″

The Denver Nuggets game against the Golden State Warriors was postponed from Friday to Monday, but only 800 brave fans managed to get to McNichols Sports Arena to see Denver win that game. The man for whom that facility was named, Mayor William H. McNichols Jr., spent his holiday weekend coordinating efforts of the newly created Office of Emergency Preparedness.

The mayor called the city's cleanup effort "herculean" and noted that the snow removal cost the city $1 million and the six-county metro area $2.5 million. The fleet of forty-five snow-removal trucks could not handle the task alone, and the city spent $150,000 a day to rent private equipment for several days. Snowstorms are tough on politicians, and despite the efforts of the mayor and the city crews, grumbling came that the snow stayed piled up way too long. "This storm should earn the mayor another term—in Cañon City," one citizen wrote to the local papers.

The storm was so severe because it stalled over the southeastern plains of Colorado, keeping the Denver area under the gun in terms of upslope winds for over twenty-four hours. This is similar to other great snowstorms, such as those on December 1913, October 1997, March 2003, and December 2006. The long duration upslope events are the ones that really pile up our snow along the Front Range. The final tally on snowfall was impressive: 25.5 inches at Stapleton, a record for

(top) Snowbound cars in central Denver on Christmas Day. (bottom) Teamwork! Pushing a car out of the snow on Christmas morning.

twenty-four hours and a record for snow depth for Christmas Day. Other parts of the city had much more: 28 inches downtown, 29 inches in Englewood, and 34 inches from Thornton to Arvada to Lakewood and Golden. Wheat Ridge had nearly 3 feet and Golden Gate Canyon reported 4 feet of snow. The northern extent of the snow was limited, though, and there were reports of folks playing golf and tennis in Greeley on Christmas Day.

The great Christmas Eve storm of 1982 was an unpleasant experience for many travelers, a time that few will forget. One group of about 250 motorists spent Christmas Eve stranded in the school gym in Deer Trail. The weary travelers were treated to a warm ham dinner by the local citizens and even had a miraculous visit from Santa Claus.

Thanksgiving Blizzard of 1983

Not even a year after the Christmas Eve blizzard, a snowstorm hammered the Front Range just in time to strand anxious holiday travelers in Denver again. Thanksgiving weekend in 1983 saw a major winter snowfall hit, just as hundreds of thousands of travelers were trying to get over the river and through the woods. The busiest shopping day of the year sent folks scurrying not for Christmas gifts but for shovels and snow chains as the flakes flew and began to pile up on the day after Thanksgiving.

The storm was colder than the Christmas Eve storm. The average temperature in the 1982 storm was 35 degrees, making that snow extremely wet and slushy. In November 1983, the average temperature was 23 degrees, so the snow was much drier and fluffier. Some 21.5 inches of snow fell, about 2 inches less than the previous storm, but the water content was much lower, only 1.42 inches compared to 2 inches. Nonetheless, a strong northerly wind blew the snow into large drifts, and the storm lasted thirty-six hours, snarling traffic by land or air during the busiest travel weekend of the year. There was some disenchantment with the forecasting of this storm as the National Weather Service erred in dropping the storm warning during a brief lull in the snowfall.

The storm picked up strength again Saturday evening and dumped several more inches of snow on the region by early Sunday morning, much to the surprise of residents. It was not as big as the 1982 storm, but coming so fast on the heels of that blizzard and hitting on another major holiday, folks felt as though nature had dealt them a solid one-two punch. Little did they know that the third blow was only a few weeks away.

Cold Christmas of 1983

There have been many terrible cold waves in the wintertime, but one of the worst hit just before the holidays just one year after the infamous Christmas Eve Blizzard. In 1983, the days before Christmas felt like Santa Claus had sent North Pole weather down as an envoy. Temperatures fell below zero for 115 straight hours in the Denver area, the longest period of subzero temperatures ever recorded in Denver, eclipsing the previous record of 91 consecutive hours set in December 1932. Denver was not alone in this subzero club. Scottsbluff, Nebraska, fell below zero at midafternoon on December 19 and did not see the plus side of zero again until 11:00 a.m. on Christmas Day—140 straight hours. Cheyenne, Wyoming, stayed below zero for 120 hours, shattering a record that had stood for 111 years. Colorado Springs set six consecutive record lows from December 19 to 25, with the Christmas morning low of −15 easily passing the previous record of −3 set in 1974.

> *December 1983, temperatures fell below zero for 115 straight hours in the Denver area, the longest period of subzero temperatures ever recorded.*

All along the Front Range, cloudy skies, light snow, and an icy fog covered the area for most of the week before Christmas. The mountains managed to block some of the heavy, cold air from flowing into western Colorado, but moderate snow and bitter cold did climb high enough to cover areas up to the Divide and into Summit County. A strong northerly flow aloft poured the arctic air down from northern Canada all the way to the Gulf of Mexico. December 1983 was the coldest December on record for more than two dozen cities from North Dakota to Colorado to Texas. In Denver, the average temperature for the month was 17.4 degrees, much colder than the previous mark of 21.2 degrees set in December 1909. This arctic express made December 1983 the second-coldest month ever in Denver, second only to the 16.9-degree average temperature in January 1930.

Ironically, the Christmas cold snap was the only one for the winter. After the bitter blast moved out, the weather pattern shifted and the prevailing winds for the rest of the winter came from the west, instead of the north, keeping Colorado rather mild from January through March.

Limon Tornado, June 6, 1990

Tornadoes are frequent visitors to the high plains of eastern Colorado. Our state averages between thirty and fifty twisters each year, mainly from late May to early July. Ninety percent of the tornadoes in Colorado occur east of I-25, with Weld, eastern Adams, eastern Arapahoe, Lincoln, Washington, and Yuma Counties leading the way.

Limon area tornado activity is higher than both the Colorado and U.S. averages.

Until the Holly tornado of 2007, there had not been a tornado fatality in Colorado since June 27, 1960, in Sedgwick County. This was due mostly to improved warnings and to good fortune as the large amount of open land over eastern Colorado has provided tornadoes with plenty of room to roam without hitting large population centers. Storm chasers have long noted that large and damaging tornadoes often occur over eastern Colorado in the late spring and early summer. Most of us are unaware of the severity of these twisters simply because they cause relatively little damage as they spin over fields and rangeland. It is only when a tornado tears up a town or causes serious injury or death that they become big headline makers. Perhaps the most famous tornado in Colorado history was the one that destroyed much of downtown Limon on the evening of June 6, 1990. The storm struck the city just after 8:00 p.m. and tore through the central part of town, destroying 80 percent of the local business district. The ten-minute rampage caused $12 million in damage; 228 homes and trailers were damaged or destroyed, leaving 117 families homeless; and 14 people were injured. The storm also knocked out the National Weather Service's radar station in Limon. Fortunately, the radar was working ahead of the storm's arrival and helped determine the strength and severity of the storm in time for adequate warnings to be issued. The Limon Tornado was rated as an F3 on the Fujita scale and was accompanied by baseball-sized hail that fell over much of the city.

(top and right) Though Colorado is ranked ninth in the nation for number of tornadoes, most are weak and cause little damage. (above) The Limon tornado was quite rare. More than 75 percent of tornadoes occur before 7:00 p.m. The Limon tornado struck just after 8:00 p.m.

Seven-Eleven Hailstorm of 1990

As the newspapers in Colorado were still covering aspects of the Limon Tornado, another major thunderstorm event was about to take center stage, this time with hail as the main event. On July 11, a large rotating thunderstorm blew up northwest of Denver and moved toward the southeast. These supercell storms, as we have seen, are common over the plains of eastern Colorado and are frequent producers of large hail and tornadoes. Supercell thunderstorms are rare right on top of Denver and along the Front Range, since the proximity to the mountains tends to inhibit thunderstorms from developing a strong rotation. When supercell thunderstorms do develop right on top of the largest metropolitan area in the Rocky Mountain region, one can expect big problems.

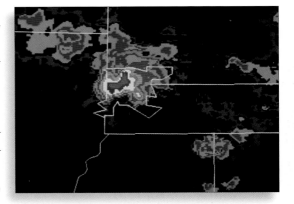

The supercell storm of July 11, 1990, proved to be the single costliest hailstorm in U.S. history as the storm stretched from north of Fort Collins almost to Colorado Springs. The hailstorm blew up in the middle of the afternoon of July 11, feeding on the combination of moist easterly surface winds and a cool pool of air aloft. The chilly air in the higher reaches of the atmosphere allowed for the formation of large hailstones. "The long-lived hailstorm traveled from Estes Park to Colorado Springs in three hours and went directly over Denver. More than six hundred million dollars in property losses were reported. Roofers had incredible business," recalled Nolan Doesken.

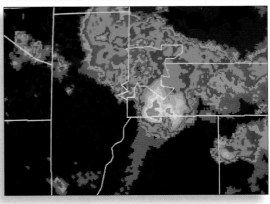

Radar images of the supercell thunderstorm of July 11, 1990.

The storm was a huge media event as all of the local Denver television and radio stations and newspapers provided extensive coverage. The hail hit quickly in the Denver area and caught some patrons at Elitch Gardens by surprise. Several injuries were reported as people were stuck on amusement rides during the storms and were cut and bruised by the large hail.

In addition to tens of thousands of damaged roofs, there was tremendous damage to automobiles. Windshields were smashed by hail that ranged in size from a marble to a grapefruit. The hoods and trunks of cars and trucks retained an eerie likeness to the surface of the moon for many months after the storm as body shops struggled to catch up.

Storm King Mountain Fire of 1994

Summer forest fires are an annual concern in our state. In certain years, the forests begin to dry not in summer but as early as late March, and early spring snows may be lacking or the weather simply warms too quickly in May, melting the snow away. In the spring of 1994, winter made an early exit and the lack of adequate late spring and early summer rainfall created extremely dry conditions over Colorado. June was a hot and dry month, with highs soaring into the 80s and 90s in the mountains, while triple-digit readings were reported

Huge plumes of smoke erupt west of Glenwood Springs.

on the plains. By early July, there were already numerous forest and grass fires developing over the central Rockies. Any thunderstorms that did develop tended to be high-based, too far above the ground to bring any meaningful moisture. Instead, high-based storms bring wind and lightning, the last thing wanted when conditions are tinder-dry. Around July 1 and 2, thunderstorms peppered central and western Colorado with over 5, 600 cloud-to-ground strikes. On July 2, lightning sparked a small fire on the flanks of Storm King Mountain, just west of Glenwood Springs. At the time, the Western Fire Coordination District was fighting dozens of fires over western Colorado and adjacent states. This fire seemed small and not a major concern, so it was not placed as a top priority.

The South Canyon fire started on a high point on Hell's Gate Ridge at the base of Storm King Mountain. In its early hours, the fire fed on piñon-juniper fuel, and it was thought that it would not spread. Rough terrain and canyons around Storm King Mountain added to the difficulty in fighting the fire.

Smoke jumpers were dispatched to fight the fire, but a large crew was not assigned to what was called the "South Canyon Fire." The science of wildfire weather forecasting is a very important one as the lives of brave firefighters are often on the line. Small-scale changes in wind patterns can send a tiny fire into a deadly firestorm in a matter of minutes. Sadly, that is exactly what happened in July 1994.

Flames from the South Canyon fire soared up to 300 feet in the sky.

Over the next few days, the fire slowly grew in size and began to worry officials in Glenwood Springs. As the blaze crept closer to homes in West Glenwood Springs, the fire district assigned additional smoke jumpers and helicopter crews to fight it. On the afternoon of July 6, fifty-two firefighters were working the fire. Most of these brave men and women were scratching away dirt and soil and cutting brush in order to create fire lines. Unknown to the firefighters, a powerful cold front was racing into western Colorado from Utah. This front did not have much moisture associated with it, but it was creating strong and shifting winds as it roared through Grand Junction and headed up the Colorado River Valley. When the front arrived at Storm King, the sudden shift in the wind acted like a giant bellows on the fire.

In only a matter of minutes, the fire exploded into a hellish firestorm. Intense flames up to 300 feet high roared across the mountainside and engulfed many of the firefighters before they could run to safety. The steep and rocky terrain made escape impossible for most of the firefighters, despite heroic efforts to get out of the way of the inferno. The tragic death toll from this fire was fourteen, the biggest single loss of life in a wildfire since a similar event in Montana fifty-five years earlier.

It was not that forecasters missed the cold front. The loss of life was due to a tragic lack of communication from fire officials in Grand Junction to incident commanders on the scene near Glenwood Springs. One positive result from this tragedy has been the revamping of forecasting and warning procedures, which with luck will prevent a similar breakdown in communication in future wildfire events.

Floods of July 1997

The first half of the summer of 1997 was hot and dry over eastern Colorado. Concern was mounting about drought conditions and fire danger through the first two weeks of July. At the same time, a massive El Niño event was building in the central Pacific Ocean. This warm water anomaly mostly manifests itself in the form of unusual winter weather, but in 1997, it was so strong that it began to affect the summertime weather patterns as well.

By late July, Colorado begins to come under the influence of the moist southerly wind pattern that brings humid air into the state. This is the monsoon flow that creates most of the mid- to late summer thunderstorm activity in the

(top) Monsoon Pattern. (left) In July and August, the annual summer monsoon develops. Moist air flows into Colorado from the south and southwest, increasing the potential for heavy rainfall. The resulting heavy rains can cause heavy flooding.

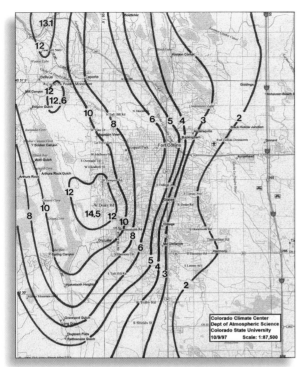

(top) Rainfall totals exceeded 10 inches across an area approximately 30 square miles in the Fort Collins vicinity. (bottom) Rescuers struggle through hip-deep waters to aid flood victims.

state. The immense heat and moisture from El Niño added fuel to the summer monsoon in Colorado. From late July through mid-August, rains fell almost daily. Many areas received more than 8 inches of rain in just a three- to four-week period. That amount is equal to about half of the average annual total for most places in eastern Colorado.

On the night of July 28, a small but nearly stationary thunderstorm began to dump heavy rains on the southwestern side of Fort Collins. This storm did not look like anything special on radar, but very light winds aloft allowed it to stay parked over the same area for several hours.

"The storm that caused this flood delivered the heaviest rain over an urban area that has been recorded in Colorado. Fourteen inches of rain were recorded in one day at the heaviest point in the storm," remarks Nolan Doesken. The heavy rain fell over a narrow drainage basin that passed under a railroad bridge. Unfortunately, the railroad bed acted as a dam for the rising water, which could not flow quickly enough through the opening under the bridge. When the railroad bed finally gave way to the tremendous pressure of the water, a giant wall of water swept into a nearby mobile home park. The result was both eerie and tragic.

Floodwaters mixed with flames as the trailers were floated off their foundations and gas lines ruptured and caught fire. Rescuers struggled amid the flames and screams to try to get people out of their homes. Despite their valiant efforts, six people died in the flood. In addition, $200 million in damage was reported on the Colorado State University campus as a result of the flooding. Thousands of valuable books were lost as the floodwaters poured into the basement of one of the campus libraries.

The following night, as eastern Colorado was still reeling from the events of the past twenty-four hours, another massive flood hit on the northeastern plains after 13 inches of rain fell in a short period. Pawnee Creek, near Sterling, flooded a large area of Logan County, wiping out many areas of crops and damaging homes.

Routt County Blowdown of 1997

The massive blizzard of October 1997 made most of its headlines for the heavy snow that paralyzed the eastern plains. Another event from the storm devastated an area near Steamboat Springs. During the early morning hours of October 25, 1997, powerful winds roared down from the Continental Divide for several hours at speeds that exceeded 120 mph and tore through the tall spruce and fir forests of Routt County just east of the town of Clark.

The tempest toppled trees along a path almost 5 miles wide and 30 miles long, flattening more than 4 million trees in the Routt National Forest. Many of the trees were simply pulled right out of the ground as the root systems, accustomed to westerly winds, were not prepared for a blast of wind from the east. Other trees were snapped off at the trunk by the leverage exerted by the wind on the tree canopy above. The blowdown was the result of a deep easterly circulation in the upper atmosphere over Colorado. Normally the winds over the mountains blow from west

The Routt County blowdown created a very abrupt change in the landscape.

to east, but the huge low-pressure system parked over south-eastern Colorado inspired a very intense easterly swirl in the air high above the northern half of the state. The winds were forced to rise over the Front Range, topping the Continental Divide west of Walden and rocketing down into the Steamboat area. Just as strong downsloping winds from the west can cause damage near Boulder and along Highway 93, these easterly cascading currents created catastrophic conditions as they roared through the forests of Routt County.

Part of the reason the winds were so strong was a layer of stable air a few thousand feet above the mountaintops. This stable air created a narrow area for the air to flow through as the wind howled over the Divide. This pinching of the winds increased their speed—known as a Venturi effect—and these greatly intensified gusts poured down from the higher terrain to the east. There were also very strong winds reported that night near Arapahoe Basin Ski Area, but much less damage was reported due to most of the winds blowing at or above tree line.

Blowdown events are rare, but not unprecedented, "much like a 1 percent chance of a one-hundred-year flood," according to research scientist and avalanche forecaster John Snook. Such devastating reverse wind events will happen again, but given the rare combination of weather needed to create the strong winds, blowdowns will remain another rarity in the wild weather of Colorado.

Drought of 1999–2004

Dry conditions have always been a worry in Colorado. The early explorers referred to the eastern plains of Colorado as the "Great American Desert." In general, all areas west of the 100th Meridian and east of the Continental Divide face water scarcity issues. The vast treeless Great Plains had an ecosystem that had been in balance for thousands of years before the plow began to carve the soil. The flora and fauna of the grasslands of eastern Colorado were perfectly suited for thriving on a mere 10–15 inches of precipitation per year. Early farmers may have been misled by a few wet seasons that occurred about the same time the first homesteads were settled on our flat eastern plains. The old saying was "rain follows the plow," an erroneous belief that turning the soil could somehow influence the heavens.

Nonetheless, despite many cycles of drought interrupted by years of plentiful rains, agriculture has flourished over the eastern plains of Colorado, the San Luis Valley, and the Grand Valley to the west. The fact that dry Colorado is a major producer of agricultural products is a testament to the skill, adaptability, and perseverance of our farmers and ranchers. The combination of good farming techniques, rainfall that is marginally adequate, and the ability to irrigate crops has made ranching and farming feasible, but certainly not easy in Colorado.

Kentucky bluegrass uses 18 gallons of water per square foot each year. Tall fescue and wheatgrass use 10 and 7 gallons of water per square foot each year, respectively.

The toughest times for agriculture are during the periodic dry spells that hit every couple of decades. In general, droughts hit about every twenty-five or thirty years in our state and across adjacent areas of the West. The most recent drought period extended from 1999 through 2004. The exact beginning and ending of a drought is hard to pin down, as some places may receive enough rain or snow to not face extremely dry conditions, while nearby the drought is in full swing.

There are three basic definitions of drought: agricultural, meteorological, and hydrological. For ranchers and farmers, an agricultural drought can begin quickly; just missing the crucial wet spring storms can mean a very poor crop over the summer. Put two years of that together and farmers will be rightly complaining about the drought. A meteorological drought is defined by the record books, when annual precipitation totals fall well below the long-term averages. Either agricultural or meteorological drought can be overcome relatively quickly. If the storm track shifts back into a position that brings soggy systems into our state, we can boost crop yields and rain gauge results in short order.

Hydrological drought is a different story. So much of Colorado's water needs are supplied by stored water. The intricate plumbing that has been installed in our mountain lakes and rivers annually brings billions of gallons of water back to the Front Range from west of the Continental Divide.

> *When drought hits the state, the water needs do not decrease; in fact, they tend to increase for cities and farms statewide.*

When drought hits the state, the water needs do not decrease; in fact, they tend to increase for cities and farms statewide. Our elaborate system of reservoirs and pipelines was built for just this reason, to store water in wet years and disperse it in dry times. Unfortunately, an extended period of drought puts an enormous strain on our water supply. Too many residents in Front Range cities desire to have a lush, green bluegrass lawn similar to those in the humid Midwest and East. This green envy is not realistic in a climate that averages only 15 inches of precipitation per year. In Colorado, we can manage to keep a bluegrass lawn alive, but to make it thrive, it needs much more water than the skies provide. For obvious reasons, years with average or above average precipitation put much less strain on our water resources. During the dry spells, homeowners are tempted to pour on the water to keep their lawns and gardens green. At the same time, farmers need to crank up the big irrigation rigs that spin across the croplands of eastern Colorado, ranchers have to water their hay fields in the mountain valleys, and the orchards of the Grand Valley and vegetable farms in the San Luis Valley are thirsty as well.

Typically, drought conditions are regional instead of local, so the water needs of surrounding states do not decrease either. The complex water treaties that cover all of the rivers flowing out of our state mean that much of the water initially locked in winter snowpack on our mountains is already spoken for by neighboring states and must be allowed to flow out of Colorado instead of being pooled in our reservoirs.

The most recent dry spell in the late 1990s and early 2000s laid bare evidence of the tremendous strain our water resources are under in Colorado. The dry weather followed several wet years from the early 1980s to mid-1990s, when our water storage was close to full but our population was growing at a tremendous rate. As the population exploded along the Front Range, acres of bluegrass replaced crops and fields of native plants. The crops certainly took their fair share of irrigation water, but the native plants and grasses were used to surviving in a semiarid climate.

Water usage was growing quickly in eastern Colorado, but the wet years did buy us some time. When the dry weather cycle kicked in around 1999, our thirst for water was high, and we were in for a rude awakening about this precious resource.

The winter of 1999 was still a fairly snowy one over the Colorado high country, but the following winters averaged below to well below normal in snowfall through 2003; much of that year's snow came in the one huge storm in March. The majority of Colorado's moisture comes from big storms, mainly moist winter storms that dump several feet of snow as they pass over the mountains. The winter months tend to drop the most snow over the mountains of northern and central Colorado, while the late winter and springtime storms bring copious amounts of moisture to the San Juans, the Sangre de Cristo, and the Front Range areas. All of this snowpack is what melts down to fill our reservoirs and to flow out of our state to fulfill water volume requirements for the rest of the southwestern United States. Although sufficient flakes did not fly during the winters from 2000 to 2004, and especially in the very dry year of 2002, the demand for water stayed high.

The most recent dry spell in the late 1990s and early 2000s laid bare evidence of the tremendous strain our water resources are under in Colorado.

A relatively dry winter can be assuaged by a generous early spring; heavy wet snows in March and April can quickly bolster the moisture supply as well as ease the need for irrigating

Horsetooth Reservoir was lowered because of drought and maintenance work.

in the early growing season. During the height of the dry pattern—the year 2002—we had both a dry winter and spring, leading into a hot summer. That trifecta was not a winning combination for any part of Colorado as extreme wildfire danger, agricultural losses, and residential water shortages made headlines from April through September.

The year 2003 looked just as bad, but the major snowstorm along the Front Range in March did an amazing job of bringing badly needed moisture to the Front Range just in time. That storm came with tremendous amount of water in the snow and brought as much as 8–10 inches of water content to areas along and east of the Continental Divide. A single storm cannot be a drought-buster, but the March 2003 storm did put a good dent into the dryness for eastern Colorado.

Although many areas in eastern Colorado were still emerging from the drought by late 2006, the overall dry pattern began to ease starting in 2004 as the San Juan Mountains experienced a very wet winter in 2004–2005. A series of soggy storms dumped extremely heavy snows in Durango, Telluride, and Silverton that season. Similarly, the winter of 2005–2006 was a winner for the central and northern mountain areas, especially around Steamboat Springs. That winter might have been one of the best in years for much of central and northern

Colorado, except that Mother Nature turned off the tap on snowfall about six weeks early. Snowstorms had been frequent and generous through February and snowpack numbers were well above average almost statewide. Unfortunately, the usually dependable March and April storms along and east of the Continental Divide failed to materialize, and warm early-spring temperatures brought the snowpack down quickly.

Nonetheless, it does appear that Colorado is past the worst of the most recent dry spell. Have we learned anything from the drought? There is no end in sight to population growth in our state, and with that comes an ever-increasing demand for water. We will need to be clever in how we deal with this issue, for clean, dependable water is a finite resource and a crucial question for the future of Colorado. Conservation will undoubtedly play a major role in making sure we have enough water for future needs.

Holiday Storms of 2006

December 2006 brought one of the most historic winter weather events in the state's history. Back-to-back blizzards struck the foothills and eastern plains of Colorado during one of the busiest ten days of the year.

It all started with a strong storm system slamming into Washington and Oregon with torrential rain and hurricane-force wind. Once onshore, the storm split into two pieces. One moved into southwestern Canada and the other slid down the Great Basin and settled into Arizona.

Back-to-back blizzards struck the foothills and eastern plains of Colorado during one of the busiest ten days of the year.

Forecasters in Denver had their eye on this storm as it hit the Pacific Northwest, and computer forecast models showed the potential for a major winter storm across eastern Colorado just before Christmas. But would it really happen?

Computer models sometimes become aggressive and forecast too much. In addition, simple climatology states that a

Blizzard conditions as seen from Aurora during the December 2006 blizzard.

major winter storm in the middle of December just isn't that common. In fact, it had been more than two decades since a snowstorm big enough to paralyze eastern Colorado and a major city like Denver hit during the Christmas holiday.

By Saturday, December 16, the area of low pressure continued to sit and spin over Arizona, orphaned from the main flow of jet stream winds aloft. It was a prediction predicament because all signs pointed to it slowly moving east-northeast, tapping into plenty of moisture from the Gulf of Mexico and gaining strength. The million-dollar question was would it really happen—and if so, when?

With the peak of Christmas travel underway, thousands watched each forecast with anticipation of what was going to happen. By Tuesday, December 19, the details became clearer with each new set of weather data: eastern Colorado faced a major winter storm that had the potential to paralyze holiday travel.

While heavy December snowfalls are not that common, they can happen. One of the most noted events was in December 1982, as 2–4 feet of snow blanketed Denver and the Front Range on Christmas Eve. That storm stopped all travel and stranded thousands. Many retail workers were stuck in their stores on Christmas Eve and were forced to make the most of the situation until the snow tapered off on Christmas Day.

Soon the watches and advisories were posted, and by noon on Wednesday, December 20, snow began to fly in the Denver area. It began falling as early as 8:00 a.m. in the foothills west of town. Snow fell along with gusty north winds for the next twenty-four to thirty-six hours, leaving much of the Front Range under 1–3 feet of snow. Heavy snow even fell across the eastern plains during the event, with as much as a foot in Washington, Logan, and Phillips Counties. Southeastern Colorado saw amounts generally between 6 and 12 inches. Gusty winds in excess of 30 mph drifted the snow between 4 and 8 feet deep in exposed areas just to the east and south of Denver.

(top) CDOT plow struggles to keep I-225 open during December 2006 storm. (bottom) A lonely look at I-70 during December 2006 storm.

The storm made national headlines as it closed Denver International Airport for two days, canceling some 2,000 flights and ruining the holiday travel plans for thousands of travelers connecting through, flying to, or flying from the Mile High City.

As the storm exited Colorado and the recovery process began, forecasters were busy tracking a second storm system following almost the same path as the first. Historically, two

The holiday snowstorm of 2006 shut down many of Denver's major roads, including Kipling Street in west Denver.

snowstorms, each having the capability to paralyze and stop a major city like Denver, were virtually absent from the weather record. The only documented event that could compare was the great storm in December 1913.

Although through the years, the 1913 storm has been characterized as one single event, it really came in two distinct waves of heavy snowfall. In that year, a storm moved through eastern Colorado, dropping 1–2 feet of snow on December 1 and 2. On December 4, a second system moved through, dropping 3–5 feet of additional snowfall on the region. Denver's total snowfall from that historical event was 45.7 inches, which remains the largest five-day snowfall in history. In the mountains and foothills west of Denver, over 80 inches of snow fell. Georgetown recorded 63 inches of snow alone on December 4. Transportation came to a standstill as gusty winds drifted the snow several feet deep.

By December 27, 2006, a new round of winter storm watches was in effect for places still digging out from the first storm. By noon on Thursday, December 28, the snow was flying across eastern Colorado, Denver, and the foothills. At first the snow rates were light, with rain mixed in across parts of the northern Denver Metro area, from Longmont to Firestone

Digging out from the 2006 holiday storms.

and extending into northeastern Colorado around Greeley. But in time, the snow filled in and the intensity picked up. By 7:00 p.m. on December 28, numerous phone calls and emails flooded 7News with reports of thunder and lightning in the northwest Denver Metro area and northern foothills. One caller from Arvada was outside shoveling when the thunder and lightning began, and she ran inside fearing for her life.

Thunder-snow is simply a thunderstorm that drops snow instead of rain. It is a sign of a very unstable atmosphere and usually indicates heavy rates of snowfall, on the order of 2–4 inches per hour in many cases. That is exactly what happened with the second of the twin holiday blizzards. Communities from Lakewood to Golden and Evergreen to Estes Park picked up 2–4 inches of snow per hour for several hours.

Once skies cleared on the eastern plains, scenes like this one from Lamar were common.

By Friday morning, the snow tapered off to showers in the foothills and the Denver Metro area as the energy shifted onto the southeastern plains, but not before dropping another 1–3 inches on the area. There was still a distinct possibility that the storm could fling more snow on Denver and the Front Range area later in the day and possibly through New Year's Eve. Everything depended upon the movement of the low pressure system centered on southwestern Kansas.

If that low tracked due north, the snow would likely wrap around the system all the way back to Denver. The local terrain effects of the foothills and the Palmer Divide would serve to focus very heavy snowfall on the western and southern sides of the metro area, perhaps bringing several more feet of snow along with extreme blowing and drifting. If the low pressure center of the storm moved to the northeast, the brunt of the storm's fury would shift to the eastern plains and western Kansas. The outcome of the storm's path was not obvious until late in the day Friday, when weather warnings were lifted for the Denver area and the eastern plains braced for a terrible winter storm.

While Denver and the foothills began the recovery process, it was only beginning for residents of eastern and southeastern Colorado. Moderate to heavy snow fell, while winds sustained at 30 mph gusted to over 50 mph at times. This continued for thirty-six hours as the area of low pressure slowly moved to the northeast over Kansas. By New Year's Eve the low was far enough east of Colorado that conditions improved for the eastern plains. However, the damage had been done. Residents found themselves buried alive in their homes. Drifts as high as the rooftops blanketed homes and farm buildings; 12–36 inches of snow had fallen during the storm, heaviest across the southeast counties. Drifts were measured at 10–15 feet deep, and up to 18 feet deep east of Sheridan Lake in Kiowa County. Thousands of head of cattle were stranded in the deep snow, and ranchers lost many of their herds, right in the midst of calving season. Despite valiant efforts by ranchers and the Colorado National Guard, hay dropping from military helicopters was not sufficient to save many of the lost cattle. Many longtime ranchers and farmers said that the late December storms of 2006 were worse than the October 1997 blizzard and as bad as any storm in memory.

In the mountains and foothills of southern Colorado, 30–48 inches of snow were measured from the storm. The storm closed all major roads for days, and smaller secondary roads for weeks. Food supplies ran low at stores once citizens could get out of their homes, and merchants were quite distressed at the timing of the storms, right in the heart of the big retail season.

The twin blizzards of 2006 did bring good news to the water supply, though. Before the storms, Denver was on track to tie the driest year ever recorded, 7.48 inches in 2002. Though 2006 stayed still in the top ten driest, ranking seventh, the storm brought a widespread 1–4 inches of liquid-equivalent moisture to the foothills and eastern plains. It also made for one of the snowiest Decembers on record, ranking just behind 1913 and 1973.

Many longtime ranchers and farmers said that the late December storms of 2006 were worse than the October 1997 blizzard and as bad as any storm in memory.

Holly Tornado March 28, 2007

About 30 to 50 tornadoes swirl across Colorado each season. Most will spin over the vast open fields of the eastern plains and do only minor damage, given the fact that small towns offer relatively tiny targets. On rare occasion, a tornado will tear through a rural community, with devastating results. On the evening of March 28, 2007, a large tornado slammed into the town of Holly, a community of just under 1,000, only a few miles from the Kansas border. Shortly before 8 p.m., the tornado first developed about 2 miles south of Holly and churned into the town from the southeast. As the twister crossed the Arkansas River on the south side of Holly, it reached an intensity of about 136–150 mph (an EF3 rating on the Enhanced Fujita Scale). The Rosales family lived in a doublewide trailer just off Santa Fe Street. They had just finished dinner when the storm roared into view. Gustavo Puga grabbed his three-year-old daughter Noelia and ran into the kitchen to hold her mother Rosemary and brace for the storm. The tornado tore the roof off the mobile

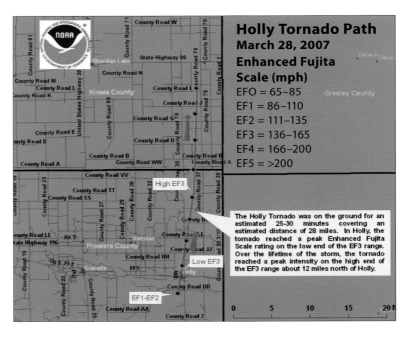

Holly Tornado Path
March 28, 2007
Enhanced Fujita
Scale (mph)
EF0 = 65–85
EF1 = 86–110
EF2 = 111–135
EF3 = 136–165
EF4 = 166–200
EF5 = >200

The Holly Tornado was on the ground for an estimated 25-30 minutes covering an estimated distance of 28 miles. In Holly, the tornado reached a peak Enhanced Fujita Scale rating on the low end of the EF3 range. Over the lifetime of the storm, the tornado reached a peak intensity on the high end of the EF3 range about 12 miles north of Holly.

home and flung it nearly a block away. The powerful winds tore both Rosemary and Noelia from Gustavo's grasp and swept them away. In the minutes to follow, a badly injured Gustavo frantically searched for his loved ones. Aided by neighbors, they found both of them wedged in broken branches of a tree. Noelia would survive, but Rosemary died later that evening of severe head trauma, and thus became the first tornado fatality in Colorado since June 1960. There were eleven other residents with injuries serious enough to be hospitalized. Nearly one month later the storm claimed its second victim, when 76-year-old Dolores Burns died in a Colorado Springs hospital from injuries sustained during the tornado.

The tornado cut a path of destruction across the small town as it reached a width of nearly 300 yards. The storm's path extended for 7 miles and the tornado reached a maximum intensity of EF3—about 150 mph, before dissipating in southern Kiowa County. In total, about 160 homes were damaged or destroyed, an estimated one third of the residences in the community.

There was little warning of the storm, even though thunderstorms were in the forecast. That evening, Colorado was on the extreme western edge of a large cold front that produced 70 tornadoes from Nebraska to the Texas Panhandle—one of the largest early season tornado outbreaks ever on the high plains. The storm that produced the Holly tornado blew up very quickly and the tornado developed only about 2 miles south of town. With the storm system racing northeast at over 30 mph, the tornado took just a few minutes before it spun into town. Holly sits in a location that is about equal distance from the various National Weather Service Nexrad Dopplers in Pueblo, Colorado, and Goodland and Dodge City, Kansas. The farther away a Doppler radar is from a storm, the less effective it is in seeing areas of potentially damaging winds. Unfortunately, despite the diligence of the radar meteorologists, the storm was simply too far at the edge of the radar and developed too quickly to allow advance warning. As such, the first knowledge that a tornado was approaching came only when the storm was spotted by the residents of Holly.

The timing of the Holly tornado was particularly cruel, coming just three months after the severe blizzard of late December 2006. Many in the area had been badly impacted by the loss of cattle during the severe winter storm and now faced even more losses due to the tornado. In some cases, long-time ranching families decided that they had finally had enough and would sell out and find another way to make a living. But in the days and weeks that followed the tornado, an amazing spirit developed in many of the residents and the town began to rebuild. The generosity of fellow Coloradans, as well as neighbors across the border in Kansas, poured into Holly as the small town recovered. Older residents recalled the flood of 1965 that swept away much of the town's commercial district. Although the tornado was worse, the resilience and independence that is a primary trait in rural communities will enable Holly to rebound and rebuild.

Aerial shots of the aftermath from the Holly tornado—about 160 homes were damaged or destroyed. The 300-yard wide tornado had winds estimated at 150 mph.

Colorado Climate Comments

Despite the occasional severity and the potential for destructive conditions, Colorado is truly a wonderland for weather. The many days of sunshine, interrupted from time to time by strong storms, make a perfect climate for weather enthusiasts. Over the years we have had many historic moments in meteorology, with record snowstorms, extreme heat and cold, raging flash floods, hail of epic proportion, devastating dryness, and fierce firestorms. Along with the severe weather, our state is famous for being the headquarters for leading weather research, with world-renowned atmospheric scientists calling Colorado home. The growing interest in our changing climate and the issues that we face, not only in Colorado but also around the nation and the world, will keep Colorado in the forefront as scientists struggle to find answers to the questions future generations will face. Regardless of where you might stand on the cause or the degree in which our climate is changing, most experts do agree that a warming climate in the western United States will be manifest by more severe weather. The severity of individual events, hot and dry or wet and stormy, will likely become greater. The length and frequency of these severe weather events will likely change as well. No doubt that the next 200 years will be highlighted by many more marks in the record books.

Despite the occasional severity and the potential for destructive conditions, Colorado is truly a wonderland for weather. The many days of sunshine, interrupted from time to time by strong storms, make a perfect climate for weather enthusiasts.

CHAPTER SIX

CHANGES IN THE AIR

"The Greenhouse Effect," "Global Warming," "Rising Sea Levels," "Our Changing Climate": these are all frequent headlines today. There seems to be as much confusion about these issues as there is concern about the longer-term effects that the changing climate will have on our future. Predicting the weather is an extremely complex problem from day to day, let alone over the course of decades or centuries. Since the mid-1970s, we have gone from worrying about the hastened arrival of a new ice age to sweating out the prospect of rapid global warming, the melting of the polar ice caps, and rising seas. Worldwide, most scientists specializing in the field of climate are increasingly in agreement that the climate is growing warmer and that humans are causing at least some of the change.

(top left) A sparse patch of tallgrass struggles in dry land east of Denver. (top right) Hurricane Emily and the moon as seen from the International Space Station. (bottom left) Hurricane Katrina shortly before landfall in 2005. (bottom right) This photo shows effects from drought in Colorado.

Long-term Climate Change

Long-term climate change is perfectly normal and a fact of nature. Earth's climate has historically cycled through warm and cold periods. Careful studies of fossils, tree rings, ice cores, and sediment layers all show that our atmosphere in the past has been both substantially warmer and colder than it is today. We know from fossil records that tropical plants once

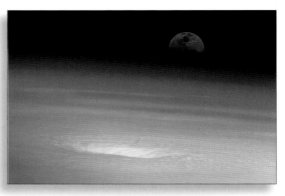

Our sun is very active. Here, a widely spreading coronal mass ejection (CME) blasts more than a billion tons of matter out into space at millions of kilometers per hour.

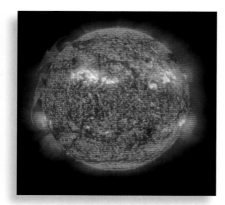

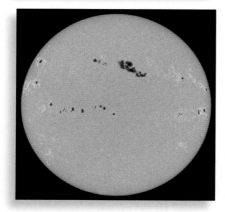

Prominences are huge clouds of relatively cool, dense plasma suspended in the sun's hot, thin corona. The hottest areas are indicated by the white color, while the darker red areas are cooler. Each sunspot is generally 5 to 10 times larger than the size of the earth. A sunspot appears to be dark only when contrasted against the rest of the solar surface because it is slightly cooler than the surrounding area.

grew in areas that today are covered with snow and ice. Some of this is due to the relentless movement of continental drift, taking certain landmasses away from polar latitudes toward the equator and vice versa. Areas that once hosted tropical life may have simply shifted location enough through plate tectonics and are now in a place far too cold. Beyond that, there are fundamental cycles that mesh like an ancient set of gears to set the thermostat of our planet.

The climate-changing mechanisms start with the sun. It is not as unchanging as once believed, and through its life cycle the sun dims and brightens, silently pouring immense and varying amounts of energy into space. If the sun's energy output drops even slightly, that can have a dramatic cooling effect on the earth. Similarly, when the sun cycles into a higher energy gear, our world will warm.

By the nineteenth century, scientists had determined that sunspot activity varied on a short-term, eleven-year cycle overlaid on a longer cycle of several centuries. Even though sunspots are slightly cooler areas on the sun, when they are in the active part of the cycle, there is actually an increase in the energy output of the sun. This increased radiation does warm the earth, although much of the energy comes in the form of ultraviolet light that warms the upper atmosphere more than the surface.

Another complicating fact is that earth does not revolve around the sun in a perfect circle; rather, its orbit is an ellipse that also shifts with time, sometimes bringing earth closer to the sun for part of the year or farther away than it has been in the last few centuries. The axis of our planet also is not constant; like a toy top spinning on a table, earth wobbles on its axis, and sometimes that wobble means that the northern and southern hemispheres are pointed more toward the sun in summer and less in winter than we are now. Over very long cycles, this has had an influence on the planet's climate.

These factors are long-term drivers of climate and help to account for the back-and-forth ticking of the global temperature over the course of millions of years. When these cosmic tumblers all happen to click together in the right combination, earth can slip back into an ice age. In the past million years there have been four major advances and retreats of glacial ice. The last of these ice ages ended between 35,000 and 20,000 years ago. In this warm interglacial period, the climate of the earth was gentle enough to allow the rise of human civilization.

Climate Factors on Earth

Active volcanoes spew immense amounts of gas and dust into the atmosphere, helping to block out sunlight. When the volcanoes quiet down, the air naturally becomes clearer, allowing more energy to reach the surface of earth. In addition, one of the biggest climate controls we have on Earth is the oceans, which occupy three-fourths of the planet. Water has an astonishing capacity to hold heat. It is estimated that to warm the North Atlantic Ocean by a mere 1 degree Celsius, it would take 15 trillion watts of power. If we could channel all of human energy, from an oxcart driver in India to the most modern atomic power plants, into just this one task, it would take two years just to raise the temperature of one small part of one ocean by that single degree.

The long-term climate of the earth is affected by changes in the orbit around the sun, the degree of tilt of the earth's axis, and the direction in space that the axis is pointed.

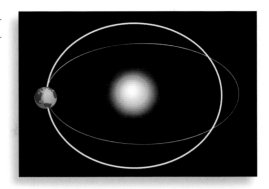

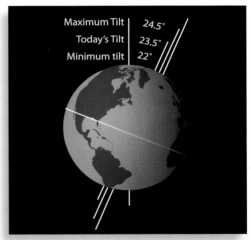

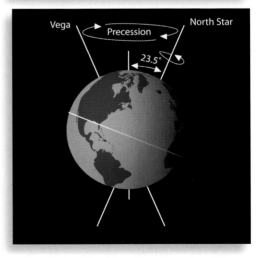

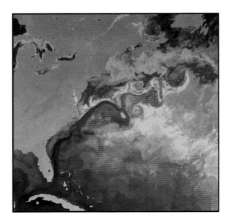

The warmer waters of the Gulf Stream not only fuel tropical systems during the summer, but also play an important role in global circulation.

Many ocean currents act as conveyor belts for warm and cold water. The Gulf Stream is perhaps the best known to Americans and Europeans. This warm oceanic river swirls northward past Florida and the East Coast and then turns toward Western Europe. The vast amount of heat that the Gulf Stream transports from tropical areas of the Gulf of Mexico and the Caribbean is what makes the climate of Great Britain, Scandinavia, and surrounding countries much more pleasant than the colder climate of inland continental Europe. Just look on a globe at the latitude of England and compare the weather there to that of Newfoundland or the Aleutian Islands, which are at comparable latitudes. The seas are crisscrossed with similar climate-controlling currents, both warm and cold, that greatly affect the weather for the nearby land areas. Ever wonder why California does not have to worry about hurricanes, for instance, while Florida does? The answer is the chilly California Current that flows down from the north along the West Coast of the United States, keeping the sea surface temperatures too chilly for hurricanes to develop—and keeping wetsuits on many surfers in central and northern California.

One huge transoceanic flow is called the thermohaline circulation (THC). This deep, very slow movement of water is driven by density changes (dense, salty water versus lighter, fresher water) and temperature (colder water is heavier). The thermohaline circulation travels through the entire world's oceans at a speed of about 1 centimeter per second—a period that takes hundreds of years. This deep ocean current is not constant and it too goes through cycles. Changes in the thermohaline circulation can have dramatic effects in a short period. About 14,500 years ago, the earth was gradually emerging from the most recent ice age. Surface temperatures were slowly climbing and the ice sheets were melting over

North America. A rush of cold, fresh, glacial meltwater into the North Atlantic caused the northern extent of the Gulf Stream to be deflected southward, weakening the thermohaline circulation that had been helping to transport warmth from the tropics northward. The post–ice age moderation in temperature came to a halt over the North Atlantic Basin, and the

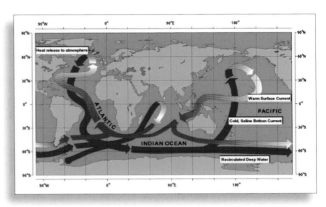

The large scale thermohaline circulation transports immense amounts of energy around the earth's oceans. Changes in the thermohaline circulation can have a major impact on climate.

climate in Greenland and Northern Europe slipped back to near ice age conditions for the next 3,000 years. In time, the thermohaline circulation strengthened—thanks to a lessening of meltwater due to the colder climate, and thus the temperatures warmed again. Ice-core samples show that Greenland warmed 10 degrees Celsius in a decade. These dramatic changes in climate are locked in the records, hard science that can be measured, so we know that our world can change quickly and dramatically.

Unusually rapid melting of the arctic ice cap and the ice sheet on Greenland is now happening. Satellite images of the polar icecap have shown dramatic changes in the past thirty years. In Greenland, the glacial ice is diminishing at a rate of 36 cubic miles per year as of 2005—an increase of 60 percent in just a decade. The melting of glacial ice on Greenland occurs in cycles too, most notably in the 1920s, but the current pace of the melting is faster than noted in previous natural cycles. The influx of cold, fresh water could slow down or temporarily halt the thermohaline current over the northern Atlantic. If this occurs, it might happen dramatically over the course of only a few years. Such a change would halt the flow of the Gulf Stream toward Western Europe and could temporarily throw Western Europe into a mini ice age that could last up to several hundred years.

Climate Change

Over millions of years, Earth's climate has experienced significant natural variability. Some shifts have occurred gradually over millennia; others have been abrupt, taking place within years. Climate change can be benign, beneficial, or disruptive, but until recently, it has always been natural. Recent evidence suggests that the climate is changing rapidly and unnaturally, and we face the huge challenge of global warming.

In 2007, the Intergovernmental Panel on Climate Change (IPCC) issued an updated report on the status of Earth's climate. We spoke with Kevin E. Trenberth, the head of the Climate Analysis Section at the National Center for Atmospheric Research (NCAR), located in Boulder, Colorado. He is a lead author of the report.

Q: What is the state of the planet?
A: The IPCC said global warming is unequivocal and that it is largely caused by humans, especially in the last fifty years. There is widespread evidence that the climate is warming. Global mean temperature and ocean temperature are rising, the sea level is rising, glaciers are melting, and the land is warming faster than the ocean.

Q: How will these changes affect the weather?
A: Water vapor is increasing in the atmosphere and precipitation intensity is generally increasing around the world, so when it rains it rains harder. Precipitation in the extratropics is increasing, partly because the atmosphere can hold more water when it's warmer. At the same time, there is widespread drought in the tropics and subtropics. Hurricane intensity is increasing. There are more extremes in high temperature and fewer cold extremes. Arctic ice is decreasing. All of these are different measures of what is going with the weather, and all are related to a warming climate.

Q: Is climate change really a bad thing? Don't we just have to adapt to a new environment?
A: Climate change isn't necessary bad. What I would suggest is bad is climate change that occurs too rapidly. The systems that we have in place, both our social infrastructure and certainly nature, are adapted to the current climate, almost by definition. It takes a long time for change to happen on a natural basis, but we are changing the climate at rates about a hundred times what occurs in nature. There are other aspects that can be regarded as bad, such as increases in drought across the tropics and subtropics and increases in the intensity of storms. Also, with the increase in temperature you get an increase in the spread of certain kinds of bugs and diseases.

Q: What are the changes we could see in Colorado's climate?
A: The biggest problems for Colorado are likely to be related to water and snowpack. We are already seeing the snowpack melt early because of warmer temperatures, and as a result there is less snowpack as we get into May and June. As a result, there is less water available when you need it most. Managing water resources is going to be a major challenge.

Q: What's the solution?
A: In the next forty years we can't do a great deal about what's going to happen. We are continuing to emit more carbon dioxide into the atmosphere. In fact, it's increasing in time, especially from countries like China and India. Even the United States has a large number of coal-fired power plants coming online in the next five years. So the prospects don't look good in the near term for even limiting the emissions that are occurring.

If we take action now, then we can make a big difference by the year 2100. It's a long-term payoff, and in the meantime we are just going to have to live with the climate change that is already going to occur. We have to plan for it.

Human Effects on Climate

Now, man-made forces threaten to disrupt this complicated climate machine. The current problem we face is simple; solving it is a challenge. Are we, the more than 6 billion people that populate planet earth, pulling on the levers that hasten changes in our climate? If we are helping to change the climate, can the changes be slowed or stopped? How will we mitigate the effects on human civilization? The study of these questions and the search for solutions is the focus for thousands of scientists and political leaders worldwide. The topic of global climate change and how much humans have to do with it is as much political science as it is physical science, and we must bring together disparate voices on this important subject toward a common goal of ensuring that we not leave our heirs a world that has been placed in peril by neglect or carelessness.

Changes in coverage of sea ice on the Arctic Ocean between 1979 and 2003.

In the 1960s and early 1970s, Dr. Reid Bryson, a founder of the University of Wisconsin Meteorology Department, was studying climate change and was concerned about what he called "the New Ice Age." At the time, evidence showed that the climate had been cooling since World War II and that the world was on a path toward longer, colder winters, shorter growing seasons, dramatic changes in rainfall patterns, and the prospect of worldwide food shortages. Bryson believed that the prime suspect affecting the cooling of our climate was a villain familiar to us in today's news: air pollution. During the early 1970s, a series of brutally cold winters had gripped North America, and it seemed plausible that we were on the edge of a steep and alarming precipice. Temperature profiles during the twentieth century had shown a great deal of variability over the previous six decades, but the overall trend was clearly downward for temperatures since the 1940s. The theory at the time was that air pollution was at least partially responsible for the cooling trend because of all the dust and particles in the air. These tiny bits of ash, smoke, and dirt—called aerosols—were blocking out incoming sunlight and keeping some of the sun's energy from reaching the surface of the earth. In fact, this does happen. Volcanoes pour vast amounts of dust and smoke into our atmosphere often, and the resultant cooling is easy to pick up in worldwide climate surveys. For instance, the eruption of Mount Pinatubo in the Philippines in 1991 resulted in a worldwide cooling of a degree or two Fahrenheit, but the cooling only lasted for about a year and a half before the volcanic aerosols settled out of the atmosphere.

Lascar, a volcano located at Mina El Laco in northern Chile, erupted on April 19, 1993. Schools as far away as 120 miles (190 kilometers) were closed because of fallout from the eruption. This volcano did not affect average global temperature significantly.

Other major eruptions in recent human history have had dramatic effects on the climate. In August 1883, the Indonesian island of Krakatoa exploded with the force of many hydrogen bombs—estimates are approximately 200 megatons. The eruption blew vast clouds of volcanic dust and smoke 50 miles high into the atmosphere, blocking out the sun for two days within 50 miles of the eruption. Global winds swept the volcanic clouds around the world within two weeks, and sunshine was reduced by 10 percent during the next three years. Colder than average winters followed the eruption at Krakatoa, and overall the earth's climate was cooler for the next five years.

With volcanic activity such an obvious culprit in short-term climate change, it is easy to see how a connection could be made as to how our industrialized society might have a similar effect in causing a cooling of earth. "Man is so industrialized, urbanized and mechanized that he has become as important as natural phenomena in the modification of weather," said Reid Bryson in 1966. "The world's cities are putting out as much particulate matter as a volcano." Bryson went on to theorize that human pollution had the effect of putting "dust on the window of our atmosphere, blocking out incoming sunlight." As the population continued to increase, the amount of fossil fuel burning would also increase, the result being a sooty atmosphere that allowed less sunlight to penetrate to the earth's surface. Gradually the atmosphere would cool, resulting in longer winters and growing ice caps at both poles. The increase in ice would add to the cooling as the reflective properties of ice and snow would mean even less of the sun's energy would be absorbed and a cycle of ever-cooling weather would develop, perhaps leading to a new ice age.

Those who doubt the role humans have in changing our climate ask, given Bryson's claim forty years ago that we might be "headed for a new ice age" because of air pollution, and now the current contrasting view that the ice caps are melting because of air pollution, is the jury still out on the matter? The truth is, there has not been as much of an about-face from cooling to warming as you might think. Rather, it was the case that all the facts were not yet in. In the early to mid-1970s there was beginning to be considerable debate about the role of carbon dioxide and the changing of the chemistry in our atmosphere. Many climate scientists at the time felt that the cooling trend since the 1940s was a short-term event and would be replaced by a warming of the global average temperature in the following decades.

Greenhouse Gases

The flip side of industrial and urban pollution from tiny particles or aerosols is the variety of gases that are belched into the atmosphere from the burning of fossil fuels. When we burn a lump of coal, we not only blow soot into the atmosphere but also produce by-product gases such as sulfur dioxide (SO_2) and carbon dioxide (CO_2). SO_2 and CO_2 are important gases in our climate equation as the sulfur emissions react in the atmosphere to form nasty smog conditions, while carbon dioxide

In the early to mid-1970s there was beginning to be considerable debate about the role of carbon dioxide and the changing of the chemistry in our atmosphere.

is an important component of the so-called greenhouse effect. Other important greenhouse gases are water vapor (H_2O) methane (CH_4), nitrous oxide (N_2O), and chlorofluorocarbons (CFCs). Since the Industrial Revolution, the atmospheric concentrations of CO_2, CH_4, and N_2O have climbed over 30 percent, 145 percent, and 15 percent, respectively. CFCs have increased by 100 percent; these are man-made chemicals that did not exist in the atmosphere before the mid-twentieth century. By careful analysis of radioactive isotopes of each gas, scientists have confirmed that the increase in these gases is primarily due to human activity.

It should be noted that overall the greenhouse effect is not in itself a bad thing; in fact, it makes life possible on earth. Without some measure of "greenhouse gases" in our atmosphere, the average global temperature would be about 60 degrees colder than at present, and earth would be frozen and lifeless. That is because CO_2 and the other greenhouse gases in our atmosphere trap some of the sun's heat by absorbing the energy and radiating the warmth back down to the surface of the earth.

It should be noted that overall the greenhouse effect is not in itself a bad thing—without some measure of greenhouse gases, the average global temperature would be about 60 degrees colder—the earth would be frozen and lifeless.

Greenhouse Effect

The incoming energy from the sun (called "shortwave radiation") arrives at the top of our atmosphere with the intensity of about three 100-watt light bulbs over every square yard. About a third of this energy is immediately reflected back into space by dust and clouds. The remaining two-thirds travels on down to the earth's surface, where some is reflected back to space by water and snow, a little is absorbed directly by the atmosphere, and the rest is absorbed by earth's surface and by the oceans. The energy that is absorbed serves to warm the ground and the water. That warmth then starts to radiate back into space, but at a lower temperature (longer wavelength) than the incoming solar energy. Various gases, including water vapor, carbon dioxide, methane, and nitrous oxide, act like a blanket by helping to keep some of this "longwave radiation" or "earth energy" from escaping back into space. It is this "atmospheric blanket effect" that we refer to as the greenhouse effect.

Our nearby planetary neighbors have greenhouse effects as well. On Mars, it is very weak and most of the incoming solar energy escapes back into space, making the planet too cold. On Venus, a very thick atmosphere composed almost totally of carbon dioxide captures more of the sun's heat, resulting in a surface temperature hot enough to melt lead. Earth is nicely in between, so we can be thankful that our greenhouse effect is just about right. But will it stay that way?

Changing the Chemistry

Since the beginning of the Industrial Revolution, mankind has been burning more and more fossil fuels and pouring an amazing amount of pollution into our atmosphere. The amount of carbon dioxide in the atmosphere has risen about 35 percent in the last 200 years, from about 280 parts per million to over 380 parts per million today. This increase has been carefully measured since the late 1950s by researchers at the Mauna Loa Observatory in Hawaii. According to climate researcher Pieter Tans, senior scientist at the Earth System Research Laboratory in Boulder, "human activity currently releases about 8 billion metric tons of carbon dioxide into the air every year, adding to the approximately 800 billion metric tons that are already there. The growth rate of atmospheric CO_2 appears to have increased to 2 parts per million (PPM) per year as an average since the year 2000. This translates to a net increase of 4.2 billion metric tons of carbon per year. Therefore, of the 8 billion metric tons of carbon released into the atmosphere, about 3.8 billion

Greenhouse gases in the earth's atmosphere absorb some of the escaping infrared radiation and release it back into the atmosphere. This warms the planet and allows life as we know it to exist. Human activities, such as burning fossil fuel and deforestation, have released more greenhouse gases into the atmosphere. This allows more infrared radiation to be absorbed and re-released. This may increase global warming and alter the earth's climate.

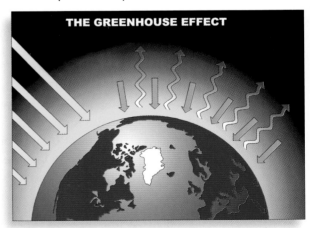

THE GREENHOUSE EFFECT

tons are absorbed by plants and the oceans." This "carbon sink" capacity complicates the issue of global warming, as the oceans may continue to have a vast holding capacity for carbon dioxide and plants actually thrive with increased CO_2. An added concern is that the oceans are growing more acidic as the increase in CO_2 is changing the pH of the water. CO_2 does not disappear from the oceans, and it may come back to the atmosphere as a result of climate change and changing biology in the oceans.

In the 1970s, the quandary was, "Why are we cooling down, when we should be warming up?" The past three decades have seen the cooling trend reverse dramatically, and the facts today show the world is indeed warming; the 1970s were just a brief blip in that trend. It is theorized that the dust and soot injected into the atmosphere through the middle of the twentieth century may have blocked out enough sunlight to cause some cooling in the 1960s and 1970s, but now the greenhouse gases have overwhelmed the "dirty window" effect to produce a steady warming of the atmosphere. In addition, the technology of burning fossil fuels has improved greatly in the past fifty years, and the United States, Canada, and Europe are not putting nearly the amount of ash and soot into the atmosphere, compared to earlier in the twentieth century. Before midcentury, the world's rapid industrialization was built largely on the burning of coal. This produced not only CO_2 and other greenhouse gases, but also tremendous amounts of soot and dust. Two world wars also created immense amounts of dust that may well have counterbalanced the increase in CO_2 and other gases in the atmosphere. After World War II, and especially in the 1960s and early 1970s, pollution controls on power plants and automobiles, along with a switch to cleaner-burning fuels such as fuel oil and natural gas for home heating, have greatly diminished to amount of man-made soot and dust in the skies over North America and Europe. Thus, the balancing act between the dirty window effect and the increase in greenhouse gases may well be tipped from the former to the latter. It also needs to be noted that the atmospheric aerosols have a much shorter life span in

The past three decades have seen the cooling trend reverse dramatically, and the facts today show the world is indeed warming; the 1970s were just a brief blip in that trend.

our air. Even if the particles settle out in just a few years, though, the increase in CO_2 will last for centuries.

The clarity of the atmosphere has improved tremendously in most major cities in Europe and the United States. Even in Eastern Europe and Russia, the trend in burning cleaner fuels has been a positive sign, and the amount of deadly smog has dropped. Sadly, such is not yet the case in the rapidly developing countries of India and China, where the rush to develop modern economies has created terrible air pollution and smog conditions.

This aerial shot of Denver from 1958 shows the foothills behind hazy skies, evidence of air pollution problems along the Front Range.

Global Warming

Global measurements show that the over the last century the average surface temperature of the earth has increased by about 1.2 degrees Fahrenheit. The warmest years of the twentieth century all occurred between 1980 and 1999. The World Meteorological Organization (WMO) and NASA concluded that 1998 was the world's warmest year on record (modern records since 1850). Since then, 2006 was even warmer for the United States. The summer of 2006 was the second-warmest June, July, and August on record for the nation, second only to the sizzling summer in the dust bowl of 1936. According to the National Oceanic and Atmospheric Administration, the 2006 average annual temperature for the contiguous United States was 55 degrees Fahrenheit, 0.07 degrees warmer than in 1998. Across the nation, the years 1997–2006 have been the warmest years on record. Furthermore, in England, across Europe, and into Asia, the past twenty-five years have seen the warmest temperatures on record. In the twelve-year period from 1995 to 2006, eleven of those years ranked among the warmest on record for global surface temperatures measured since 1850.

The warming so far may not seem like much, but in global terms the warming that has already occurred and, more importantly, the projected warming of another 2–6 degrees Fahrenheit would be much larger and faster than any of the climate changes over the past 10,000 years. It only took a degree of cooling to create the Little Ice Age in Europe during the period from 1570 to 1730. This period of unusual cold created famine in Europe from crop failures and caused glaciers to greatly expand in the Alps. It may have been related to a substantial decrease in sunspot activity called the Maunder Minimum. When sunspots are at a low point in their various cycles, the mean output of energy from the sun drops, and the result is less heat reaching Earth. The upshot here is that even a small change in average temperature (up or down) can have far-reaching effects.

Mickey Glantz, senior scientist and program director of the Environmental and Social Impacts Group at NCAR, puts the effect of small things into perspective: "A man weighing two hundred pounds does not need two hundred pounds of arsenic to kill him." The key is, small amounts do matter.

Now, some people say that carbon dioxide is just a trace gas in the atmosphere, amounting to a mere 3 to 4 parts in 10,000 to other gases that make up our air. How can such a tiny fraction of the atmosphere cause so much trouble, especially when water vapor is much more abundant and is also a highly effective greenhouse gas? Mickey Glantz, senior scientist and program director of the Environmental and Social Impacts Group at NCAR, puts the effect of small things into perspective: "A man weighing two hundred pounds does not need

(bottom left) Ice and snow on Kilimanjaro, February 17, 1993, and (bottom right) February 21, 2000.

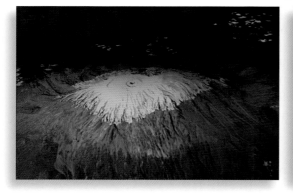

two hundred pounds of arsenic to kill him." The key is, small amounts do matter—and with our atmosphere, even with all of the major gears and cycles previously mentioned, it is very possible that our tinkering with the subtle chemistry of the air will have large long-term effects. Have we reached a tipping point where the injection of all of the fossil carbon from burning coal, gas, and oil will interact with the normal natural mechanisms to fundamentally change the course of our future climate?

There are ominous signs that climate change is accelerating. In Kenya, the famed snows of Kilimanjaro are decreasing so fast that they may soon be merely a literary reference. Since 1968, 30 percent of the glaciers have melted away in Glacier National Park in Montana. Glaciers are shrinking at an alarming rate in Alaska, where the Columbia Glacier used to tower 200 feet over Prince William Sound, calving huge blocks of ice into the water. In the past thirty years, the front of that glacier has retreated more than 9 miles from the sound. Between Valdez and Fairbanks, huge expanses of spruce forest are dead and gray, killed by a population explosion of bark beetles that are thriving on warmer temperatures. A similar invasion of pine bark beetles is in progress in Colorado. Areas of permafrost in central Alaska are thawing and forests there are drowning as they sink into the soggy swamp that is forming beneath them. Scientists at the University of Alaska say that the temperatures in Alaska, Siberia, and northwestern Canada have risen an average of 4 degrees since the 1950s, with the warming most pronounced in the winter—about 7 degrees Fahrenheit warmer. Arctic temperatures increased at almost twice the global average rate in the past 100 years.

Have we reached a tipping point where the injection of all of the fossil carbon from burning coal, gas, and oil will interact with the normal natural mechanisms to fundamentally change the course of our future climate?

Satellite images of the polar icecap show a dramatic loss of sea ice in the past thirty years, and the polar bear may be added to the list of animals considered threatened on the endangered species list. Sea-ice extents have decreased in the Arctic since 1978, particularly in spring and summer (7.4 percent per decade), and patterns of the changes are consistent with regions showing a temperature increase, although changes in winds are also a major factor. Sea-ice extents were at record low values in 2005, which was also the warmest year since records began in 1850 for the Arctic north of 65 degrees north. There have also been decreases in sea-ice thickness. In contrast to the Arctic, Antarctic sea ice does not exhibit any significant trend since the end of the 1970s, which is consistent with the lack of trend in surface temperature south of 65 degrees south over that period. However, along the Antarctic Peninsula, where significant warming has occurred, progressive breakup of ice shelves has occurred beginning in the late 1980s, including the breakup of the Larsen-B ice shelf in 2002.

Rising Seas

According to the United Nations Environment Programme, global mean sea level has risen 4 to 10 inches over the past century, mainly because water expands when heated, but also due in part to the melting of glaciers. The result of this rise, if it continues, will be a major concern for coastal flooding along the shores of the United States and will be an alarming problem for many island nations around the world. Global average sea level rose at an average rate of 1.8 mm per year over 1961 to 2003. The rate was faster during 1993–2003, when truly global values have been measured from altimeters in space, at about 3.1 mm per year. Hence, about 60 percent of this is from ocean warming and expansion, and 40

Arctic sea ice. Polar bear navigates broken ice and sometimes open waters.

percent is from melting land ice, adding to the ocean volume. The observation of consistent sea-level rise over several decades, and also an increasing rate of sea-level rise in the last decade or so, is probably the single best metric of the cumulative global warming that we have experienced to date. There is really no explanation other than global warming for the observed sea-level rise.

Droughts and Floods

In addition, a warmer climate will likely produce more severe variations in the precipitation patterns. According to the U.S. Office of Science and Technology Policy, "Since the beginning of the 20th century, precipitation in the United States has increased by about six percent, while the frequency of intense precipitation events (heavy downpours of more than two inches per day) has increased by twenty percent. Such events can cause flooding, soil erosion, and even loss of life. In some mid-continent areas, increased evaporation has led to drought because the heavy rains fell elsewhere." Long-term trends from 1900 to 2005 have been observed in total precipitation amounts over many large regions. Significantly increased precipitation has been observed in eastern parts of North and South America, northern Europe, and northern and central Asia. Drying has been observed in the Sahel, the Mediterranean, southern Africa, the western United States, and parts of southern Asia. Precipitation is highly variable, so robust long-term trends have not been observed for other large regions. The pattern of precipitation change is one of increases generally at higher northern latitudes (because as the atmosphere warms it holds more moisture) and drying in the tropics and subtropics over land. Basin-scale changes in ocean salinity provide further evidence of changes in the water cycle, with freshening at high latitudes and increased salinity in the subtropics.

Producing a typical lunch—hamburger, french fries, and a soft drink—uses 1,500 gallons of water. This includes the water needed to raise the potatoes, the grain for the bun and the grain needed to feed the cattle, and the production of the soda.

What does this mean for Colorado? Climatologist Philip Mote and colleagues note one probability:

This huge iceberg, called B15, broke off the Ross Ice Shelf in March of 2000. Measuring 11,000 square kilometers (4,400 square miles) it broke into two pieces in 2006, according to data from satellites above the frozen southern continent. The state of Delaware is about half the size of the original iceberg.

Much of the Mountain West has experienced declines in spring snowpack, especially since mid-century, and despite increases in winter precipitation in many places. Analysis and modeling shows that climatic trends are the dominant factor, not changes in land use, forest canopy, or other factors. The largest decreases have occurred where winter temperatures are mild, especially in the Cascade Mountains and Northern California. In most mountain ranges, relative declines grow from minimal at ridge top to substantial at snowline. Taken altogether, these results emphasize that the West's snow resources are already declining as Earth's climate warms.

Extreme Weather

Recent computer simulations run by researchers at the National Center for Atmospheric Research in Boulder show that global warming will likely continue at a steady rate over the next several decades, but a gradual increase may not be the biggest weather worry. New research points to the extreme weather conditions—intense storms and severe droughts—not the increasing averages, as the real concern. NCAR scientist Claudia Tebaldi and colleagues used simulations from nine different climate models for the periods 1980–1999 and 2080–2099. The simulations were created on supercomputers at research centers in France, Japan, Russia, and the United States. Each model simulated the 2080–2099 interval three times, varying the extent to which greenhouse gases accumulate in the atmosphere. These three scenarios were used to account for the uncertainty over how fast society may act to reduce emissions of CO_2 and other greenhouse gases in the coming

"Warming of the climate system is unequivocal" and it is *"very likely due to human activities."*
—**IPCC Assessment, Paris 2007**

decades. The results of the modeling showed a significant increase in very warm nights and longer heat waves over nearly all land areas across the globe. In addition, most areas above 40 degrees north will see a significant jump in the number of days with heavy precipitation (at the expense of moderate precipitation). At the same time, dry spells could lengthen significantly across the western United States, southern Europe, eastern Brazil, and several other areas. Finally, the growing season could increase significantly across most of North America and Eurasia.

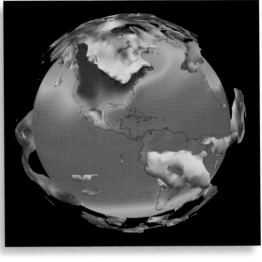

Although a temperature fluctuation of just over 1 degree Fahrenheit seems small, it amounts to a global rate of change much greater than has been known to occur over the past 10,000 years. Such a change increases the moisture in the atmosphere by 4 percent, but it also increases the rate of evaporation, resulting in larger fluctuations in precipitation. In short, as the climate continues to warm, droughts will become more severe, but so will flood events. Storm systems will have more moisture to work with, raising the possibility of more severe outbreaks of thunderstorms, hail, and flooding rains in the warm months, and major snow events during the cold season. The hurricane question is a tricky one as tropical systems already cycle through periods of higher and lower activity. But it seems intuitive that warmer temperatures overall may add fuel to the fire and increase the long-term frequency and strength of tropical storm systems.

Climate system modeling as seen on its debut in 1996.

Climate Change in Colorado

The Rocky Mountain Climate Organization (RMCO) estimates that a warmer climate in Colorado will create the following conditions. The frequency of extreme summer heat would increase, as would intense rain events in the spring and summer.

In the summer, the overall rainfall would decrease—with the exception of local severe storms that could cause localized flooding. Mountain snowpack will decrease, and the spring snowmelt will occur earlier. The normally arid southwestern United States is dependent upon the winter snows for its water supply. The vast majority of our water supply comes from winter snowpack that melts to fill our rivers. The Colorado River Basin is projected to see a 24 percent drop in snowpack in the years 2010–2039 and another 6 percent drop from 2040–2069.

Colorado is a headwater state, meaning that all of our rivers, with the sole exception of the Green River in the northwestern corner of the state, begin in and flow out of Colorado to other states. The mountain snowpack is the source for waters that flow out of our state in many directions—the Colorado River to the southwest, the Rio Grande to the south, the Arkansas to the east, and the South Platte to the northeast. These major rivers are a vital resource not only for our state, but also for vast parts of the nation. A constant worry for Colorado and all of the southwestern United States is water. As our population increases, so does the strain on our limited water resources. A warmer climate will mean increased evaporation and a greater need for water during the summer months. Stream flows will drop, as will lake and reservoir levels. This will place a greater burden on the ecosystems associated with these bodies of water. When the rains come, they will do so in a big way, raising the risk of severe flooding events such as the Big Thompson Flood in 1976 and the flash floods in Fort Collins in 1997.

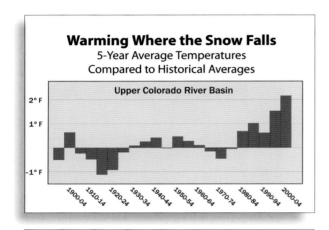

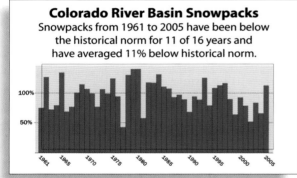

(top) A record of the warming temperatures over the Colorado River Basin. (bottom) Snowpack measured in the Colorado River Basin since 1961.

In Colorado, agriculture contributes nearly $16 billion to the state's economy each year. Almost half of the crop acreage is irrigated. A warmer climate could reduce grain yields by 8 to 33 percent, according to the Environmental Protection Agency (EPA). Yields could fall, causing greater amounts of land to be put into production, but the need for irrigating that land will also increase. The amount of water needed for irrigation in Colorado and across the southwestern states has already pushed the supply to the limit. The waters of the mighty Colorado River are already spoken for downstream in other states by a variety of compacts and treaties, each taking its share of the supply. During many years the river is so used up that by the time it reaches the border of Mexico, the current is reduced to a trickle, and the remaining water sinks into the hot sand instead of flowing into the Gulf of California.

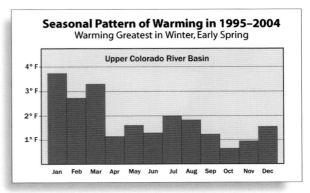

The increase in average monthly temperatures over the Colorado basin since the mid-1990s.

Trees and fauna will change with the climate as some of the species in the affected areas decline and others flourish. Estimates are that the treeline will rise by roughly 350 feet for every degree Fahrenheit of warming. Mountain ecosystems such as those in Rocky Mountain National Park could shift upslope, reducing habitat for many subalpine species. Many of the mountain wildflowers and other delicate plants will have difficulty adapting to warmer and drier conditions and may disappear from once beautiful meadows. Changes in precipitation patterns will alter stream flows, possibly accelerating the growth of nonnative plants. Coldwater fish such as trout could lose important habitat, and endangered species such as the Colorado pikeminnow, already stressed by the change in habitat due to dams and controlled flows, will have difficulty adapting and could be in greater danger of extinction.

Hotter and drier weather along the Front Range in the summertime may increase the risk of wildfires. For example, as the climate warms, the general health of ponderosa and lodgepole pines has declined, introducing the terrible invasion of pine

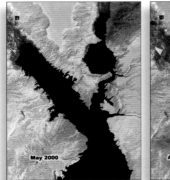 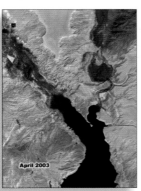

beetles that is decimating the mountain forests, especially in central Colorado. Although the pine beetle infestations do occur in natural cycles, the recent warmer winters have allowed the number of these insects to skyrocket. Very cold winter temperatures in the past have served to kill many of the larvae, keeping the damage to trees at a smaller level. The weakened forests will become an even greater fire threat—at the same time that the human population continues to grow in the forested areas just west of Denver. The risk of a catastrophic fire with great loss of life and property will continue to increase along with the temperatures.

This pair of images shows the dramatic reduction in water levels in Lake Mead, Nevada, during recent years. Located about 25 miles southeast of Las Vegas, Lake Mead stores Colorado River water for delivery to farms, homes, and businesses in southern Nevada, Arizona, southern California, and northern Mexico. (below, left) Damage from flash flooding near Crestone in July 2006. (below, right) Urban flash flooding at Ward Road and Interstate 70 in Wheat Ridge.

The warmer climate may allow for an increase in mosquito populations, accompanied by a greater threat of diseases such as Western Equine Encephalitis. Similarly, the recent increase in the deer mouse population and the associated increase in the risk of hantavirus may be linked to a warmer climate.

Skiing is a huge industry in our state, and already the major resorts are taking action in response to a warming climate. Most of the resorts have added snowmaking to counter the lessening snowpack in the early part of the season. Many resorts are establishing themselves as year-round playgrounds,

offering plenty to do in the warm season, as a buffer as the ski season grows
shorter. In addition, several resorts have
recently "gone green," buying wind and
solar energy credits to balance their
output of carbon dioxide.

Slowing Climate Change

What to do about the changing climate
is an even harder question than whether
the climate change is being hastened by
mankind. At the International Summit on Climate Change,
held in Kyoto, Japan, in December 1997, a treaty was signed by
most nations around the world. The United States participated
in the conference, but it has still not signed the treaty, and it

(top) Snowmaking can
help counter warm and
dry conditions at ski areas.
(below) Cleaning up the
debris in and around
Sterling from the 1997 flood.

does not appear likely that it will. The purpose of this treaty was to impose limits on the production of greenhouse gases—chiefly carbon dioxide—below levels produced in 1990.

Here is where science really meets politics. The United States, per capita, is by far the largest producer of greenhouse gases in the world, and to some businesses and utilities, the idea of cutting back on our consumption of fossil fuels or adding expensive pollution controls and CO_2 management systems has been a bitter pill to swallow. In addition, developing countries feel that they have a right to exploit their supplies of coal, oil, and forests in order to grow their economies, much as the growing United States did. Deforestation is a double contributor to greenhouse gases, as the burning of wood releases more CO_2 and the loss of forests reduces the uptake of CO_2 from plant photosynthesis.

Attempting to establish international policies on the reduction of greenhouse gases will be a great political problem for years to come and will require bold political leadership and determination. It is not an easy task because the sheer growth of world population and the exploding economies of many developing nations will make it difficult to reduce even the rate of increase of greenhouse gases, let alone the amount already in the atmosphere. The reduction of greenhouse gas emissions may well have a major impact on the environment, but there is also little uncertainty that a drastic cutback in the use of fossil fuels will have a profound impact on society. A major issue will continue to be the tremendous growth of the economies in India and China. As stated earlier, China is the world's largest producer of coal, and 80 percent of its electric needs are supplied by coal-fired power plants—mostly inefficient and dirty. The growing economy in China is requiring hundreds of new coal-fired power plants to be brought on line, vastly increasing the contribution China makes to global CO_2 levels. From the perspective of the United States, is it in our best interest to cut our own CO_2 levels if other major CO_2 producers do not act in similar fashion? On

(top) A coal-fired power plant in Pueblo. (below) Damage from acid rain.

the other hand, as the world's only superpower and still a leading producer of CO_2 and other greenhouse gases, is it not our responsibility to attempt to lead the way in the reduction of these gases and be an example to other countries of the world? In addition, reducing our contribution to greenhouse gases will bring major increases in fuel economy, a decline in our dependence on foreign oil, and many health benefits. Finding the answers will also stimulate the growth of whole new industries in the United States.

Technology May Be the Answer

There is some hope that the cause could be the cure. Technology has enabled us to develop into a very mobile, affluent, and highly advanced society. We are a cleaner society as well, as advancements in technology have increased the efficiency of our automobiles and industries. Cities are much cleaner today, considering the population increases, than they were fifty years ago. We have in recent years been able to find real solutions to major atmospheric problems such as acid rain and ozone depletion. The acid rain issue is an important one as the emission of sulfurous gases, mainly from power plants, can change the pH of rain and snow, creating conditions that kill plants and fish in areas that receive precipitation downwind from those power plants. Advanced smokestack scrubbers can remove the sulfurous gases from the power plant smoke. It is expensive for the utility and eventually for the consumer, but it is technology that is available today and has been implemented at many power plants.

The significant problems we face cannot be solved at the same level of thinking with which we created them.

—Albert Einstein
(attributed)

There has been one very notable success in reversing the problems we ourselves create. In the mid-1970s, two researchers at the University of California at Irvine, Sherwood Rowland and Mario Molina, found evidence that Earth's protective ozone layer was being destroyed by chemicals called chlorofluorocarbons (CFCs). These chemicals were thought to be inert and harmless, but in fact interact with other chemicals high in the stratosphere to destroy ozone molecules. The ozone layer is a thin but vital layer of ozone gas (O_3) that blocks out harmful ultraviolet light from the sun. Without the ozone layer, there would be a dramatic rise in skin cancer, a reduction in agricultural yields due to sun-caused damage to plants, and a disruption to the food chain as plankton in the ocean died. The Nobel Prize–winning research of Rowland and Molina led to the Montreal Protocol in 1987. This agreement called for a dramatic reduction in the use of CFCs worldwide. These chemicals were used in air conditioners, as cleaners for electronics, and as aerosol propellants. The alarming loss of ozone, especially around the South Pole, where strong winter wind circulation and extremely cold temperatures enhanced the ozone-eating effects of the CFCs, has continued and has produced an actual "hole" in the ozone layer. This hole reaches its greatest extent each September (spring in Antarctica) and grows to be about the size of the continental United States. Alarm over such a dramatic example of mankind's destructive power and the Montreal Protocol have prompted industry to find safe alternatives to CFCs. In the years since the Montreal Protocol was signed, CFC pollution has dropped substantially and the thinning of the ozone layer has slowed. While it will take a century or so for the ozone to completely replenish, the results are already noticeable. This serves as an example of how technology coupled with political willpower can together rise up and meet a global environmental challenge.

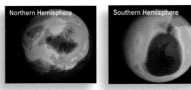

The depletion of the ozone layer happens at both poles, but is more pronounced over the South Pole.

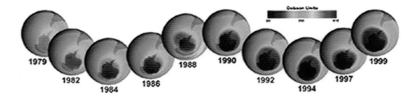

This time series shows the depletion of the ozone over the South Pole during the 1980s and 1990s.

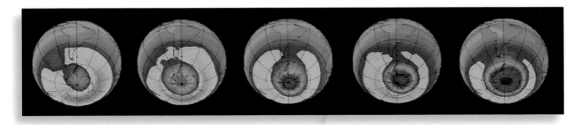

Going Green

Seasonal timed sequence of the ozone hole over the Antarctic. The hole reaches it's maximum expanse (indicated by area in purple) in September—the Antarctic spring.

Many major corporations are already jumping on board the "eco-friendly" bandwagon and embracing the challenge of "green" industry. In business, there is a rising awareness that increasing efficiency and decreasing the environmental impact of industry can mean greater profitability—not only from overall production costs, but also from a marketing advantage. Consumers want to buy products from companies that are forward-thinking and kinder to the environment. From automobiles to retail to utilities, major corporations worldwide are rapidly realizing that to win you had better "go green."

In the years since the Montreal Protocol was signed, CFC pollution has dropped substantially and the thinning of the ozone layer has slowed.

We can meet our needs with less energy. Actions we can take to save ourselves money can also save the climate. Aspen Skiing Company put fluorescent light bulbs in the parking garage of its Little Nell Hotel. Savings paid for the bulbs in a year and a half, and profits have now increased by $11,000 a year. The bulbs can save about 30 dollars in electricity cost over their lifespan and will reduce the amount of energy needed to light your home. Some of the overall environmental savings are limited by the higher amount of energy needed to manufacture compact fluorescent bulbs compared to traditional incandescent bulbs, but taken on the whole, switching to these bulbs will reduce carbon dioxide emissions.

Keeping your car's tires properly inflated costs less than a dollar. If we all check our tire pressure monthly, we would eliminate 2 percent of all carbon dioxide emissions from the nation's cars.

There are two challenges that face us in the years ahead. First, it behooves all of us to increase our "environmentality." In other words, we need to read and study, to learn as much as we can about environmental issues that face Colorado, the United States, and the world. We can then ask questions and challenge our political leaders to face these issues. We should be wary of what we read. We need to try to discern the motives of the author of whatever we are reading—for example, who may be paying the author to have a certain agenda. If an author claims that we should not worry about mankind's influence on the environment, and yet that person is working for an industry with a poor environmental track record, be wary! Be watchful of politicians who are beholden to the fossil fuel industry, thus clouding judgment on policy. Be aware of the pundits and talk-radio personalities who have little real knowledge of science, but certainly have their own agendas. Similarly, watch out for doomsday prophecies from some re-

The sun sets over a Colorado wind farm.

Mike Nelson and his hybrid Toyota Highlander and Prius—great mileage and very good performance even in the mountains!

searchers whose motivation may be a greater supply of grant money or draconian solutions from extreme viewpoints.

Consider, too, becoming a member of the Rocky Mountain Climate Organization (www.rockymountainclimate.org), a non-profit organization whose mission is to spread the word about what climate disruption means for Colorado and what can be done about it. RMCO members are very diverse, from NCAR scientists, city managers, and ski resort operators to municipal water utilities, farmers, and ranchers. The main focus of the RMCO is on the local effects that a changing climate will have on our state and what we can do to mitigate them.

It is also a good idea to be a modest consumer. Technology will improve energy efficiency and that will help limit the release of greenhouse gases, but it will take time. In the short run, we all can do the simple things that we deep down already know about—reduce, reuse, and recycle. It may sound trite, but the reduction in miles driven, lights turned on, and the level of your thermostat all are things we can do immediately to reduce the amount of greenhouse gases produced. Reusing and recycling will cut down on the consumption of fossil fuels needed to produce various products, as well as lessen the need for additional landfill space, which of course comes with its own set of environmental problems.

Support clean technologies, both politically and with your pocketbook. An example of this is Xcel Energy Company's Wind Source program. By electing to spend just a few cents more on your monthly bill, you finance the development of wind-generating power stations at various places around Colorado. There are a number of companies that offer a "carbon offset" program where consumers can purchase renewable energy credits to counter the amount of carbon dioxide one's car or home produces by supporting an equal amount of clean renewable energy.

> More than 200 years ago, George Washington believed that the key to national security for our young, fledgling nation was independence from the need for foreign resources.

Consider hybrid technology for your next car, truck, or SUV. The combination of gas and electric propulsion is a solid proven technology and results in only a moderate increase in the cost of a vehicle. The more consumers demand this fuel-saving technology, the more the auto manufacturers will jump on the hybrid bandwagon and the lower prices will be. Hybrid technology saves fuel and cuts down on air pollution, especially in slow city traffic where the battery does most of the work and the engine shuts off. The more exotic hydrogen fuel cell cars of the future will not be truly viable for many years, and there is little infrastructure for hydrogen cars. Hybrid cars, trucks, and buses work right now and can be of great benefit to our environment and our national security as higher fuel economy means less imported oil. New technologies are developing in plug-in hybrids, cars, and trucks that will have larger batteries and will actually be plugged in at night, much like a golf cart, and get 70 to 100 miles per gallon.

Renewable Energy

Right here in the Denver area, the National Renewable Energy Laboratory (NREL) is working on improving clean-energy technologies such as photovoltaic cells that produce electricity directly from sunlight. Their goal is to reduce the price of energy produced by photovoltaic cells, extend their lifetime, and increase their efficiency. As far back as 1996, the Olympic swimming events in Atlanta took place under lights powered by photovoltaic cells. At 7News, we teamed up with NREL to create the first Doppler radar system powered by the sun. The

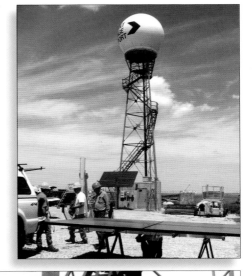

John Thornton, P.E. of NREL, and Mike Nelson survey the installation of solar panels at the 24/7 Live Doppler radar site.

radar is still connected to the power grid, so during dry, sunny days it produces more electricity than it uses and returns the excess power to the Xcel Energy grid. At night and on overcast days, the radar uses standard power from the grid. Solar energy researchers at NREL determined the annual power requirements for the radar and built the properly sized solar array to supply all of the average power needs—day and night, cloudy or clear—for an entire year. They based their estimates on the average annual sunlight at the radar site, plus added a little more reserve, so that in the course of a year, the solar panels will produce more energy than the radar will use. As a result 24/7 Live Doppler is the only truly

"green" weather radar, outputting zero net greenhouse gases. As the cost of production for photovoltaics continues to drop and the efficiency increases, solar power will become much more competitive as a source of energy.

Research in photovoltaic cells has already resulted in new roofing shingles that can actually produce electricity. The cost is high compared to a conventional roof, but with growing demand and further research, this type of shingle may become as common as asphalt shingles are today. Entire neighborhoods could become power plants just by having photovoltaic roofing. Some of the rooftops might not face in the perfect direction to be generating power at maximum efficiency, but taken as a whole a subdivision full of acres of rooftops could create a lot of electricity instead of the rooftops simply trying to dissipate the heat from the sun's rays. This idea is especially attractive because on the hottest days of the year, when power grids are straining to keep up with the demand from air conditioners, the solar rooftops would be at their most efficient.

The Department of Energy and NREL are also working with private industry to develop technologies to make biofuels from the inedible parts of plants. The most promising technologies take plant matter—corn stalks, switchgrass, wood waste, and other agricultural crop by-products that are usually discarded—and produce ethanol fuel.

Nearly all ethanol produced today is made from the kernels of corn. Production of ethanol from corn kernels is straightforward technology, and the use of these fuels fits well within our present infrastructure; in fact, almost all the gasoline sold in Colorado contains some ethanol. Many agricultural states are heavily promoting "E-Fuels" as a means of cutting our consumption of foreign oil and boosting the local farm economies. Still, there are some questions as to whether biofuels really provide much more energy than they take to produce, given that fuel is needed to cultivate the crops in the first place.

The energy balance question is resolved when ethanol is made from the nonedible parts of plants or from plants grown specifically to convert to ethanol. While some technical chal-

As the cost of production for photovoltaics continues to drop and the efficiency increases, solar power will become much more competitive as a source of energy.

lenges remain, demonstration biorefineries—similar to an oil refinery, but using biomass in the place of oil—are expected to be up and running in about three years with the goal of using the leaves, stalks, and stems of corn plants as well as the kernels to make ethanol and other products. Commercial-scale biorefineries are expected by 2012.

The Department of Energy and NREL are also continuing to research the development of clean geothermal energy. Using the heat of the earth, steam can be produced to run electrical turbines as well as directly heat water to heat buildings. This type of technology is most useful in certain areas where geothermal heat is close to the surface, but it is completely free from producing greenhouse gases. Research is also being done to capture the relentless power of the ocean tides and waves. An ingenious system of floats and baffles can channel tidal energy and use it to turn electric generators. Obviously, such technology cannot be used everywhere, but it offers another option to consider in an overall "energy portfolio."

Coal and Nuclear Energy

Coal is still an extremely abundant resource in the United States, a proven reserve that will last for hundreds of years. Coal is dirty; mining it causes many environmental problems, and burning it blows out a lot of CO_2 and a host of other pollutants. However, new technologies are being developed that will make coal burning far less damaging to the environment. Coal gasification is a process that allows many of the pollutants, including particulates, mercury, and sulfur, to be removed before the coal is burned. Research is also promising in coal CO_2 sequestration—taking out the CO_2 after burning the coal and injecting it deep into the earth for storage. At this writing, Xcel Energy is proposing that a new coal gasification and sequestration plant be built in eastern Colorado. The technology will initially be more expensive, but since coal still offers the attractive aspect of a huge domestic supply, gasification shows promise and should be supported as a way for Colorado to lead in the development of this type of power plant.

Nuclear energy has a bad reputation because of the terrible accidents at Three Mile Island and Chernobyl. It is right that we are wary of nuclear fission, because any accident would be devastating. However, there still is a place for nuclear fission as a source of large amounts of electricity. More modern designs for fission reactors have eased many of the concerns about catastrophic accidents, as newer designs do not depend upon complex pump systems to keep the reactor core cool in the event of an emergency. Some designs employ a simple gravity feed for cold water to bathe a hot reactor core. Since the force of gravity is always constant, the risk of a core meltdown due to lack of cooling water is greatly diminished. Much of the electric power in France is produced by fission reactors that have been operating safely for many years. There are still major issues to adding more fission reactors in the United States: extremely high building costs, the threat of terrorism, and the problem of disposing of spent fuel are all huge obstacles to overcome. The attraction of nuclear power is in its lack of greenhouse gas production and the capacity to generate very large amounts of power regardless of whether the wind is blowing or the sun is shining.

Nuclear fusion is another matter. Instead of splitting large atoms of uranium, which creates tremendous problems with nuclear waste, nuclear fusion does the opposite. Fusion creates helium from the combination of two hydrogen atoms; it is the way the sun produces energy. Because hydrogen is the most common element in the universe, the power supply is limitless and the radioactive by-products are minimal.

As far as we know, out of the vastness of the universe, the planet earth is the only place that harbors life.

It sounds great, but the problem is that we know only how to create fusion in the laboratory or through the explosion of a hydrogen bomb. Many years of research are still needed before we can truly harness the "power of the sun." The public should not be afraid of fusion research; it is

the ultimate long-term answer to the power needs of mankind. Supporting the continued research of controlled fusion through our universities and by pressing our political leaders to invest in larger-scale research will be important if we hope to harness this power by the end of this century.

Earth's atmosphere is a very thin and fragile envelope of air. This is a view from 100 kilometers (62 miles) above the surface.

Energy Independence

It will likely be several generations before nuclear fusion, wind power, biofuels, ocean tides, geothermal energy, and photovoltaic cells replace most fossil fuels as our energy sources. In the interim, we must continue to support even more research on climate change as well as learn better ways to efficiently use our fossil fuel resources. We must urge our political leaders to focus on, not ignore, the critical issues of our changing climate. Whether the weather is changing all by itself, or more likely, that we are helping speed the change, we are going to have to learn to adapt in order to survive and thrive. We should not shrink away from this challenge, but rather embrace it and use our intellects to seek new and better ways to produce, use, and conserve energy. This is not simply a matter of having enough power for business and industry; it is a matter of national security. Far too much of our current fuel of choice—oil—comes from parts of the world and political regimes that do not like us very much. Every barrel of oil purchased from these areas weakens our country by adding to greenhouse gases, by increasing our national debt, and by funding international movements that have dangerous agendas. We can develop better methods and use the resources we have here at home to regain our position as the world's leader in a new energy economy.

It seems prudent, patriotic, and reverent that we do everything we can to conserve and protect the fragile envelope of air that allows us to live on planet earth.

Other nations, especially Germany and the Scandinavian countries, have been ahead of us in the development of wind, solar, and wave power. We need to create a sense of national urgency, on the level of the space program or the Manhattan Project, to greatly increase our fuel economy, greatly decrease our dependency on foreign oil, and lead the way in the development of alternative energy choices. This is the time to act, not ignore the problem and hope it goes away.

In the unlikely event it turns out that humans are just too feeble to affect the climate, we will still be better off, as will our grandchildren, that we helped advance the technology to produce clean, renewable energy sources that reduce pollution and our dependency on foreign energy resources.

More than 200 years ago, George Washington believed that the key to national security for our young, fledgling nation was independence from the need for foreign resources. In that light, Washington sought to use his home, Mount Vernon, as an example of self-reliance. Washington developed methods of planting, recycling, and local manufacturing of materials so that he would not need to import them from overseas. He realized the importance of this nation being self-sufficient. It is vitally important that we strive again to win our independence—this time from foreign and sometimes hostile sources of energy.

In his thoughtful and erudite book *The Pale Blue Dot,* Carl Sagan noted that when Soviet cosmonaut Yuri Gagarin, the first human in space, reached the top of our atmosphere and gazed out across the edge of the earth, he was terrified by how thin and frail our atmosphere appeared against the cold black of outer space. Gagarin later said that he had always been taught that we lived at the bottom of a great ocean of air, but to him it looked like a very shallow puddle. As far as we know, out of the vastness of the universe, the planet earth is the only place that harbors life. Someday we will likely find other worlds that provide an environment gentle enough to enable life to form, but for now, this is it, our lonely outpost in a corner of a galaxy. It seems prudent, patriotic, and reverent that we do everything we can to conserve and protect the fragile envelope of air that allows us to live on planet earth. The legacy we leave future generations depends upon the actions we take in the coming years. Our heirs will be the judges of our success.

Earthrise from Apollo 8, December 1968.

CHAPTER SEVEN

Bringing the
WEATHER
HOME

It seems to be a common thread with meteorologists. Whenever National Weather Service forecasters, NCAR researchers, TV weathercasters, or storm chasers get together, almost without fail, the same quote can be heard: "I've wanted to be a meteorologist since I was a kid." Most weather enthusiasts seem to catch the fever at an early age. Often the catalyst was a memorable storm—a tornado, blizzard, or hurricane—that caught a schoolchild's imagination. Weather is all around us, and children are outside in it more than just about anyone else. As a result, it should not come as much of a surprise that a lifelong fascination with the wonders of weather would begin before the age of ten. From the first stormy memory, the newly minted weather nut will begin to pay more attention to the skies, watching for signs of impending weather changes. At the dinner table, mom, dad, and siblings begin to get used to the ever-increasing weather babble from this fledgling forecaster!

Local Heroes

In addition to watching stormy skies, most aspiring young meteorologists closely watch their local weathercasters on TV. To a young weather wannabe, the local television meteorologist can be as big a hero as the sports stars from football and basketball are to student athletes. The author of this book speaks from experience. For local weather nuts in the Denver area in the 1960s and 1970s, a school visit by Weatherman Bowman, Larry Green, Stormy Rottman, or Bill Kuster would have been a very exciting day indeed! Truly the television meteorologist is the most visible personification of the science of meteorology for most people. It is unusual, in Colorado, that we have so many different types of meteorologists, climatologists, theorists, numerical modelers, tropical researchers, avalanche forecasters, geologists, hydrologists, and other experts in the various fields of meteorology and the earth sciences. With all of the

Both the author of this book (above) and lead researcher (Chris Spears, right) started checking the weather at an early age.

Longtime Denver weathercaster Bill Kuster started his career at WGAL-TV in Lancaster, Pennsylvania in the late 1950s and moved to Philadelphia in the 1960s. Through the mid-1970s, weather conditions were displayed on large maps using grease pencils or magnetic weather symbols.

research facilities in Boulder and Fort Collins, as well as the local institutes for teaching meteorology, there are likely more meteorologists per capita in this area than in most places around the nation. It is important that the role played by the television meteorologist is done with a strong emphasis on accuracy and professionalism. The television meteorologist truly represents a small but very visible piece of an important and varied profession here in Colorado.

Early TV Weather

From the 1950s to the 1970s, television weather did not change dramatically in the way that it was presented. The main challenge was to come up with a way to display the basic meteorological information in a manner that would be easy enough for the audience to understand. This was usually accomplished by taking the raw weather data from teletype and facsimile machines and then simplifying it by displaying the information on a big map on the wall. A giant mural of the United States was painted on a wall of the studio, and then the weather features were put over the map with hooks,

(left) Mike Nelson presenting weather around 1980. (right) Mike Nelson's first weather cast on WKOW-TV, July 4, 1979, in Madison, Wisconsin.

magnets, or water-based paint. Some stations tried to be more creative by putting the map on a glass wall and having the weathercaster stand behind the glass and draw the weather live. Unfortunately, this required not only art skill, but also the ability to draw backward so that the audience could read it. The glass map method had limited success owing to the dexterity needed for the job.

In the 1970s, weathercasters decided to experiment with other methods of drawing their maps for TV. Some of the first efforts involved hardcopy base maps that were printed on paper or lightweight pieces of cardboard. These maps would show the basic outlines of the state, region, or nation, and the weathercaster could then draw the fronts and other features on the map. The art supplies typically included a variety of felt-tipped markers in different colors, with press-on lettering from a drafting store and something called Zipatone—a thin, translucent, plastic film available in a variety of colors. By cutting the film with an Exact-o knife, a television meteorologist could create cloud shapes, radar representations, and temperature bands and apply those colors to the base map. Gradually a series of different maps would emerge, and each could then be literally taped to the wall of the TV studio, shot with a camera, and superimposed behind the weathercaster. It took a lot of effort: the preparation time for a single weather report was many hours, and the hardcopy maps were difficult to update once they were complete. In addition, there were technical complications. Sometimes, for instance, the little pieces of masking tape used to hold the map on the wall would let go, sending the United States falling to the floor in the middle of the weather report. Try explaining that one in the middle of a live newscast! Once, a prankster on the studio crew had some fun by lighting the paper map on fire—reminiscent of the start of the old *Bonanza* TV series. Then there was the time a fly landed on the map and crawled back and forth behind the flustered forecaster as he tried to deliver the weather report. Remember that these maps were made on small pieces of light cardboard, perhaps 8 inches by 12. The map was then electronically enlarged and superimposed behind the weathercaster. Typically the map was blown up about twenty times bigger than its real size. Of course, that meant the fly was too, so the effect was like Flyzilla versus the Weatherman!

Hardcopy weather maps from the mid- to late 1970s. To complete just a few simple maps sometimes required hours of effort.

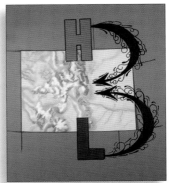

The frustration felt by many a forecaster in trying to get an accurate, updated, and understandable weathercast on TV was not only a local issue. It was happening all across the country. At a small ABC affiliate in Madison, Wisconsin, a local meteorologist named Terry Kelly was trying to figure out a better way to produce his weather report. As it turned out, he was quite a visionary and entrepreneur. In addition to his television career, he had started a weather consulting company called Weather Central in 1974. This private weather firm provided forecasts for radio stations, highway departments, agribusiness, ski areas, and other enterprises that needed specialized weather information that the National Weather Service did not provide.

Terry Kelly

Computer Weather Revolution

In early 1979, Terry Kelly teamed up with Richard Daly, a computer scientist at the University of Wisconsin, to begin a new venture: computerized weather graphics for TV. There had been a few attempts by others around the country to try to use computers to generate weather maps, but the high cost of the hardware and the crude stage of software had limited the success of such technology. Kelly and Daly formed a company called ColorGraphics Weather Systems. The initial systems were based upon some of the minicomputer display breakthroughs at the University of Wisconsin's Department of Space Science and Engineering, where Kelly and Daly had been working. A system had been developed there called McIdas (an acronym for Man-Computer Interactive Data Access System). The McIdas system used a large and powerful (for the time) PDP-11 minicomputer to allow meteorologists to draw and analyze satellite cloud data directly on a computer screen. By today's standards, it was like Pong or Space Invaders compared to the current high-end video games, but at the time it was indeed the leading edge. The McIdas system was designed for use in research and National Weather Service satellite and data display, and it was vastly too expensive for a television station to buy.

Terry Kelly and Richard Daly envisioned creating a weather computer system that would be easy to use, affordable, and capable of producing attractive images to show on TV. The first ColorGraphics system was based upon an Apple II home computer! It was capable of generating six different color choices over a color background. The resolution of the maps was very blocky, and the fonts were pretty hard to read. The system could not be plugged directly into the TV station's routing switcher, so a camera had to be aimed at a computer monitor in order to get the image on the air and home to your TV. It all sounds pretty lame by today's standards, but the first ColorGraphics computer was an amazing leap forward for television weather.

It was not long after the debut of the television weather computer that the concept caught on, and television stations nationwide sought to become the first in their market with computerized color weather. ColorGraphics began to install the computers at TV stations all over the country and to train the local weathercasters how to use the fancy new weather systems. So, by the early 1980s, meteorologists and computer trainers were traveling around the nation with the weather computers and teaching the weather personnel how to best use this new technology. By the mid-1980s, most television weathercasters were using computers to generate their weather graphics, replacing the various weather boards, cardboard base maps, and glass screens that had to be drawn on in reverse. In five years, a generation of old weathercasting techniques had pretty much become obsolete; it truly was a revolution in the television industry.

Mike Nelson working on paper maps (left) and an early TV weather computer (right) at Weather Central. (bottom) The first generation of television weather graphics, circa 1979.

The weather computers, like calculators and personal computers, continued to grow in power and shrink in cost. At the same time, as computer development continued, the quality of the graphics grew enormously during the mid- to late 1980s. By the beginning of the 1990s, the pixel resolution and color choices had zoomed ahead from the very blocky and crude looking images that had been so impressive only a decade earlier. In addition, many other features became available beyond just simply drawing a weather map. Improvements included high-resolution satellite imagery, frame animation, color cycling to make the maps move and thus allow weathercasters to show jet stream simulations, and national radar images, enabling weathercasters to depict severe weather in other parts of the country.

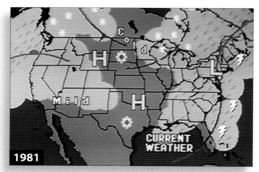

Computer graphics technology improved rapidly through the 80s.

Through the 1990s, weather computer systems continued to improve in their graphics quality, animation features, and ease of use. The graphics power of computers was limited in the 1970s and 1980s, unless the user could afford a "paint system" that could run well over $200,000. There were, however, some small computer companies in the 1980s that specialized in graphics systems (including elementary "3D" graphics) that were on the lower end from the fancy paint systems, but robust enough for TV weather. These small companies have mostly faded into computer history today, but at the time, they provided the platforms that allowed TV weather graphics to continue to evolve through the 1980s and early 1990s. Today, with the advent of very powerful graphics platforms using PC hardware, we once again use off-the-shelf equipment and run specialized graphics software to create high-quality weather graphics. Virtually

Mike Nelson and weather producer Chris Spears, preparing the forecast and graphics for the evening weather. (right) Putting the graphics in sequence before show time.

every TV weathercast that you may watch anywhere in the country, and in many areas around the world, will utilize the newest, most powerful generations of the weather computer that truly started as a cottage industry in the late 1970s. The company that Terry Kelly founded is still based in Madison and is the leading supplier of television weather computer equipment in the world. In the 24/7 Weather Center at 7News, our meteorologists are surrounded by the latest generation of this system and use it to produce the weather graphics that you see every day on 7News, Comcast Channel 247, and TheDenverChannel.com.

The computers still are not cheap. Many of the systems used by TV stations tally far into six figures, but they have become the mainstay of the television weather business. If you travel around the country, it is very rare to find anyone using an old weather board, even for a small part of the weathercast. Those old-fashioned "weather walls" could make a comeback of sorts, kind of like a flashback to disco music, but the weather computer business should be robust for many years to come.

Graphics Innovations

Of course, now weathercasters have all sorts of fancy things they can do with the graphic displays: time-lapse cloud animation, lightning detection, Doppler radar, and fly-through animations, all brought to you by the weather computer. Time-lapse is actually not new; back in the early 1970s, Terry Kelly used an old Bolex film camera to take a single frame of film every ten to thirty seconds. This film had to be rushed out to be developed in time for the nightly weather reports, and sometimes a beautiful sunset would end up jammed and ruined in the developing machine. Today, the weather computer simply grabs a single frame off a weather camera every few seconds and stores it for playback. Television weathercasters can now turn around a time-lapse display in no time at all, not only

(below) Temperature plot with contours. (bottom) State-of-the-art weather graphics in 2007.

(top) Cloud-to-ground lightning strikes create a brief but intense radio signal called a sferic. This signal can be measured and used to pinpoint the location of the lightning strike. (bottom) The lightning-strike locations can then be plotted on a map. It is not uncommon for Colorado to receive 10 to 15 thousand lightning strikes on a stormy summer day.

time-lapsing the clouds and sunsets but also focusing the camera on highways, skiers, construction equipment, window washers, or anything else that might be fun to see in high-speed motion.

Lightning detection is fascinating to most viewers; how it works was detailed in Chapter 3. The first lightning system in Denver was installed back in 1982. The system has been changed and modernized considerably in the past twenty-five years, but it still remains a mainstay of the summertime weathercast. One of the interesting things about lightning is that it will sometimes begin well ahead of the precipitation in a thunderstorm. Since weather radar only "sees" precipitation, the lightning detector can provide a ten- to twenty-minute advance notice about developing thunderstorms. Occasionally there is lightning even in the wintertime. Cold season lightning is indicative of a large amount of turbulence in the atmosphere and is a sign that heavy snowfall of several inches per hour may be developing.

Weather Radar

Radar remains one of the big guns in the arsenal of TV weather. In the 1950s and 1960s, weather radar was very crude, basically a camera pointed at an electron tube display that had an eerie greenish glow and a slowly fading sweep line that looked like something from an old war movie. In the mid-1970s, these radar displays were replaced by the biggest innovation of the time, color radar. In a colorized display, each intensity level for the precipitation (light to heavy) was assigned a different color. Usually light blue or green marked the light showers, while the heavy downpours were shown in orange or red. With some exceptions, that part of the radar display for television remains unchanged. Radar works by sending out a burst of microwave energy, similar in frequency to a microwave oven. At this particular wavelength (about 5 to 10 centimeters) the energy tends to pass through clouds, but bounce or echo off rain, snow, or hail. By timing the signal from when it leaves the radar to when it bounces back, the location of the precipitation is determined. The intensity of the precipitation is determined by the strength of the echo. This type of radar has actually been around since World War II; today it is referred to as *conventional radar*. The technology for conventional radar is basically the same, whether it is displayed with the old circular greenish scope of the 1950s or the colorized version of the 1970s.

Conventional Radar

Conventional radar signals pass through clouds but reflect off of rain, snow, or hail. Location and distance can be determined by timing the return of the reflected radar signal.

Doppler Weather Radar

In the 1980s, technology made another jump with the introduction of Doppler weather radar. Doppler radar sees not only precipitation but also the wind. Of course, wind is invisible, but the Doppler radar can analyze the movement of raindrops and snowflakes inside clouds. Those cloud particles are being blown around by the wind, so in essence, by seeing them we can see how fast the winds are blowing and in what direction. Doppler is actually the name of a nineteenth-century physicist, Christian Doppler, who first formally described a phenomenon with which we are all familiar. If you have ever noticed how the sound from an approaching car or train changes as it passes by, then you have experienced the "Doppler shift." As the vehicle moves closer, the sound waves coming from the car or train are being picked up by your ear. Because the object is moving toward you, the sound waves tend to bunch up, and their frequency increases. That is why the tone or pitch seems to rise as the car or train gets closer. When it passes by, the sound waves are still coming from the vehicle toward your ear, but because it is moving away,

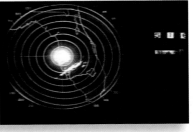

Conventional Radar

(top) Early weather radar circa 1960. (middle) The first hook echo ever seen on radar, April 9, 1953. (bottom) Early weather radar, WTTV, Tampa Florida. (left) Doppler radar sends out more signals very quickly. These reflected signals show not only precipitation but also movement of the precipitation. This movement provides information on wind currents and speeds, which allows detection of windshears and tornadoes.

Just as sound waves from a moving vehicle change in pitch, or frequency, radar signals shift slightly if the precipitation is quickly moving toward or away from the radar. This shift can be measured to detect wind shears and help pinpoint areas where tornadoes may be developing.

The Doppler Shift

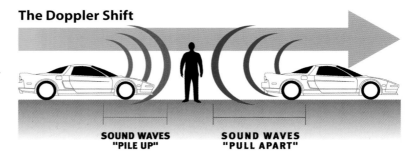

SOUND WAVES "PILE UP"   SOUND WAVES "PULL APART"

the sound waves are farther apart, the frequency is lower, and the pitch drops. The faster the object approaches and moves by, the greater the change in pitch or frequency. Measuring this change provides a very good idea of how fast an object is moving. This Doppler shift can work with sound waves or with microwaves. In radar, a large number of pulses of radar or microwave energy are sent out from the radar antenna; those signals bounce off an object (such as a raindrop) and return to the radar at slightly different times, depending on whether the object is moving toward or away from the radar antenna. This shift in the frequency of the radar return signals can be measured and used to determine how fast the object is moving toward or away from the radar. Doppler radar also is used by the police to give you that speeding ticket! It is also the way that we determine how fast a pitcher is throwing a baseball or how fast a hockey slap shot is moving.

In weather forecasting, Doppler radar provides two major improvements over conventional weather radar. First, it eliminates most of the confusing false echoes that used to clutter up the radar screen. Older radars had a problem with the signal bouncing off buildings and trees and sending back the impression that there was precipitation in those locations. This was, of course, very misleading to the viewer, as they thought it was raining or snowing in that area. Plus, when it really was raining or snowing, the precipitation area was "caught in the clutter" and was very hard to see. The Doppler

24/7 Live Doppler showing precipitation over northern Colorado.

radar eliminates ground clutter by simply seeing what is moving. If that building stays in the same place long enough, the clutter suppression program in the radar computer simply eliminates the echo. There can still be a little bit of clutter on a Doppler display because sometimes the signal will bounce off moving objects, so that a little tiny pixel of green on our radar might be an airplane flying by your house. The biggest benefit of Doppler weather radar is the fact that it allows us to have X-ray vision to peer into the heart of severe thunderstorms. By seeing how the rain and hail are being blown around inside a storm, we can look for areas of very strong winds and possible tornadoes. Doppler radar enables meteorologists to find places in the storm cloud where the winds are blowing very rapidly in one direction, and nearby areas where they are blowing very rapidly in the opposite direction. These areas of rapidly

The 24/7 Doppler Network consists of four National Weather Service Doppler radars located in Colorado and surrounding states. The combination of several radars enables 7News to monitor stormy weather anywhere in the central Rockies.

changing winds contain what is called shear, the greater the shear: the better the chance that a tornado or downburst may be forming. By using Doppler radar, forecasters can catch a glimpse into the storm and pinpoint these areas much earlier than ever before. Doppler radar allows meteorologists to issue earlier, better, and more useful tornado and severe thunderstorm warnings. More advanced notice can save lives.

Doppler radar became available for television in the mid-1980s. By the beginning of the 1990s, most TV stations in larger cities were equipped with their own Dopplers. These radars are not cheap; most installations cost between a quarter-million and nearly a million dollars. That is part of the reason that TV stations always come up with such fancy names for their radar. After making such a large investment, the station management wants to get the most for their money, so they come up with important sounding names: Super Doppler, Double Doppler, Doppler 4000, Doppler Max, Mega-Doppler, High Definition Doppler, and so forth. All of the Doppler radars used around the nation are very good radars. Some have more features than others, but the upshot is that the competition

(above) A 3-D display of 24/7 Live Solar Doppler tracks afternoon thunderstorms building over the foothills west of Denver. (right) Street level radar mapping showing strong storms just west of Denver.

between TV stations ultimately benefits the viewer. By each station having an excellent radar display, the viewer has more choices and better weather information in the event of dangerous storms. In 2005, the 24/7 Weather Center at KMGH-TV teamed up with scientists at the National Renewable Energy Lab in Golden and developed the first solar-powered Doppler radar for television. In cooperation with Xcel Energy, the 24/7 Live Solar Doppler is the first radar that is carbon-neutral, not adding any greenhouse gases to the atmosphere. In fact, the solar panels, located on the radar tower, actually produce more electricity in a year than the radar requires. The radar system puts more energy back into the power grid than it takes out, making it the most environmentally friendly weather radar in the world.

In recent years there have been a few more improvements on the Doppler radar. These improvements are mainly in the display aspect, making the radar easier to understand. For many years, the center of the radar sweep marked the center of the radar map. This worked well if the radar was located in the middle of town. If the radar was located somewhere else, the audience could be confused by thinking the middle of the map was the center of town, when actually it was simply the radar site. New computer technology has allowed meteorologists to remap the radar echoes onto any size or scale of map. The most interesting part of this improvement is that it allows remapping the radar onto a very small map, right down to the city streets. It is now possible to show a thunderstorm cell that literally is raining on one side of the street and not on the other. This type of close-up mapping is very helpful with the type of small, fast-moving storms common in Colorado. The software enables the meteorologist to click on the radar screen with a mouse and actually have the name of the street pop up. In addition, it is possible to click on a storm cell and show its speed and direction, and to have the radar calculate what cities will be affected by the storm and at what time. This "storm path analyzer" function is very useful with squall lines and has provided important advanced notice of approaching severe thunderstorms and tornadoes in many TV markets around the country.

3-D Weather

Another important innovation in television weather graphics has been the development of 3-D fly-through weather. The first 3D weather systems came on line in the mid 1990s as graphics capabilities reached a point where a computer could remap the weather over a three-dimensional background. This allowed the user to change vantage points, elevation, and angle, and look at the weather from all kinds of different perspectives. The computer had to be powerful enough to draw the map background, topography, and weather very quickly in order for the system to be really useful. The whole idea was to start at a certain viewpoint, say right over the foothills west of

The first 3D weather systems came on line in the mid 1990s as graphics capabilities reached a point where a computer could remap the weather over a three-dimensional background.

Denver, and then "fly" across the country. The computer would then interpolate between the starting point and the end point and render an animation graphic, frame by graphic frame. It is the cyber equivalent of drawing a stick figure on a set of flash cards and changing the position of the figure slightly on each card. Then, flipping through the cards quickly, one gets the illusion of the figure moving.

Early innovators of these television systems had to be careful to not go overboard and take their viewers on too much of a roller-coaster ride. Around the country, some of the weather flights got a little wild. Television forecasters had to curb their enthusiasm for zooming through the weather as the audience found it difficult to follow. That might be an understatement, since some of the viewer complaints indicated that the flights were making viewers nauseated. Rather than doling out Dramamine, prudent prognosticators opted to tone down the fast spins and quick turns.

In time, most television meteorologists have learned to use the fly-around capability much more effectively, moving gently from one part of the country to another. This capability also allows animation of a weather feature or the pulling of some video out of certain locale to show what the weather is doing in that area. Three-dimensional weather has become a mainstay in television weather graphics, and most weathercasters around the country are now using some form of it for at least part of their report. Another recent development is the 3D analysis of radar images, allowing us to fly through live radar. Some of the latest computer software now allows a forecaster literally to spin the radar image around a thunderstorm, showing the structure of the storm from all sides. Some of this capability may be beyond the scope of a normal weathercast as it could be too confusing to the viewer, but for the meteorologist, it actually is valuable to scan critical areas of a

(top) 3-D radar display of storms east of Denver. (middle) 3-D display of satellite imagery over the western U.S. (bottom) Weather Alert for flooding over northeast Colorado.

thunderstorm to look for signs of developing tornadoes or areas of large, damaging hail. It is important for weathercasters to remember that they can spend many minutes looking at these 3D images, but the viewer may only see it for a matter of thirty seconds; it is important to not overuse technology that can actually make it harder for the audience to understand.

High Definition

With the rapid increase in the number of consumers purchasing high-definition (HD) televisions, the next great wave in technology is in high-definition weather graphics systems. During the next few years, weather computer systems will again make a quantum leap into the next generation of graphics. HD weather graphics are incredibly detailed and provide viewers with an amazing degree of clarity for satellite and radar data. The huge amount of detail in HD graphics requires far more computer power and memory, for the graphics files are enormous compared to earlier systems. Despite the hurdles in handling the data needed to create much high-definition weather graphics, history has shown that the computer wizards at the weather graphics companies will again find a way to make the new systems work. Viewers will approve of the beautiful new images, and the inherent competition between TV stations will drive the development and deployment of the next round of "latest and greatest" in local television weather.

(top) Seven-day forecast graphic. (left) High-definition computer images will make television weather graphics as high resolution as a quality computer monitor.

The Green Screen

The one aspect of the television weather report that still surprises most people is the fact that the weathercasters do not actually stand in front of a weather map. When viewers watch on TV at home, it looks like there is a giant weather map behind the forecaster. In fact, there is nothing back there except a big blue or green wall. In the television studio, weathercasters simply stand in front of this wall, talking and pointing into thin air. The camera, located about 10 feet in front of the presenter, is set up with the chroma key. This type of special effect works very simply: the camera "sees" the weathercaster and the blue or green wall. The camera is set up in a special way so that wherever the camera sees the color, it shows a weather map to the viewers at home. Basically, the rule is: any place the camera sees blue or green it looks like a weather

Mike Nelson delivers his afternoon weathercasts in the chroma key, also known as a green screen.

map. Because all there is behind the weathercaster is a colored wall, how do they know what to point at? Just on the edge of the wall—at a position called "off camera"—is a TV monitor. The weathercaster looks at that monitor and will see the same picture that the audience at home sees. It is a little strange to be watching oneself on TV while actually being on TV, but that is how weathercasters know what they are pointing at. It is hard to do at first, a bit like patting your head and rubbing your tummy at the same time, but with practice, it becomes second nature. By the way, the reason that blue or green is used is due to the way that the color television signal is produced, which mixes red, blue, and green pixels to form all the other colors. It is possible electronically to take one of these primary TV colors and process it in a way that any video source can be superimposed over it. Chroma key is widely used in movie production, and often Hollywood action movies are filmed with actors going through fight scenes or flying through the air, all acted out in front of a giant green wall. Most of the time, the green color is preferred as the key color, since most folks do not choose bright green shirts and suits.

(top) Monitors on both sides of the chroma key and on the camera allow Mike to see what he is doing while interacting with the viewer at home. (bottom) The "24/7 Weather Experience" is a traveling version of the 7News 24/7 Weather Center. Anyone can stand in front of the chroma key and see what it is like to report the weather on TV.

Obviously, one cannot wear the same color clothing as the wall behind them, or the clothing will end up having weather maps superimposed over them. Red could also be used as the key color, but that is not practical because there are so many reddish tones in our skin, and female weathercasters wearing red lipstick might find weather maps appearing on their lips!

Something else viewers may notice is the little "clicker" that weathercasters hold in their hand while doing the weather. This clicker is a small electronic control unit that is rigged up to change the weather map or add special effects. When the forecaster hits the button, the signal goes to the weather computer and tells it to jump to the next map. The early clickers were garage door openers, with the signal receiver simply plugged into the back of the computer. Today, the computers are so sophisticated that weathercasters actually have four or five different buttons on the clicker, each for a different function. The latest generations of weather computers have special software that enables the presenter to hold down a button on the clicker and actually draw on the weather map live on the air. This technology is very useful for highlighting certain aspects of a thunderstorm, or literally drawing a cold front over a satellite image in real time.

The weather clicker is used to advance the maps on the weather computer while in the chroma key.

The last thing viewers may have wondered about is the little hearing aid device that weathercasters wear in their ear. This is the IFB, or program interrupt. It basically is just a little walkie-talkie that allows the behind-the-scenes staff in the control room to give the on-air person instructions. The producer and director of the newscast often need to convey things such as how much time is left: "one minute / thirty seconds / wrap it up." They also can provide information about breaking news or technical problems, such as "the tape machine just ate your time-lapse!" In the movie *Broadcast News*, Holly Hunter's character fed questions and information to the anchorman played by William Hurt. Although most producers and directors do not tell the weathercaster what to say, they do frequently send time cues or other information during the weather report.

Ready for Primetime

In general, it takes about an hour of preparation of forecasts and graphics for each minute that a weathercaster is on the air. When meteorologists go on TV, they have to laugh and joke with the anchors, get up from the news desk, walk about 30 feet to the chroma key, point at something that is not really there, remember who's hot, who's cold, where it's raining, where it's snowing, where it's all going, click the button at the right time, keep track of what map will come up next, and do all of this in about three minutes while someone is talking in their ear! All of that does not even include getting the forecast right! Unlike news anchors, most weathercasters do not read their script off the teleprompter; instead, virtually all television weather reports are delivered as an ad lib. This is not as difficult as it might seem because meteorologists have spent several hours pouring over forecasts and developing the maps and graphics, so by the time they go on TV, they pretty much know what

With computers, map walls are becoming rare. But 7News Chief Meteorologist Mike Nelson and his staff maintain a map wall with all the latest weather charts. The 24/7 Weather Center sits within feet of the news desk.

they want to say. In fact, trying to read off a teleprompter while also concentrating on the chroma key and the clicker would be more difficult than ad-libbing the weather report. The last task is going on the air and delivering the weather in a clear, upbeat, and, with luck, accurate manner. The weather presentation can be as pretty as a picture, but if the forecast is wrong it does not serve the audience very well.

That last paragraph was not designed to drum up sympathy. Forecasting the weather on TV is a great job, and most meteorologists in the profession love it. However, remember that the weather is the only part of the newscast that predicts instead of reports. There may be a big difference between a snowstorm and sunshine as far as the audience is concerned, but meteorologically it may have been just a slight change in the storm track. The one part of the weather report that each weathercaster on every channel always agrees upon is what the high and low temperatures actually were for the past day.

> *"If we could land on the moon, how come we can't better predict the weather?" The answer is that it is easier to land on the moon!*

Those numbers are facts. Just as with news reporting, the facts are much easier to provide than the forecast. The job of a meteorologist is much more like that of a stockbroker: ask five different brokers specifics about the market and you will likely get five different forecasts. When people say, "If we could land on the moon, how come we can't better predict the weather?" The answer is that it is easier to land on the moon! A mission to the moon is a matter of propulsion and supplies. Take enough rocket fuel, food, and oxygen, and you should be able to get there and back. Weather forecasting involves the future motions of a complex mix of gases on a swirling, irregularly shaped planet.

Take everything we have discussed previously into consideration, and the result is a chaotic mix of sun, clouds, and storms that meteorologists try to track and project into the future. Advances are being made constantly, but the atmosphere is so complex that forecasters will likely never succeed in pinpointing the exact weather several weeks in advance. However, we are getting much better at nailing down short-term, dangerous, severe weather events and at predicting the general trends for an entire season. These improvements can save lives and tremendous amounts of money by providing valuable advance notice of local events such as tornadoes or hailstorms, medium-length episodes such as El Niño, and the long-term concerns of our changing climate. In addition, the accuracy of weather forecasting in the two- to seven-day span is improving. In fact; recent studies show that weather forecasts of three to four days are now as accurate as a two-day forecast was only twenty years ago.

Mike Nelson putting the finishing touches on the weather graphics shortly before going on the air.

Television meteorologists serve many masters. The goal is to provide accurate and timely information in a lively and, hopefully, enjoyable manner. We need to cover the local scene, but also to give the folks in the rest of Colorado the information they need. Weathercasters attempt to give an overview of national weather, since viewers want to know what the weather is like for "Aunt Flo" in New Jersey, but they also try to educate the viewer about important events in weather history or about new research about global climate change or ozone depletion. As weathercasters we could probably fill five to eight minutes on the subject each night, but news and sports have plenty to say as well, so we do what we can with the time allotted. The Internet offers another avenue to expand upon the coverage, and our website on TheDenverChannel.com provides a great deal of in-depth coverage about our weather and the environment each day. The site is constantly evolving and constantly being improved upon, and the email box is always open if you have an idea about how we can make the weather more relevant to your life.

We hope that this book has provided some insight into the sometimes mild, but often wild, weather we get here in Colorado. Everyone who lives in this beautiful state are lucky, but weather enthusiasts are perhaps the luckiest of all. The many days of lovely sunshine, the great variety in the clouds, the brilliant colors throughout the seasons, the fast changes and the intensity of our storms, all combine to make Colorado an especially wondrous place to watch the skies.

When all the preparations are done, it is time to go ON-THE-AIR! The control room at 7News is "Mission Control" for putting the entire newscast together and broadcasting it throughout Colorado.

Anne Trujillo joins Mike Nelson during the weather segment of an evening newscast.

Credits

Cover: Gregory Thompson (front); Tony Laubach (back top, middle); John F. Weaver (back bottom)

P iii: Flint Glassier

P. 1: Red Sunrise

P. 5: 2007 Copyright, © University Corporation for Atmospheric Research

P. 6: Mark Montour-Larson

P. 7: Mark Montour-Larson

P. 8: Mark Montour-Larson

P. 9: Mark Montour-Larson

P. 13: Mark Montour-Larson

P. 17: Mark Montour-Larson

P. 20: 2007 Copyright, © University Corporation for Atmospheric Research

P. 21: Mark Montour-Larson

P. 22: 2007 Copyright, © University Corporation for Atmospheric Research

P. 23: Linda Ford

P. 24: Linda Ford

P. 25: Mark Montour-Larson

P. 27: Mark Montour-Larson

P. 28: Mark Montour-Larson

P. 29: Mark Montour-Larson

P. 34: 2007 Copyright, © University Corporation for Atmospheric Research

P. 37: Mark Montour-Larson and Andrew Williams

P. 38: Tony Laubach

P. 39: Patrick Belt (both)

P. 40: 2007 Copyright, © University Corporation for Atmospheric Research (both)

P. 41: 2007 Copyright, © University Corporation for Atmospheric Research (both)

P. 42: KMGH-TV

P. 44: Sharon Noel (top); 2007 Copyright, © University Corporation for Atmospheric Research (bottom)

P. 46: Rob Dow (top); Dale Lyman (bottom)

P. 47: Klaus Girk (top left); Dewey Anderson (top right); Kathy Fenton (bottom right)

P. 48: Kathy Fenton

P. 50: Kathy Fenton (top); Matt Sugar, Winter Park Resort (left); Mike Lane (center)

P. 51: R. W. Flubacker (top); Rich Day (bottom)

P. 52: Linda Ford

P. 53: Mike Chalek

P. 55: Mike Lane

P. 59: Wayne Edlin

P. 64: Mark Montour-Larson

P. 68: Andrew Williams

P. 71: Mark Montour-Larson

P. 73: Mark Montour-Larson

P. 74: Ken Langford

P. 75: Mark Montour-Larson and Andrew Williams

P. 76: Carl Valentine (left); Nora Rudnick (right)

P. 77: M. Owen

P. 78: Linda Ford

P. 79: Ken Langford

P. 80: Colorado Avalanche Information Center

P. 81: Linda Ford

P. 82: Raymond Mumford

P. 83: Raymond Mumford (both)

P. 84: Tony Laubach

P. 85: KMGH-TV (both)

P. 87: National Ice Core Lab (both)

P. 88: Tony Laubach (both)

P. 90: Mark Montour-Larson

P. 92: KMGH-TV (both)

P. 93: Courtesy Denver Water Board, 2007 (both)

P. 102: 2007 Copyright, © University Corporation for Atmospheric Research

P. 105: Linda Ford (both)

P. 106: Tony Laubach

P. 107: Tony Laubach (top left); Roger Hill (top right); www.agweb.com (bottom right)

P. 109: Linda Ford (top); Tony Laubach (bottom)

P. 110: Mark Montour-Larson

P. 111: Tony Laubach (top); Linda Ford (bottom)

P. 112: Roger Hill (top); Tony Laubach (bottom)

P. 113: CoCoRaHS (left); M.Lepper (right)

P. 114: Tony Laubach

P. 115: Mark Montour-Larson

P. 116: Jim Bliss (left); Bill Fortune (right)

P. 117: Colorado River Water Conservancy District (top); Susanna Gross (bottom)

P. 119: TheDenverChannel.com

P. 122: 2007 Copyright, © University Corporation for Atmospheric Research

P. 123: Linda Ford

P. 124: Linda Ford

P. 126: Ken Langford

P. 127: Jonathan Moreno

P. 129: Tony Laubach (both)

P. 130: Ken Langford (top); Tony Laubach (middle, bottom)

P. 131: Ken Langford

P. 136: Linda Ford

P. 137: Linda Ford

P. 138: Tony Laubach

P. 139: Jonathan Moreno

P. 140: Andrew Williams

P. 142: 2007 Copyright, © University Corporation for Atmospheric Research

P. 143: NASA Windshear Airborne Sensors Program

P. 144: Northern Colorado Water Conservancy District Archives

P. 146: Jonathan Moreno

P. 148: Northern Colorado Water Conservancy District Archives (all)

P. 149: Colorado State University (top); John F. Weaver (bottom)

P. 150: John F. Weaver

P. 151: Ken McDowell

P. 152: Jon Van de Grift

P. 153: KMGH-TV

P. 154: Jon Van de Grift

P. 155: Chris L. Peterson

P. 156: Jon Van de Grift

P. 158: Andrew Williams

P. 160: Tony Laubach

P. 163: Tony Laubach

P. 164: Tony Laubach

P. 165: Tony Laubach

P. 166: Roger Hill (both)

P. 167: Tony Laubach

P. 168: Tony Laubach (top); Dustin Wilcox (bottom)

P. 169: Roger Hill

P. 170: Jonathan Moreno

P. 171: Linda Ford

P. 172: Pat Porter

P. 173: Carsten Peter (top); Gene Rhoden (right)

P. 174: Roger Hill (top), Tony Laubach (bottom)

P. 175: Tony Laubach

P. 176: 2007 Copyright, © University Corporation for Atmospheric Research (top); Sandy Pethan (bottom)

P. 177: Adam Ball (top); Roger Hill (bottom)

P. 178: Caleb Kimbrough (top); Sam Dienst (middle); Dan Bush (bottom)

P. 179: Caleb Kimbrough (top); Tony Laubach (bottom)

P. 181: Linda Ford

P. 182: Tony Laubach (left); Ken Langford (right)

P. 183: Roger Hill (all)

P. 184: Tim Samaras

P. 189: Linda Ford (left); Ken Langford (right)

P. 190: Henry Reges

P. 192: Jon Van de Grift (left); NCAR (top right)

P. 193: Odie Bliss

P. 195: Denver Public Library Western History Department

P. 198: Denver Public Library Western History Department

P. 200: Henry Reges

P. 201: Denver Public Library Western History Department

P. 202: Dorothy Capraro

P. 204: Denver Public Library Western History Department (both)

P. 206: Colorado Historical Society

P. 209: Colorado Historical Society (all)

P. 210: Denver Public Library Western History Department (left); Douglas County Public Library (right)

P. 212: Denver Public Library Western History Department

P. 214: Robert Duncan (both)

P. 216: Douglas County Libraries/ Douglas County History Research Center; Accession# 1993.006.036; Creator: Charles W. Love; Date: June 1965 (top); Douglas County Libraries/ Douglas County History Research Center; Accession# 1997.043.011; Creator: Roberta Moore; Date: June 1965

P. 219: Big Thompson Flood Memorial, Inc.

P. 220: Big Thompson Flood Memorial, Inc. (both)

P. 221: Linda Ford

P. 222: Northern Colorado Water Conservancy District Archives

P. 223: Big Thompson Flood Memorial, Inc.

P. 226: Linda Ford

P. 228: KMGH-TV (both)

P. 231: KMGH-TV

P. 232: Eugene W. McCaul, Jr. (top); KMGH-TV (bottom left); Eugene W. McCaul, Jr. (bottom right)

P. 233: Dr. Alexander MacDonald

P. 234: KMGH-TV

P. 235: KMGH-TV

P. 236: KMGH-TV

P. 237: Linda Ford (top); John Weaver (bottom)

P. 238: Nolan Doesken (top); John Weaver (bottom)

P. 239: USFS

P. 244: Northern Colorado Water Conservancy District

P. 246: Tony Laubach

P. 247: KMGH-TV (both)

P. 248: Tony Laubach

P. 249: Tony Laubach (both)

P. 250: Jilane Hixson

P. 252: NOAA

P. 254: Monte Tinnes (both)

P. 256: NASA

P. 258: NCAR (top left); Stormcenter Communications & NASA (top right); NCAR (bottom right); Stormcenter Communications & NASA (bottom left)

P. 259: Solar and Heliospheric Observatory – NASA

P. 260: Solar and Heliospheric Observatory – NASA (both)

P. 261: Linda Ford (all)

P. 262: NOAA

P. 263: NASA

P. 265: NASA

P. 266: 2007 Copyright, © University Corporation for Atmospheric Research

P. 269: Andrew Williams

P. 271: Denverskyscrapers.com

P. 272: NASA's Earth Observatory (both)

P. 274: 2007 Copyright, © University Corporation for Atmospheric Research (left); NOAA Climate Office Program, NABOS 2006 Expedition (right)

P. 276: Stormcenter Communications & NASA

P. 277: 2007 Copyright, © University Corporation for Atmospheric Research

P. 278: Rocky Mountain Climate Organization (both)

P. 279: Rocky Mountain Climate Organization

P. 280: Stormcenter Communications & NASA (top left and right): Keno (bottom left); Tony Laubach (bottom right)

P. 281: Mike Lane (top); Ken McDowell (bottom)

P. 282: Xcel Energy (top); 2007 Copyright, © University Corporation for Atmospheric Research (bottom)

P. 284: NASA (all)

P. 285: NASA

P. 286: Gary Zolnosky

P. 287: Cindy Nelson

P. 289: NREL (all)

P. 293: NASA

P. 295: NASA

P. 296: Van A. Truan

P. 298: Mike Nelson (left); Chris Spears (right)

P. 299: Bill Kuster

P. 300: Mike Nelson

P. 301: Mike Nelson

P. 302: Weather Central, Inc.

P. 303: Mike Nelson (all)

P. 304: Mike Nelson (all)

P. 305: KMGH-TV (both)

P. 306: KMGH-TV

P. 307: KMGH-TV

P. 308: Andrew Williams

P. 309: Weather Central, Inc. (top, bottom); Illinois Water (middle); Andrew Williams (left)

P. 310: Linda Ford (top); KMGH-TV (bottom)

P. 311: KMGH-TV

P. 312: KMGH-TV (both)

P. 314: KMGH-TV (all)

P. 315: KMGH-TV (top); Tom Stillo (bottom)

P. 316: Mark Montour-Larson

P. 317: Mark Montour-Larson (top); Eaton Middle School (bottom)

P. 318: Mark Montour-Larson

P. 319: Mark Montour-Larson

P. 321: Mark Montour-Larson

P. 322: Mark Montour-Larson

P. 323: Mark Montour-Larson

Bibliography

"A Climate Conundrum." *Weatherwise.* March/April 2006.

"Among Global Thermometers, Warming Still Wins Out." *Science*, Vol. 281, September 25, 1998.

Aviation Weather. U.S. Dept of Commerce. Washington, D.C., 1975.

Anderson, Bette Roda. *Weather in the West.* Palo Alto: American West Publishing, 1975.

Anthes, Richard. *The Atmosphere*, 2nd Edition. Merrill Publishing Co.,1987.

Armstrong, Robert E. *Flood, Mud and Misery.* Denver: Mountain Bell, 1965.

Bader, M.J., G.S. Forbes, J.R. Grant, R.B.E. Lilley, and A.J. Waters. *Images in Weather Forecasting.* Cambridge: Cambridge University Press, 1995.

Boote, Kenneth. "The Greening of the Planet Earth." The Institute for Biosphere Research, Inc., videotape.

Boyd, Jill. "Bracing for a Blaze." *Water News.* Northern Colorado Water Conservancy District, May 2006.

Branley, Franklyn M. *It's Raining Cats & Dogs.* Boston: Houghton Mifflin, 1987.

Bryson, Reid A., and Thomas J. Murray. *Climates of Hunger.* Wisconsin: University of Wisconsin Press, 1977.

Buckley, Bruce, Edward J. Hopkins, and Richard Whitaker. *Weather—A Visual Guide.* Richmond Hill, Ontario, Canada: Firefly Books, 2004.

"State of the Climate in 2006." Bulletin of the American Meteorological Society, Vol. 88, No. 6, June 2007.

"Sizzling Summer Statistics." Bulletin of the National Weather Association, January 2007.

Burroughs, William J., Bob Crowder, Ted Robertson, Eleanor Vallier-Talbot, and Richard Whitaker. *A Guide to Weather.* San Francisco: Fog City Press, 1996.

"Chasing Tornadoes." *National Geographic.* April 2004.

Chaston, Peter R. *Weather Maps.* Kearney, MO: Chaston Scientific, Inc., 1995.

"Climate Change—Scientific Certainties and Uncertainties." National Environment Research Council, September 1997.

Colorado Avalanche Information Center (CAIC). "Avalanche Wise—Your Guide to Avalanche Safety in Colorado." Special Publication 48.

Dickinson, Terence. *Exploring the Sky by Day.* Ontario, Canada: Camden House, 1988.

Doesken, Nolan J., Robert J. Leffler, Raymond M. Downs, Grant Goodge, Keith Eggleston, and Dr. David Robinson. "Evaluation of the Reported January 11-12, 1997, Montague, New York, 77 Inch, 24-Hour, Lake-Effect Snowfall." U.S. Dept. of Commerce Special Report, March 1997.

Dunlap, Storm. *The Weather Identification Handbook.* First Lyons Press, 2003.

Durham, Louise E. "Paleo Markers Can Be Deceiving." *American Association of Petroleum Geologists Explorer.* July 2006.

Engardio, Pete. "Beyond the Green Corporation." *Business Week.* January 29, 2007.

Environmental Protection Agency. "Cool Facts About Global Warming." EPA 320-F-91-001, July 1997.

———"Climate Change and Colorado." EPA 230-F-97-008f, September 1997.

EOS, Transactions, American Geophysical Union. "North Pacific Interdecadal Oscillation Seen as Factor in ENSO-Related North American Climate Anomalies." EOS Vol. 79, No 52, January 1999.

"Facing a Warmer Future." *Nature Conservancy.* Vol. 55, No. 3, Autumn 2005.

Facklam, Howard, and Margery Facklam. *Changes in the Wind: Earth's Shifting Climate.* San Diego: Harcourt Brace Jovanovich, 1986.

Fields, Alan. *Partly Sunny: The Weather Junkie's Guide to Outsmarting the Weather.* Boulder: Windsor Peak Press, 1995.

Flannery, Tim. *The Weather Makers.* New York: Atlantic Monthly Press, 2005.

Foggitt, Bill. *Weatherwise: Facts, Fictions and Predictions.* Philadelphia: Running Press, 1992.

Forrester, Frank H. *1001 Questions Answered About the Weather.* New York: Dover Publications, Inc. 1981.

Freier, George, D. *Weather Proverbs.* Tucson: Fisher Books, 1992.

Glantz, Michael H. *Currents of Change.* Cambridge: Cambridge University Press, 1996.

———"Making Climate Serve the People." WMO Bulletin 55(2) pp 116–125, June 2005.

———"Review of the Causes and Consequences of Cold Events." NCAR Workshop Report pp 15–17, July 1998.

"Global Climate Change: An East Room Roundtable." Washington, D.C.: Office of Science and Technology Policy, July 1997.

"Global Warming." *National Geographic.* September 2004.

"Global Warming: Can it be Stopped?" *The Week.* Feb. 16, 2007.

Green, Kenneth. "A Plain English Guide to the Science of Climate Change." Reason Public Policy Institute, December 1997.

"Greenhouse Wars: Why the Rebels Have a Cause." *New Scientist.* July 19, 1997.

Greenler, Robert. *Rainbows, Halos and Glories.* Cambridge: Cambridge University Press, 1980.

Haltiner, George J., and Frank L. Martin. *Dynamical and Physical Meteorology.* New York: McGraw-Hill, 1957.

Hansen, James E. "Climate Forcings in the Industrial Era." The National Academy of Sciences, Vol. 95, pp 12753–12758, October 1998.

Hansen, Wallace R., John Chronic, and John Matelock. *Climatology of the Front Range Urban Corridor and Vicinity, Colorado.* Washington D.C.: U.S. Government Printing Office, 1978.

Henson, Robert. *Television Weather-casting: A History.* Jefferson, NC: McFarland and Company, Inc., 1990.

Hess, Seymour L. *Introduction to Theoretical Meteorology.* New York: Holt Rinehart & Winston, 1959.

Holton, James R. *An Introduction to Dynamic Meteorology.* New York: Academic Press, 1972.

"How Was the Weather?" *American Heritage Magazine.* June/July 1986.

Intergovernmental Panel on Climate Change. Fourth Assessment Report of the IPCC, February 2007.

International Geosphere-Biosphere Programme (IGPB). A Study of Global Change of the International Council of Scientific Unions (ICSU), 1997.

Solar Energy. International Solar Energy Society. Vol. 80, No. 9, 2006.

Johns, Robert H. "Meteorological Conditions Associated with Bow Echo Development in Convective Storms." *Weather and Forecasting.* American Meteorological Society. Vol. 8, No. 2, June 1993.

Johns, Robert H. and Charles A. Doswell. "Severe Local Storms Forecasting." *Weather and Forecasting.* American Meteorological Society. Vol. 7, August 1992.

Keen, Richard A. *Skywatch: The Western Weather Guide.* Golden, CO: Fulcrum, Inc., 1987.

Kerr, Richard. "Greenhouse Forecasting Still Cloudy." *Science*, May 1997 pp 1040–1042.

———. "Among Global Thermometers, Warming Still Wins Out." *Science*, Vol. 281, September 25, 1998.

Kessler, Edwin, Ed. *The Thunderstorm in Human Affairs*. Norman, OK: University of Oklahoma Press, 1983.

"Killer Hurricanes." *National Geographic*. August 2006.

Lang, J. Stephen. *The Complete Book of Bible Trivia*. Wheaton, IL: Tyndale House Publishers, 1988.

Lee, Albert. *Weather Wisdom*. Garden City, NY: Doubleday and Company, 1976.

Lehr, Paul E., R. Will Burnett, and Herbert S. Zim. *Golden Guide to Weather*. New York: Golden Press, 1975.

Leslie, Jacques. "Running Dry—What Happens When the World No Longer Has Enough Fresh Water?" *Harper's Magazine*. July 2000.

Ludlum, David M. *National Audubon Society Field Guide to North American Weather*. New York: Chanticleer Press, 1997.

———. *The American Weather Book*. Boston: Houghton Mifflin, 1982.

Lyons, Walter A., Ph.D. *The Handy Weather Answer Book*. Detroit: Accord Publishing Ltd., 1997.

MacLean, John N. *Fire on the Mountain: The True Story of the South Canyon Fire*.

Marshall, Tim. "Tornado Damage Surveys." Presented in Denver at National Storm Chasers Convention, February 2003.

McKee, Thomas B., Nolan J. Doesken, and John Kleist. "A History of Drought in Colorado: Lessons Learned and What Lies Ahead." Colorado Water Resources Research Institute: Water in the Balance, No. 9, Second Edition, February 2000. Colorado State University.

Michaels, Patrick J. "Is the Sky Really Falling?: A Review of Recent Global Warming Scare Stories." Policy Analysis No. 576. The CATO Institute, August 23, 2006.

Miller, Albert. *Meteorology*, Third Edition. Columbus, OH: Charles E. Merrill Publishing Company, 1976.

Moore, Patrick. *The World's Weather and Climate*. London: Orbis Publishing Limited, 1974.

National Assessment Synthesis Team. *Climate Change Impacts on the United States*. Cambridge: Cambridge University Press, 2000.

Nelson, Michael P. *The Colorado Weather Book*. Englewood, CO: Westcliffe Publishers, 1999.

Novy, Chris and Greg Stumpf. *Getting Ready to Spot Severe Storms—A Field Guide*. Norman, OK: National Severe Storms Laboratory.

Parzybok, Tye W. *Weather Extremes of the West*. Missoula, MT: Mountain Press Publishing Co., 2005.

Ponte, Lowell. *The Cooling*. Englewood Cliffs, NJ: Prentice Hall, 1976.

Rinehart, Ronald E. *Radar for Meteorologists*. Columbia, MO: Rinehart Publications, 2004.

Robinson, Arthur E., Sallie L. Baliunas, Willie Soon, and Zachary W. Robinson. "Environmental Effects of Increased Atmospheric Carbon Dioxide." George C. Marshall Institute, Washington D.C., January 1998.

Sagan, Carl. *The Pale Blue Dot—A Vision of the Human Future in Space*. Ballentine Books, 1994.

Sawkins, Frederick J. and Clement G. Chase. *The Evolving Earth—A Text in Physical Geology*. New York: Macmillan Publishing Co., 1978.

Schaefer, Vincent J., and John A. Day. *Atmosphere: Clouds, Rain, Snow, Storms*. Houghton Mifflin Co., 1981.

———. *A Field Guide to the Atmosphere*. Houghton Mifflin Co., 1981.

Schneider, Stephen H. *Global Warming*. New York: Vintage Books, 1989.

Siemer, Eugene G. *Colorado Climate*. Published by the Colorado Experiment Station, December 1977.

Singer, Fred S. "The Scientific Case Against the Global Climate Treaty." The Science and Environmental Policy Project." Fairfax, VA, 1997.

"Storm Chasing." *Weatherwise*. April/May 1996.

The Big Thompson Disaster. Drake, CO: Big Thompson Canyon Flood Memorial, Inc., 2006.

"The Truth About Tornadoes." *Weatherwise*. May/June 2001.

Trenberth, Kevin. "The Use and Abuse of Climate Models." *Nature*, Vol. 386, March 13, 1997.

———. "What Is Happening to El Niño?" *Encyclopedia Britannica: Yearbook of Science and the Future*, 1997.

"Our Ozone Shield. Reports to the Nation On Our Changing Climate." University Corporation for Atmospheric Research, 1992.

Vasquez, Tim. *Extreme American Weather*. Garland, TX: Weather Graphics Technologies, 2004.

———*Storm Chasing Handbook*. Garland, TX: Weather Graphics Technologies, 2002.

———*Weather Forecasting Handbook*. Garland, TX: Weather Graphics Technologies, 2002.

Williams, Jack. *The Weather Book*. New York, NY: Vintage Books, 1997.

Wilson, William E. *Georgetown Weather Observations, A Historical Perspective*.

Newspaper Sources

Rocky Mountain News

"Xcel's plans for clean-coal plant may grow." March 1, 2007.

"Climate debate grows heated during House hearing." February 9, 2007.

"Wind turbine facility planned." January 20, 2007.

"Western droughts could become norm, say climate scientists." February 3, 2007.

"A far different planet in 100 years, climate scientists warn world." March 2, 2007.

"Humans 'very likely' ignited global warming, panel says." February 2, 2007.

"Climbing Temps likely to erode ski season." February 2, 2007.

"A sea change coming." February 17, 2007.

"Put blame on El Nino, expert says." October 27, 2006.

"Necessity of new reservoirs debated." February 22, 2007.

"Fiercer water wars seen for west." February 22, 2007.

The Denver Post

"Grim Assessment on Climate." February 2, 2007.

"Climate Report on deadline." February 18, 2007.

"Interview with Michael Potts." April 1, 2007.

"Colorado River Basin forecast not good." February 22, 2007.

"Rain-gauge fund dries up before slide threat does." November 13, 2006.

"Global warming? Them's fightin' words." September 24, 2006.

"Global call to action." February 4, 2007.

"Capitol Hill pledges climate-change laws." January 31, 2007.

"Coal-site plans stir warming concerns." January 31, 2007.

"Energy ambitions converge." January 27, 2007.

"Has Bush noticed the cherry blossoms are out?" January 21, 2007.

"Congress and global warming." February 9, 2007.

"Climate Panel heats forecast." February 2, 2007.

"PelosióExpect House global-warming bill by July." February 9, 2007.

The Wall Street Journal

"Fuel Interests Split on Coal." January 26, 2007.

"If the Cap Fits." January 26, 2007.

World Meteorological Society (WMO) Press Release

"WMO Statement on the Status of the Global Climate in 2006." December 14, 2006.

327

Index